Reformation and the Culture of Persuasion

15.99
06/2005

message ✓ Woodcut as promoting the Reformation

Why did people choose the Reformation? What was it in the evangelical teaching that excited, moved or persuaded them? Andrew Pettegree here tackles these questions directly by re-examining the reasons that moved millions to make this decisive and traumatic break with a shared Christian past. He charts the separation from family, friends and workmates that adherence to the new faith often entailed, and the new solidarities that emerged in their place. He explores the different media of conversion through which the Reformation message was communicated and imbibed – the role of drama, sermons, song and the book – and argues that the potency of print can only be understood as working in harmony with more traditional modes of communication. His findings offer a persuasive new answer to the critical question of how the Reformation could succeed as a mass movement in an age before mass literacy.

ANDREW PETTEGREE is Professor of Modern History and founding Director of the Reformation Studies Institute at the University of St Andrews. He is the author of a number of studies of the European Reformation, sixteenth-century Europe and the history of the printed book.

Reformation and the Culture of Persuasion

Andrew Pettegree

CAMBRIDGE
UNIVERSITY PRESS

CAMBRIDGE UNIVERSITY PRESS
Cambridge, New York, Melbourne, Madrid, Cape Town, Singapore, São Paulo

Cambridge University Press
The Edinburgh Building, Cambridge, CB2 2RU, UK

Published in the United States of America by Cambridge University Press, New York

www.cambridge.org
Information on this title: *www.cambridge.org/9780521602648*

© Andrew Pettegree 2005

First published 2005

Printed in the United Kingdom at the University Press, Cambridge

A catalogue record for this book is available from the British Library

ISBN-13 978-0-521-84175-7   - hardback
ISBN-10 0-521-84175-5   - hardback
ISBN-13 978-0-521-60264-8   - paperback
ISBN-10 0-521-60264-5   - paperback

For Bruce, Rona and Charlotte

Contents

Illustrations

Preface

This book was conceived in 1991, when I made my first visit to Lutherstadt-Wittenberg, as it was then called. Standing in front of one of the display cases in the Lutherhalle Museum, I came face to face with a cascade of *Flugschriften*. The visual impact of this great heap of Reformation writings, piled up seemingly at random, was very strong, and set me musing on the contemporary impact of such literature: the extraordinarily innovative manner in which the Reformation made its appeal for public support, and the manner, perhaps very different, in which this appeal was received. I have been ruminating on these questions ever since, even as other writing projects have directed my immediate attention to more specific tasks. This book is an attempt to give these thoughts some sort of systematic expression. With the passage of years since 1991 I have obviously read and learned a very great deal, working primarily on the experience of Reformation in four main areas: Germany, the Netherlands, France and the two kingdoms of Britain, England and Scotland. Much of this has been learned through the guidance of friends and professional colleagues, and it is a pleasure to acknowledge here the help and inspiration of scholars on both sides of the English Channel and the Atlantic Ocean. Many people have guided my exploration of the various literary disciplines and media explored in this volume. Specific debts are acknowledged at appropriate places in the text, but I should also express my gratitude to the three anonymous readers for Cambridge University Press, who gave the first proposal for this project a rigorous workout. A more general debt is owed to the many students and scholars whose work I have heard at conferences, particularly the Reformation Colloquium, the European Reformation Research Group and the Sixteenth Century Studies Conference. Reformation scholars are especially well served by our conference culture, but this would not be so without the heroic efforts of those who devote so much time to organizing these meetings. Two friends, Alastair Duke and Peter Marshall, were kind enough to read the whole text of this book in draft, and their observations helped me greatly as I prepared the final text for publication. I also owe a special debt to my wife Jane, whose expertise in the fields of music and early modern drama have immeasurably increased my knowledge in preparing the chapters devoted to these topics here. My two daughters Megan and Sophie also helped me understand the process of learning, not least the enduring power of rote learning, the importance of melody, and the fantastic power of the human memory. Over the years my graduate students have taught me an enormous amount about diverse topics, and all of them will see a little bit of themselves reflected here. In recent years I have also benefited greatly from the opportunity of sustained field-work with members of the St Andrews French Book Project team, especially my two principal colleagues in that enterprise, Alexander Wilkinson and Malcolm Walsby. A first draft of this text was test-driven by my third-year Reformation Honours course at St Andrews, and I am grateful to them for their perceptive comments. Finally, one cannot be for twenty years, as I have been, a friend, and latterly colleague, of Bruce Gordon without learning an enormous amount of Reformation history. The impact of his conversation, his versatile mind and deep learning, have over the years been more profound than I can easily acknowledge. For this reason I dedicate this book to Bruce, and to his family, Rona and Charlotte.

1   The dynamics of conversion

Why did people choose the Reformation? What was it in the evangelical teaching that excited, moved or persuaded them? How, and by what process, did people arrive at the new understandings that prompted a change of allegiance, and embedded them in their new faith? These are questions central to an understanding of the Reformation movement, but they are far more often approached obliquely than answered directly. We know that Luther and other evangelicals preached a powerful doctrine of redemption and salvation; we know that they conjured a sense that the Reformation would address long-standing discontents about the relationship between clergy and people; and we know that large parts of Europe would ultimately accept the new Protestant churches. But precisely what moved people – either as individuals, or as part of a community – to abandon one allegiance and embrace another is a complex and difficult question.

What we can be certain is that, in the first generation of evangelical agitation, the decision to adhere to the Reformation was often a very painful one. It involved difficult choices and life-changing decisions. It involved exchanging the familiar round of traditional observance for a new order which was untested and largely unknown. It involved accepting the good faith and charismatic authority of preachers who had often emerged from a comparatively lowly position in the local clerical hierarchy, ignoring the counter-charges of those who denounced them as false prophets. It involved embracing novelty in an era that despised and distrusted innovation, and validated all change by its compatibility with the inherited wisdom, custom and teaching of the ages. This was a particular problem of which the reformers were all too aware, as we can witness in their frequent attempts to validate the renovation of religion as a return to the pure Gospel principles of the early church: restoration not innovation.[1] Theirs, they urged, was

---

[1] Bruce Gordon, 'The Changing Face of Protestant History and Identity in the Sixteenth Century', in his *Protestant History and Identity in Sixteenth-Century Europe* (2 vols., Aldershot, St Andrews Studies in Reformation History, 1996), pp. 1–23.

the true church, which they had rescued from the perversions of papal tyranny and the accretion of false tradition. But this was a justification articulated by Protestant theologians and historians largely after the event. In any case, new adherents could hardly avoid being struck by the large element of unfamiliarity in the new churches – in their experience of worship, their public festivities, and their relationship with the much-changed clerical order. Change, for all that it was so widely distrusted, was a universal and very obvious consequence of the Protestant revolution: in dress, in the working round (cleansed of extraneous festivals), most of all in the experience of religion.

Many were drawn to embrace the new vision of the evangelical ministers by particular elements of a complex programme; their choice may sometimes have been whimsical or ill considered. Yet ultimately the renovation of religion involved the loss of much of the old structure of worship that had given comfort and pleasure. Some could only accommodate this transformation by putting psychological distance between the religious lives they had lived and that they were choosing. They turned on aspects of this now rejected religious system with a savagery that would have been unthinkable only a few years before.[2] Others simply incorporated loved elements of their old religious lives within the fabric of the new, often incongruously and to the frustration of their new preachers.[3]

This recognition, that the process of conversion was an extended and evolving process, brings us up against the first, and very substantial, interpretative question. Are we right to assume that adherence to the Reformation was a conscious choice for more than a very small number of articulate, educated individuals? Are we guilty of using a single word – conversion – to mask a complex process of psychological adjustment that requires far more careful analysis?

Here it may be helpful to distinguish the experience of the first generation from the extended process of reorientation that followed, once new churches were in existence. For the first years of the Reformation we have plentiful evidence that the decision to adhere to it involved conscious choice. This evidence comes from very many contemporary testimonies: the reformers themselves, all important converts; correspondence, chronicles, martyrologies; the records of the state authorities struggling to contain the consequences of these religious perturbations. These diverse records make clear that for many, even from

---

[2] Carlos Eire, *The War Against the Idols* (Cambridge, 1986).
[3] Susan C. Karant-Nunn, *The Reformation of Ritual. An Interpretation of Early Modern Germany* (London, 1997).

comparatively humble stations in life, the religious alteration was one pregnant with consequences. For many in the first generation the choice was a lonely one, made individually or with a small group of fellows who thus excluded themselves from the fellowship of societies not yet ready to accept the evangelical message. For these men and women, to embrace the Gospel was to court calamity. Religious divisions ended friendship, caused division between neighbours and kin, damaged relations with parents beyond repair, sometimes even caused rejection by a spouse or children. Some paid the ultimate price for their decision to embrace the new teaching. During the course of the Reformation century several thousands were put to death for the crime of heresy.[4] Many others died as a consequence of the religious wars that engulfed Europe in the second half of the century.

Later, as the churches of the Reformation became institutionalized, it became possible to adhere to Protestantism with little real choice, and without any real mental engagement. Even here, however, there is reason to doubt whether such utter passivity would have been the normative experience. The practice of worship was now so thoroughly different that the peoples of these new churches were in very real ways changed. And through a course of years many came to value these new practices and invest in them a real sense of loyalty and affection. This process, too, forms part of our study – if only because it is so vital to an understanding of how Protestantism could become, in a real sense, a popular religion.

What did people choose when they adhered to the evangelical teaching? This is a question with which the reformers were themselves obviously greatly concerned, and to which they offered contrasting answers. To Luther and others, adherence to the Gospel message was, in the first instance, an acceptance of a call to repentance. The church must be cleansed, and this would only be possible if Christians embraced the obligation – perhaps even a last opportunity – to witness to their faith and accept the assurance of their salvation. It was a message that was from the beginning freighted with complex implications. It addressed both the individual Christian, called to accept a personal assurance of salvation, and the church community, directed to restore a vision of apostolic service. Within this complex of competing messages the

---

[4] William Monter, 'Heresy Executions in Reformation Europe, 1520–1565', in Ole Peter Grell and Bob Scribner (eds.), *Tolerance and Intolerance in the European Reformation* (Cambridge, 1996), pp. 48–64. William Monter, *Judging the French Reformation. Heresy Trials by Sixteenth-Century Parlements* (Cambridge, Mass., 1999), pp. 28–54. Brad S. Gregory, *Salvation at Stake. Christian Martyrdom in Early Modern Europe* (Cambridge, Mass., 1999).

reformers envisaged a real process of conversion, a choice that became more stark and urgent once it became clear that the call for reform would lead to divided, competing churches. At this point the process of evangelical awakening became not just an acceptance of salvation, but also a choice of loyalties. It was in this context, of churches drifting into separation, that the reformers began to articulate individual religious choice in terms of conversion. Each offered the inspiration of his own conversion narrative. Luther in fact offered two: the moment when, caught in a storm, he first accepted his religious vocation, and the moment when he recognized his great theological breakthrough, the so called 'Turmerlebnis'.[5] These recollections are relevant, not because we wish to rejoin the extended historical debate about where in his career Luther's new understanding of justification should be placed, but because they show the importance the reformers placed on the classic conversion models in framing a discussion of their own experience of spiritual enlightenment. For Luther knew that conversion was both a sudden life-changing moment and a marvellous example of God's intervention in the lives of men: thus the Lord had called Paul, Saul the persecutor, on the road to Damascus; thus had Augustine described his own life-changing repudiation of early frivolity. The strength of this model is evident in the careful, rather oblique account offered by Jean Calvin of his adherence to the evangelical movement, which seems, in truth, to have occurred rather gradually over a period of years while Calvin was living in Paris in the 1530s.[6] This quite understandable human experience of gradual awakening to compromising and ultimately unorthodox beliefs was clearly not acceptable, recalled twenty years later in the very different atmosphere of reformed Geneva. Rather, Calvin chose to relate how, having been mired in papist superstition, God had by a sudden conversion (subita conversio) recalled his mind to a more teachable frame.[7]

Such framing, while demonstrating the very powerful strength of the conversion paradigm, should also warn us of the pitfalls of too credulous a use of contemporary documentation. For generations of Protestants would similarly come to frame their own experience of spiritual awakening in such terms. Such narratives inevitably lay great

---

[5] W. D. J. Cargill Thompson, 'The Problem of Luther's "Tower Experience" and its Place in his Intellectual Development', in his Studies in the Reformation. Luther to Hooker (London, 1980), pp. 60–81.

[6] Alister E. McGrath, A Life of John Calvin (Oxford, 1990), pp. 21–50.

[7] The autobiographical reflections come in the preface to his Commentary on the Psalms (1557). McGrath, Calvin, pp. 69–78.

stress on the motivating power of theology, particularly Luther's teaching of justification, in building support for the Reformation, an explanatory framework also eagerly embraced by many generations of historians. It is fair to say that such an approach to writing the history of the Reformation, placing the primary emphasis on the appeal of Luther's Reformation teaching, was largely unchallenged until the middle part of the last century. The boom in social history in the three decades from the 1960s has to some extent called this into question, though most recent work, which stresses the strengths of the old church and downplays the importance of anticlerical feeling as a motive force for change, has gone some way towards restoring the value of the older tradition. This synthesis finds eloquent expression in a formula recently proposed by Diarmaid MacCulloch: 'The old church was immensely strong, and that strength could only have been overcome by the explosive power of an idea'.[8] That idea was justification.

In their own day the reformers were very aware that the reform of the church was a task of great complexity that required the active engagement of many classes of people. Luther was every bit as fine a polemicist as he was a theologian. They also had a complex and refined sense of the process of Christian conversion. On the one hand, there was the dramatic moment of acceptance; then again, the creation of a Christian people required a process of long, hard unrelenting struggle. The Luther whose early published works had included a torrent of apocalyptic invective against a corrupt church hierarchy, had within a very few years turned to the process of Christian education. A people had to be led to right understanding and right living: to this process he contributed sermons, psalms, his Long and Short Catechisms (1529), and his translation of the Bible. Other of his colleagues contributed church orders, one of the great, and thus far much understudied, innovations of Protestant church life. It is this part of the conversion process, the slow, painstaking creation of active Christian citizens, that has engaged the attention of scholars particularly in the last thirty years. This engagement has, it must be said, been very often from a perspective of profound scepticism. Ever since in 1978 Gerald Strauss published his *Luther's House of Learning*, a highly critical analysis of the Lutheran attempt to create a reformed society, the terms of debate have been radically revised.[9] Whether or

[8] Diarmaid MacCulloch. *Reformations. Europe's House Divided, 1490–1700* (London, 2003), p. 110.
[9] Gerald Strauss, *Luther's House of Learning. Indoctrination of the Young in the German Reformation* (Baltimore, Md., 1978). The subsequent debate on this question is reviewed by Strauss in his 'The Reformation and its public in an age of orthodoxy', in R. Po-Chia Hsia (ed.), *The German People and the Reformation* (Ithaca, N.Y., 1988), pp. 194–214.

not we accept Strauss's largely negative appraisal, there is now a wide-spread acceptance of a chronology of evangelical renewal that encom-passes the generations necessary to embed new beliefs and new religious practice. The process of building a new church required much more than conversion. Education, assimilation, familiarity and the creation of new enemies – a new dialectic of belonging and rejection – all played their part.

This present study seeks to explore the process of persuasion by recognizing this as a layered and complex process, proceeding in differ-ent ways, and at different points in the political process by which states or cities made a choice of confessional allegiance. It might be helpful to our discussion here to postulate a tiered hierarchy of commitment, all parts of which played a role in the process of commitment.

This schematic representation may shape our discussion, though it is not suggested that this represents a necessary chronology in the process of conversion. But it may offer some useful pointers to the way in which people reacted to the new evangelical teachings, before ultimately com-mitting themselves to Protestantism. Obviously, in order to adhere to the

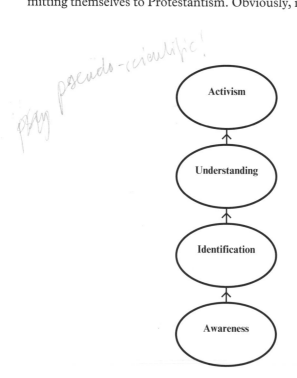

Figure 1.1. The Protestant conversion process.

new Gospel teaching, one had first to be aware of it. This would not necessarily lead to commitment – for some, knowledge of Luther's teaching led ultimately to rejection and a confirmed loyalty to familiar beliefs. But for those who would ultimately join the Protestant churches awareness led to some form of personal identification: as witnesses to Christ, or as members of Protestant churches. A more controversial question is whether membership of the church involved any real degree of understanding of the core doctrines of the faith. If historians have been sceptical on this question, then they have been able to draw on many gloomy contemporary assessments, often by disenchanted evangelists lamenting that their ceaseless activism had made so little impact on the ignorance of their flock.[10] Ultimately, however, and in whatever ways, Protestantism did succeed in engaging the loyalties of large numbers of Europe's citizens. This is reflected in a tradition of activism that represents here the last stage of our pyramid of engagement and commitment. This activism might take many forms: in the first generation acts of iconoclasm, in later days a determination to defend a Protestant culture against enemies within and without. But it was very real, even if those that professed this loyalty might not have satisfied the most demanding catechists, or the most persistently inquisitive compilers of the German visitation reports.

The investigation of this tiered anatomy of commitment proceeds through the examination in turn of different media by which the Reformation message was communicated and imbibed. This too reflects different patterns of investigation and scholarship in the last decades. The classic formulation of the Reformation process gives pride of place to the printed book. Ever since Elizabeth Eisenstein published her study of *The Printing Press as an Agent of Change*, scholars have built their interpretations on two apparently solid pillars: the identification of the technology of the book with an optimistic progress-orientated agenda of change; and an association of the book with Protestantism, the new religion.[11] Protestantism was the religion of the book; the book was a Protestant instrument.

This is an attractive and influential vision, though it should be recognized that it involves layers of assumptions that have not always been accurately tested. That Protestantism dominated the world of the printed book is certainly true for Germany in the 1520s, but it would

---

[10] Christopher Haigh, 'Puritan Evangelism in the Reign of Elizabeth I', *English Historical Review*, 92 (1977), pp. 30–58.

[11] Elizabeth Eisenstein, *The Printing Press as an Agent of Change* (2 vols., Cambridge, 1979).

not always be so. The book had been an effective servant of traditional religion before the evangelical controversies broke out in Germany, and it would be again. Once Catholic authors found their voice, the printed book would be a cornerstone of the Catholic counter-attack against Protestantism; in some parts of Europe, such as France, Catholics comfortably out-published their evangelical opponents almost from the first days of the Reformation movement.[12]

Our perception of the book is also shaped by certain much deeper assumptions about the role of print in intellectual culture. It is always assumed, for instance, that books are purchased for the words they contain, by people anxious, and able, to understand their contents. Put another way, it is accepted that analysis of the contents of books is an acceptable means of analysing the understanding of those for whom they were written. This is a gigantic, if perfectly understandable, assumption, but it really needs to be tested if we are to place the book correctly in the culture of persuasion. Perhaps unconsciously, by elevating the book in this way as a primary instrument of change, we are promoting a view of reading that is essentially modern (and academic). We conceive a world of private reading and private, largely individual decision making. But this essentially modernistic reconstruction of the process of religious choice goes very much against the grain of sixteenth-century society. In the early modern world most information was conveyed in public, communal settings: the market place, the church, a proclamation from the town hall steps. And it was conveyed by word of mouth, sometimes subsequently reinforced in print.

Religious choice may still be personal – as it often was – without being private. Decisions were often arrived at in a communal context. Much of the culture of persuasion in the sixteenth century was based on an assumption that decisions would be arrived at collectively. If the Reformation were to succeed, the culture of persuasion would have to work with the grain of this society. Reformers recognized a necessary double process of engagement: with the individual Christian, and with a collective religious consciousness that also had to be nurtured and reinforced. Hence in this study an attempt is made to relocate the role of the book as part of a broader range of modes of persuasion that used every medium of discourse and communication familiar to pre-industrial society. Preaching, singing and drama would all play their part, alongside the careful private tutelage of the new Protestant family in catechism class and Bible reading. But, in the first decades of evangelical agitation, that

[12] Andrew Pettegree and Matthew Hall, 'The Reformation and the Book: A Reconsideration', *Historical Journal*, 47 (2004), pp. 1–24.

lay very much in the future. The first explosive impact of the challenge to traditional religion was felt in public places: in the market place where news was exchanged and the first pamphlets were passed around, in the taverns, and, of course, in the churches. For it was here, through the traditional and time-honoured practice of preaching – always an event of special significance in every era of church history – that many of Europe's Christian people would first have been aware of the explosive ideas that would wreak such havoc on the comfortable practices of their forebears.

2   Preaching

Luther and his colleagues would make much play with the concept of the new evangelical sermon. We should certainly not underestimate the element of novelty, and the surprise of the new. The priest who commandeered the pulpit – often his own pulpit – to launch a bold attack on time-honoured practices and the doctrine of the community he served was bound to cause a sensation. The impact on his congregation, moved, excited, troubled or appalled, was clearly profound. But it was so precisely because the sermon was so fundamental a part of church life. It also played an important role in the wider information culture of pre-modern society. In a world where most information continued to be conveyed by word of mouth, few could doubt that preaching represented one of the primary means of communication with a wider public.

This was a world the reformers instinctively understood. Few doubted that, if they were to reach their audience, it would be through the medium of the word: and that meant in the first instance the word preached, as much as their published works. Many of those who would make up the first generation of the leaders of the Reformation had made their reputation first as preachers; they owed both their local reputation and the opportunity to contribute to the new evangelical movement to their skill in the pulpit. All, without exception, regarded preaching as fundamental to their duty as pastors, and to their evangelical mission.

The evidence, if any were necessary, lies in their conduct of their public careers. All the major reformers preached incessantly; in most cases almost to the last days of their life. From early in his career in Wittenberg, Luther preached both to his Augustinian order and (from 1514) in the town church, a torrent of sermons that came to form the cornerstone of his pastoral publications. Mark Edwards estimates that of 1,800 editions of Luther's works printed before 1526, some 40 per cent were published sermons.[1] Between 1519 and 1522 Ulrich Zwingli

---

[1] Mark U. Edwards Jr., *Printing, Propaganda and Martin Luther* (Berkeley, Calif., 1994), p. 27.

in Zurich delivered expository sermons that covered the Gospel of Matthew, the book of Acts and several of the Epistles. His call to be People's Priest in Zurich in 1518 was the proof of a singular talent, and the basis of the charismatic authority that sustained the Reformation in Zurich through its first tumultuous years. In the second generation, the commitment to preaching was, if anything, even more intense. Between 1531 and 1537 Zwingli's successor at Zurich, Heinrich Bullinger, preached six times weekly; in the course of his forty-four-year ministry he is thought to have preached over 7,000 sermons, covering every book of the Old and New Testaments. His zeal was more than matched by that of Jean Calvin in Geneva: preaching twice on a Sunday and on weekdays, Calvin preached as many as 286 sermons a year, a total of around 4,000 sermons through his whole ministry.[2]

For all this overwhelming evidence of the importance attached to preaching, the sermon nevertheless remains a problematic genre. For our investigation the core of the problem lies in the relationship between the written record and the aural form: the distance that seems to exist between the sermon as a literary genre and the preached word. This is a problem that faces all students of sermon literature from the mediaeval period onwards. Most sermons survive as epitome (in a manuscript or printed form), or as pastoral or polemical writings that have gone through a profound reshaping during the editorial process. From these evidential remains it is extremely difficult to reconstruct the sermon as event: some scholars have argued, indeed, that it is essentially impossible.[3] That may seem to be unduly pessimistic, for there is a wealth of valuable, if scattered, evidence for the impact of sermons during the Reformation century. This evidence will need to be carefully sifted if we are to address the central question that animates this present project: how did sixteenth-century people receive the preached message? What part did preaching play in the process of Reformation – first in the process of evangelization, later in church building and catechismal instruction?

To attempt to address these questions it is necessary to collect evidence for *how* the reformers preached, as well as what they said; and how their audiences reacted to their exhortations. These reactions were in turn conditioned by expectations of the sermon as genre, reaching back into the mediaeval tradition: a tradition which was also deeply influential in shaping the Reformation sermon. This mediaeval heritage was, as in so much, both rich and complex.

---

[2] James Thomas Ford, 'Preaching in the Reformed Tradition', in Larissa Taylor (ed.), *Preachers and People in the Reformations and Early Modern Period* (Leiden, 2001), p. 68.
[3] See, for instance, Larissa Taylor in her introduction to *Preachers and People*, p. x.

The sermon tradition

Much as the reformers might wish to pour scorn on the church they sought to reform, they could hardly deny that it had always directed considerable energy towards preaching the word. Luther and his followers would come to believe that much of this energy had been directed towards the promotion of false theological precepts; but the influence of the preaching tradition on the life of the church also exercised a profound influence on their own rhetorical and professional development. In the centuries before the Reformation, preaching was one of the most obvious, and often most spectacular, means of engagement between clergy and people. Some scholars would make much larger claims. For Corrie Norman, preaching lay at the centre of Italian culture and devotion. For David d'Avray, this development was institutionalized in European culture two centuries even before this: already by the thirteenth century 'preaching was becoming a system of mass communication'.[4] This communication process was far from one-way: mediaeval sermons called for a high level of participation on the part of large and eager audiences. People came in large numbers and expected a show: 'People at least in the major urban areas, expected that they and their societies would be dazzled, entertained, informed, even transformed, on a regular basis by preaching'.[5] In this, perhaps the most critical element was transformation. People expected to be moved, and all the theatrical or rhetorical elements of preaching – the careful preparation, the solemn opening, the whole choreography of emotion reaching a shattering climax – were all means towards this primary goal. To achieve this required enormous effort, careful thought and a high level of skill.

There can be little doubt that preaching constituted a powerful and prominent component of mediaeval religion. It is equally certain that its impact would have been very uneven. For most parishioners preaching was an occasional event, rather than part of the daily or weekly norm of religious observance. Town dwellers were more likely to have more frequent access to sermons, and to the most celebrated preachers. The Protestant reformers were very conscious that, if they were to transform society, then they would also have to transform the mediaeval culture of preaching. There were substantial differences between the way that the reformers perceived the role of preaching and the inherited mediaeval experience.

---

[4] Corrie Norman, 'The Social History of Preaching: Italy', in Taylor, *Preachers and People*, pp. 125–91. D. L. d'Avray, *Medieval Marriage Sermons. Mass Communication in a Culture without Print* (Oxford, 2001), p. 1.

[5] Norman, 'The Social History of Preaching', p. 125.

Most studies of the mediaeval preaching tradition stress two salient facts: that sermons were more likely to be given and heard during the penitential season of Lent than at any other time of the year; and that preaching was regarded as a special skill, possessed most particularly by members of the mendicant orders. Many of the most famous preachers of the day were either Dominicans or Franciscans, and members of these mendicant orders also dominated the emerging genre of the printed sermon epitome, from which we draw so much of our information as to what was preached in the pre-Reformation church. It is also customary to distinguish between sermons delivered as special events, and those that formed part of the routine of worship during the regular church year. Of the special sermons, it is the revivalist preaching of the most famous Italian preachers, Bernardino of Siena and Savonarola, that have caught the eye. While Savonarola's sermons electrified late fifteenth-century Florence, it is perhaps Bernardino's itinerant ministry that most encapsulates the mediaeval preaching tradition. From the time that he inaugurated his missionary ministry at Milan in 1417, Bernardino ranged the length and breadth of the peninsula, attracting crowds, celebrity and the hostility of clerical critics in almost equal measure. Bernardino's experience would prove indicative that the peculiar capacity of the sermon to rouse and unsettle would often prove unwelcome to established authorities. Between 1458 and 1463, the Franciscan Johannes Brugman, a sort of northern Bernardino, established a widespread peripatetic mission throughout the Netherlands: he visited some thirty-six places and travelled over 1,200 miles. Clearly Brugman's preaching had a huge impact. The proverbial expression, 'praten als Brugman', meaning to speak eloquently and persuasively, still current in contemporary Dutch usage, was already in use before the end of the fifteenth century.[6] Brugman was generally welcomed, but after one particularly lively performance in Amsterdam the town council forbade him to return. Forewarned and forearmed, the town council had sent agents to join the crowd and report anything untoward, which is why we are particularly well informed on what occurred.[7] On this occasion Brugman ended his sermon by raising his crucifix, and asking those in the audience who supported him to raise their hands (most did). The Amsterdam town council had particular reasons for concern (they

---

[6] A *stadsprotocol* of Amsterdam in 1492 mentions the expression: 'al cost ghy praten als Brugman'. Alastair Duke kindly provided me with this reference.

[7] R. B. Evenhuis, *Ook dat was Amsterdam; de kerk der hervorming in de goude eeuw* (2 vols., Amsterdam, 1965–7), vol. I, pp. 17–18. Jelle Bosma, 'Preaching in the Low Countries, 1450–1650', in Taylor, *Preachers and People*, pp. 333–6.

feared Brugman's promotion of the Observant movement might threaten the local religious houses), but their careful monitoring of a charismatic preacher set a precedent that would also have echoes in the Reformation era.

The concern for public order that characterized this incident seems to have been relatively unusual. There is considerable evidence that through the fifteenth century local demand for preaching was increasing. Many towns, far from discouraging preaching, expended city funds to hire preachers to give special sets of Lenten sermons, and competition for the most celebrated preachers could be intense. We know far less about preaching outside these times of special religiosity, though here too the evidence suggests that preaching was on the increase. The most significant strand of evidence lies in the growth, particularly in the cities of Germany and the Swiss Confederation, of endowed preacherships. These positions, quite separate from and supplementary to the normal structure of the parish ministry, were established in a large number of cities in the half-century before the Reformation. The funds were normally provided by the city or local princely ruler. The holders of these positions might be expected to preach up to one hundred sermons a year: in these places sermons could be expected to be regularly available. Even where there was no specific position founded to promote preaching, the efforts of preaching clergy were supported by the growth of the new printed genre of model sermon collections. These were intended, according to the most intense recent study of this literature, 'for preaching to the laity by fairly ordinary clergy in fairly ordinary places'.[8] This genre of literature proved enormously successful: to judge by surviving editions, it was one of the most important classes of pre-Reformation religious books. The most successful, a collection of over 200 model sermons for feast days and regular preaching throughout the year, was the achievement of the German Dominican Johannes Herold. This went through no fewer than eighty-four printed editions between 1470 and 1520.[9] Although no other single works matched this for enduring popularity, a number were significant bestsellers; the success of the genre is also indicated by the speed with which it moved from stately folio editions to the more practicable and portable octavo and quarto.

These collections did not contain sermons as they would have been delivered. They were intended, rather, to convey the essence of what was considered worth preaching in a very usable form. This qualification

---

[8] Anne T. Thayer, *Penitence, Preaching and the Coming of the Reformation* (Aldershot, St Andrews Studies in Reformation History, 2002), p. 7.
[9] Ibid., p. 17.

raises a problem that we will meet repeatedly in dealing with sermon literature: that published sermons give us little sense of the sermon as event; they leave little evidence of the life and spirit once in them. Some epitomes were quite short. But we know that many preachers preached for as many as four or five hours at a time.[10] In this case the printed epitome would have served as little more than a prompt or shell for a performance that would have derived much of its impact from repetition and sheer endurance (on both sides, when we remember that for sermons the audience usually stood throughout). To learn more about the manner and style of preaching to which clergy were intended to aspire we need to turn from the sermon collections to preaching manuals, another popular and developing genre in the period. Nevertheless, these model collections of sermons, of which several thousand survive from the pre-Reformation era, would have an enduring impact, not least on the reformers themselves. The genre lived on in an active tradition of model sermons, intended to be preached by those who lacked confidence or talent to devise their own. Many of the leading reformers made contributions to this literature, the most prominent and successful examples being Luther's Postils and Heinrich Bullinger's *Hausbuch* (known in England as the *Decades*). In some parts of the Protestant tradition, such as England, such authorized model sermons would be an enduring part of the landscape of the new reformed church.

When considering the impact of preaching in the pre-Reformation church, two qualifications must be entered. Firstly, even at the mundane and everyday level represented by the published sermon collections, hearing sermons was most likely an overwhelmingly urban experience. The survival of these collections tells us little about the penetration of preaching beyond the major centres of population where it was easiest to draw an audience.

Secondly, preaching was by and large not embedded in the fabric of routine worship. Even in towns where many sermons were preached, the sermon remained largely separate from the Mass. Indeed, in towns that moved towards the creation of an endowed preachership, there was considerable capacity for tension and rivalry between town preachers, with their special role and obligations, and the parish priests conducting their routine round of Masses. Alongside these workaday observances, the sermon service had a rhythm and tradition that was largely its own,

---

[10] In the case of one Italian Observant friar who routinely records the average length of his sermons, they average four and a half hours. Norman, 'Social History of Preaching', p. 141.

albeit some way short of a separate rite. In the years before the Reformation the sermon never lost its sense of being a special event.

What can one say about the content of pre-Reformation sermons? All the evidence points to the overwhelming concentration on the doctrine of penitence. The skilful preacher had first to move his audience to a consciousness of sin, and then to present a path to redemption. To this end the preacher would expect to draw both on a repertoire of shared scriptural knowledge, and on the hearers' everyday experience and concerns. In this respect the sermon was expected to do more than impact on the congregation's sense of their expectations in the next life: at its best the sermon could have a transforming effect on society, by calling men and women to lead a better life.

Within this general context there was room for a degree of variation, or even regional differences across the churches of Europe. A detailed examination of the model sermon collections suggests that, while all laid emphasis on the importance of contrition, there was considerable variation in identifying the place in the penitential process where forgiveness would take place. For some preachers confession was the cornerstone of the penitential process. Others offered more spiritual help via clerical ministrations, and understood forgiveness to require a combination of personal contrition and priestly absolution.[11] Many preachers did not spare their listeners from graphic enunciations of the consequences should they ignore their strictures. Several scholars have argued that preachers in the German lands presented a particularly bleak view of the consequences of persistence in sin; but such 'pulpit terrorism' would have had to be fiery indeed to match the impact of the Florentine Savonarola, the most famous of all pre-Reformation preachers. For Savonarola the consequences of sin were direct, terrifying and imminent:

O Italy, O princes of Italy, O prelates of the church, the wrath of God is over you, and you will not have any cure unless you mend your way . . . O noblemen, O powerful ones, O common people . . . Do penance while the sword is not out of its sheath, and while it is not stained with blood![12]

It is hard to judge whether it would have been the more protean, everyday preaching represented in the sermon collections, or the celebrity theatricals of Savonarola, that had the most enduring impact.

[11] Thayer, *Penitence*.
[12] Girolamo Savonarola, 'On the Renovation of the church', in John Olin (ed.), *The Catholic Reformation: Savonarola to Ignatius Loyola* (New York, 1992), pp. 14–15. On Savonarola see especially Donald Weinstein, *Savonarola and Florence* (Princeton, N.J., 1970).

Certainly, Savonarola's reputation continued to cast a long shadow into the sixteenth century. Luther had a more than grudging admiration for the great Florentine, and Savonarola's sermons were reprinted and read by Protestants until late in the sixteenth century. Against this, editions of the mediaeval revivalist Bernardino of Siena were dwarfed by the popularity of more humble practitioners like Herold, for all that the latter is scarcely known today. And the example of Savonarola was far from straightforward. While churchmen could take inspiration from his apocalyptical fervour and uncompromising asceticism, magistrates would draw from the Florentine experience a sense of the obvious dangers that flowed when a popular preacher with access to a prominent public platform moved from generalized strictures on immorality to specific criticisms of the ruling powers. In this respect, too, the Florentine stirs would provide a cautionary example.

The Reformation, as we shall see, would ultimately transform the office of preaching; the reformers nevertheless drew from the pre-Reformation heritage important lessons which they would apply to their own ministry. These were, not least, a sense of the sermon as performance; a belief that preaching could transform the lives of those who stood before them; and a belief that the spirit of God was embodied in the preacher, and that the preacher's rhetorical skill worked with divine grace. All of this remained vital to the preacher's art, as the Reformation moved the sermon to the heart of worship.

Reformers in the pulpit

By his own account Luther was initially a reluctant preacher. Speaking in later life to family and friends, he recalled that when first approached by his superior, Johannes Staupitz, to take up the office of preacher in his own Augustinian monastery, he recoiled in horror. He could hardly sustain such an office, he protested, when his own spiritual doubts were not yet resolved. But Staupitz was not to be denied, and so began a career in the pulpit that lasted until the last months of his life. From 1514 Luther was called also to preach in the town church, and it was no doubt this double office, ministering to both his clerical brethren and the city population, that helped prepare Luther for his extraordinary success as both a learned writer and a popular polemicist.

In the first years of the Reformation Luther's skills as a preacher and disputant would help sustain his challenge to authority in a number of highly charged and difficult situations: at the meeting of the Augustinian chapter at Heidelberg in 1518, at Leipzig in 1519, on the way to the Diet of Worms the following winter. But it was to the congregation at

Wittenberg that he preached the vast bulk of the 2,000 sermons that survive (perhaps a third of all he preached). In Wittenberg, after the institution of a reformed church order, the three services on a Sunday were all built around a sermon; there were also weekday services with sermons on the catechism and the Gospel. From 1522 Luther shared the main part of this burden with Johannes Bugenhagen, who succeeded him in the office of town preacher, but those who came to Wittenberg to hear the master were seldom disappointed. In most years Luther preached at least once a week, and sometimes much more. In 1528, despite countless other activities, he preached over 200 times.

Luther's preaching activity has left an extensive written record. Nevertheless, to hear Luther's voice in the pulpit this has to be used with some care. Luther, like most of his contemporaries, did not preach from a text. By all accounts he prepared his sermons with great care, but carried with him into the pulpit only the barest written outline. This *Konzept* has only very rarely survived; where it does it offers little more than a series of headings. The texts that have come down to us are based most often on notes made by student disciples sitting in the congregation (notes they often took in Latin, though Luther's sermons were obviously delivered in German). The vast majority of the sermons edited in the standard editions of Luther's writings – twenty-two volumes in the Weimar edition – are based on recensions of these contemporary records. It is questionable just how much of Luther's pulpit style would survive such a process, though sometimes Luther would be more involved, particularly if he intended to adapt a sermon for publication. Enough material with his personal involvement has survived for us to be able to capture something of Luther's authentic pulpit manner, particularly if we allow the published sermons to be augmented by Luther's later remarks on the printer's art in his Table Talk and correspondence and advice to friends.

Central both to Luther's concept of the preacher's art and his extraordinary skill was careful preparation, above all through reading the Scriptures. 'Some preachers', he wrote in 1542, 'are lazy and no good. They do not pray, they do not study, they do not read; they do not search the Scripture . . . In truth, you cannot read too much Scripture, and what you read you cannot read too carefully'. Luther's sermons were built round a careful exposition of the Scripture text. He followed the text from first to last, usually in a continuous sequence of sermons that dealt over a longer period with a whole book or Gospel. This method would become the leitmotif of the great reformers, many of whom have left, as a principal legacy of their writings, great series of such expository sermons. It was not necessary, within such a structure, to give equal attention to all parts of the text. Luther, in particular, is distinguished by a relentless attention to the central message, the heart or kernel of the text, to which he would return again and again. To Luther this method of preaching became a living vindication of the central principle of the Gospel movement, the return to Scripture, *Rein Evangelium*.

In his later reflections on preaching Luther would scorn what he regarded as the oratorical tricks of the pre-Reformation church. He spoke scathingly of the rhetorical repertoire of those who preached to impress the great: alliterative phrases, plays on words, balance and polish. He was particularly merciless in denouncing those who looked for popularity through a wild theatricality of delivery: a preacher should strive rather for simplicity and clarity. Above all he must realize that he spoke with God's voice. The fear of the young priest, overwhelmed with the responsibility of representing the Almighty through his words, never entirely left Luther.

It was not then Luther's pulpit manner that most obviously impressed contemporaries (though his celebrity no doubt gave his appearances in the pulpit an unmistakable aura). Luther conquered his audience through the careful, systematic exploration of Scripture in terms finely tuned to their lives and understanding. Luther's sermons are intercut with imagined dialogue, often with both parties represented in the first person. Here, for instance, is Luther on marriage, imagining the horrified objections of a reluctant inner voice, Natural Reason:

Takes a look at married life, she turns up her nose and says, 'Alas, must I rock the baby, wash its diapers, make its bed, smell its stench, stay up nights with it, take care of it when it cries, heal its rashes and sores, and on top of that care for my wife, provide for her, labour at my trade, take care of this and take care of that, do this and do that, endure this and endure that, and whatever else of bitterness and drudgery married life involve? What, should I make such a prisoner of myself?'

. . . And what does Christian faith say to this? It opens its eyes, looks upon all insignificant, distasteful and despised duties in the Spirit, and is aware that they are all adorned with divine approval as with the costliest gold and jewels.[13]

This search for the common voice was entirely intended: Luther advocated simplicity in preaching with all the authority of a man who had debated with the best technical minds on equal terms. 'He who teaches most simply, childishly, popularly, that's the best preacher.'

---

[13] Martin Luther, *The Estate of Marriage* (1522). Cited in Susan C. Karant-Nunn and Merry E. Wiesner-Hanks (eds.), *Luther on Women. A Sourcebook* (Cambridge, 2003), p. 107.

Complicated thoughts and issues we should discuss in private with other clever people. I don't think of Dr Pomeranius [Bugenhagen], Jonas, or Philip in my sermon. They know more about it than I do. So I don't preach to them. I just preach to Hansie or Betsy.[14]

Nevertheless, for all this search for simplicity, Luther's sermons were not without their evident stylistic traits. We have observed two in the example above: the copious heaping up of linked examples, and the establishment of antithesis through imagined dialogue. In both structure and exposition, Luther made continuous use of paired opposites: Law/Gospel, sin/grace, God/Satan. This went to the very heart of his belief, an expression of his dialectic conviction of the apocalyptic struggle that fuelled his assault on the papacy and continued to shape his life. Sometimes the tensions of the unrelenting obligations to act as God's instrument spilled over in a torrent of pessimistic invective: for Luther, for all that he devoted endless care to engaging his audience, certainly did not spare them. In 1530 the unregenerate nature of Wittenberg society brought him to crisis, and a dire warning:

I am sorry I ever freed you from the tyrants and papist. You ungrateful beasts, you are not worthy of the Gospel. If you don't improve, I will stop preaching rather than cast pearls before swine.[15]

His lament was one that would become a familiar refrain for the Reformation preacher: even in places exposed to the true Gospel, people continued to live a life of dissipation. In Wittenberg, Luther charged, the Reformation had brought no rush of generosity of spirit.

In times past people gave for temples and altars, now everybody scrapes everything together for himself. There is nothing going on but scraping and scratching. But in two years the Turk will be at your door. Just don't think you are safe. If you were pious you would accept the Word, trust God, do good to your neighbour, and take heed to your calling.[16]

Luther suspended his preaching for nine months before his spirits revived. But the tensions exposed in this interlude – the preacher as pastor, the pastor as prophet – would become familiar to all those who laboured as preachers in the Reformation period.

For Ulrich Zwingli, preaching was the cornerstone, not only of his work as the reformers of Zurich, but of his whole career. Zwingli's

---

[14] Fred W. Meuser, *Luther the Preacher* (Minneapolis, Minn., 1983), p. 53.
[15] Ibid., p. 29.
[16] Ibid., pp. 29–30. For Luther's preoccupation with the Turkish threat, see Gordon Rupp, 'Luther against "The Turk, the Pope and the Devil"', in Peter Newman Brooks (ed.), *Seven-headed Luther* (Oxford, 1983), pp. 255–73.

appointment in 1518 as People's Priest in the Great Minster was an outstanding promotion for a man whose extended apprenticeship at Glarus and Einsiedeln had not been free of controversy.[17] The canons who swayed the appointment no doubt chose him because of his outspoken views on the incendiary issue of mercenary service (he had supported the Zurich position). It was a highly sensitive appointment, and even before taking office Zwingli had to explain to the canons his concept of the preaching function. Once installed, Zwingli adopted a practice close to that of Luther, of serial exposition, beginning with the Gospel of Matthew. Only gradually did Zwingli move towards the harsh denunciation of clerical abuses that underpinned his call for root and branch reform.

No text survives for any sermon preached by Zwingli before 1522. But we know from later accounts that the People's Priest swiftly extended the range of his targets to encompass many of the practices and much of the personnel of the old church: monks, tithing, the cult of saints. In this campaign for renewal and reform the pulpit was Zwingli's major weapon. Each stage in the gathering conflict in Zurich, the symbolic breaking of the Lenten fast, the subsequent confrontation with the bishop, was framed by Zwingli's advocacy in the pulpit. A significant moment was reached in November 1522, when Zwingli was formally released from all the normal duties of his office (such as hearing confession and saying Mass) and allowed to devote himself wholly to preaching – a sure sign that his supporters were gaining ground among the city council. From this point the pressure for decisive action became unrelenting. When in 1523 the council summoned delegates for the first public meeting intended to resolve the conflicts raised by the evangelical criticism, they cited as their primary motivation the evident dissension among the preachers. If this was so, it was dissension they had done much to foment.

Zwingli's career as a preacher was comparatively short. The spectacular defeat of Zurich forces as the battle of Kappel in 1531 exposed the dangers of his relentless pursuit of reform. Even those who had not paled at the full implications of his visions of a purified church within Zurich were now exposed to the consequences of his reckless desire to extend the Reformation throughout the Confederation. That the Zurich Reformation survived owed much to the determined, understated leadership of Heinrich Bullinger, Zwingli's friend and successor. Bullinger's fond admiration and unflinching defence of his predecessor did not disguise a

---

[17] G. R. Potter, *Zwingli* (Cambridge, 1976), pp. 22–46. Bruce Gordon, *The Swiss Reformation* (Manchester, 2002), pp. 46–51.

huge temperamental difference. Bullinger was prepared to work with the bruised and humiliated city fathers to restore trust in the project of reform.[18]

Preaching, inevitably, played a large part in this process. Bullinger shared with Zwingli a clear sense of the centrality of the preaching office: the minister had a clear obligation to preach the Gospel to an earthly community consisting of both the elect and the damned. The minister, distinguished by his calling, and marked by ordination, employed his training in biblical exegesis to rouse the inner Word present in the community. The changing times, however, called for some differences of emphasis. The task of consolidation and rebuilding implied a more settled relationship between minister and congregation. On the side of the minister Bullinger and his colleagues laid greater stress on formal training and ordination; on the part of the congregation the need was for patience rather than a relentless call to arms:

The sermon ought to be held with great warmth and fervent love for the listeners, for their improvement and edification in God as takes place among the pious. Thus the sheep of Christ hear the voice of their Lord, the true shepherd. They follow it because they recognize it. Through coarse onslaughts the gentle hearts will only become embittered and ravaged. Then our sermons only give rise to irritable, hostile, rebellious and harmful people.[19]

Of all the great reformers, Calvin was perhaps the least prepared, by temperament and training, to undertake the preaching office. Wrested from a life of scholarship to assist the process of Reformation in Geneva, Calvin initially struggled to make sense of the demands of his office, and the peculiar constraints of the serpentine local politics. Three years of enforced exile in Strasbourg provided the belated in-service training the young scholar had previously lacked. He returned to Geneva in 1541 far better equipped for the heavy burdens of a preaching ministry.

For the next twenty years Calvin sustained a preaching regime that would have been remarkable even in a man in robust good health (which he was not).[20] He preached twice every Sunday, and on every weekday in

---

[18] Gordon, *Swiss Reformation*, pp. 135–49, 173–87. On Bullinger see also now Bruce Gordon and Emidio Campi (eds.), *Architect of Reformation. An Introduction to Heinrich Bullinger, 1504–1575* (Grand Rapids, Mich., 2004) and Emidio Campi (ed.), *Heinrich Bullinger und Seine Zeit, Zwingliana*, 31 (2004).

[19] Wolfgang Capito quoted in Bruce Gordon, 'Preaching and the Reform of the Clergy in the Swiss Reformation', in Andrew Pettegree (ed.), *The Reformation of the Parishes. The Ministry and the Reformation in Town and Country* (Manchester, 1993), p. 78.

[20] T. H. L. Parker, *Calvin's Preaching* (Edinburgh, 1992). Charles L. Cooke, 'Calvin's Illnesses and their Relation to Christian Vocation', in Timothy George (ed.), *John Calvin and the church. A Prism of Reform* (Louisville, Ky., 1990), pp. 59–70.

alternate weeks. This was in addition to his scholarly lectures, delivered in the Auditorium next door to his church. Like other preachers of the Reformation, Calvin followed a principle of sequential exegesis, moving steadily through books of the Old and New Testaments.

Calvin was, by all accounts, a remarkable preacher. His command of the Scriptures and a prodigious memory combined with his early training in the law and classics to produce a masterpiece of concise and lucid exposition. We know a great deal more about Calvin's preaching than is the case with most sixteenth-century figures, because in 1549 a group of admirers decided that his sermons should be systematically recorded.[21] A skilled stenographer was employed to take down the sermons as they were delivered. Huge volumes of these sermons, written up in fair copies, were then deposited in the town archives, where they remained until disposed of in the nineteenth century. Only a relatively small proportion survive, but enough to allow us a fascinating view of a master preacher at the height of his powers.[22]

Calvin was never wholly comfortable with the recording of his sermons. In his own mind there was a clear distinction between the scholarly lectures, which he willingly edited for publication, and sermons preached for a particular local audience. It is far from accidental that even while Calvin was a massively popular author – sometimes his published output would approach half a million words in a year – few of his sermons were authorized for publication in his lifetime. In his sermons Calvin had in mind very much the needs of his local audience, the mixed congregation of native Genevans and fellow French exiles standing patiently before him. He was not afraid to allude to local issues or to take sides in controversial questions. For the magistrates, arrayed in the front rows, Calvin's sermons had an uncomfortable unpredictability. William Naphy, exploring the records of the Genevan city archives, has found several instances where, as the congregation spilled back onto the streets, different factions came to blows, as some took offence at Calvin's

---

[21] The copyist was paid by the Bourse française, the fund established to care for the immigrant poor. Jeannine E. Olson, *Calvin and Social Welfare. Deacons and the Bourse française* (Selinsgrove, Pa., 1989), p. 34.

[22] The full story of the disposal of Calvin's sermons in 1805 is told by Bernard Gagnebin, 'L'histoire des manuscrits des sermons de Calvin', in *Jean Calvin, Sermons sur le Livre d'Esaie, chapitres 13–29* (Supplementa Calviniana, vol. II, Neukirchen, 1961), pp. xiv–xxviii. The corpus of surviving works has, however, been materially increased by the recent discovery in London of three volumes of the sermons on Isaiah, preached between 1557 and 1559. Max Engammare, 'Calvin Incognito in London: The Rediscovery in London of Sermons on Isaiah', *Proceedings of the Huguenot Society of London*, 26 (1996), pp. 453–62.

words and others revelled in their discomfiture.[23] But no one was truly spared. This is Calvin in 1551, reflecting (with shades of Luther) on the lack of impact made by a decade of Gospel preaching:

When a city becomes renowned for having received the Word of God, the world will reckon that the city ought to be, as a result, so much better governed, that such order will prevail as to accord right and justice to one and all. Therefore, if things turn out to be no better than anywhere else, or worse than this, as if the truth of God were not to be found there at all, what is one to say? Will they not appear to be the worst people in the world? Listen to the papist talking! 'Oh the Genevans! They claim to be better than everybody else, because they want to reform the whole world; anyone would think they are angels themselves. But just look at the way they actually behave! If you go to Geneva you will find just as many tricks and petty frauds as ever in their shops. You will be robbed and fleeced, not only in business dealings but in everything else as well'.

How sad it is that nowadays there is among us more unbelief and impiety than has ever been seen before, and that this is so plain to be observed. In truth the Lord makes his Grace available to us in as much abundance as one could ask, but we trample it underfoot. We have such malicious impiety in us that it looks as though we have decided deliberately and on purpose to despise God. Everywhere around, there is nothing to be seen but blasphemies, scandals and ruin; the world is so disorderly that the impiety I can see in Geneva today is of such enormity that it is like seeing down a chasm into the very mouth of Hell.[24]

The year 1551 was a period of crisis for Calvin's relations with the City Council, and this sermon may reflect an unusually pessimistic moment. Even so, it is an unfamiliar perspective on the city John Knox would famously experience within a few years as the 'the most perfect school of Christ that ever was in the earth since the days of the apostles'. Perhaps, though, we are misled if we imagine that sixteenth-century peoples would share a modern sensibility or indignation at such outspoken criticism. We certainly err if we interpret such statements as a piece of cool historical analysis of the success or failure of the Reformation to this point. For all Luther's contempt for rhetoric or flamboyant theatricals, people still expected the Reformation preacher to stand in the established prophetic tradition: they looked for shades of Jeremiah or John the Baptist, if not of Savonarola.

In Calvin's case we know that his reputation as a preacher spread far beyond the borders of Geneva. The Catholic historian Florimond de

---

[23] William G. Naphy, *Calvin and the Consolidation of the Genevan Reformation* (Manchester, 1994), pp. 159, 161.

[24] Calvin's sermons on Micah, cited in Alastair Duke, Gillian Lewis and Andrew Pettegree, *Calvinism in Europe. Documents* (Manchester, 1992), pp. 30–4.

Raemond offers a revealing anecdote of a Savoyard nobleman, returning from the wars, who decided to make a detour through Geneva to hear the celebrated preacher. Arriving in church he settled to observe the sermon, only to find, to his astonishment, his own wife and daughter sitting elsewhere in the congregation. Surprise turned to horror as his wife, spying him as they left the church, ran to Calvin for protection. 'Oh sir save me', she exclaimed, 'It is Monsieur my papist husband who has come to get me!' It was left to Calvin to subdue the hubbub and find a satisfactory resolution.[25]

Florimond de Raemond tells the story to warn against the flighty susceptibility of those too easily seduced by the siren call of the reformed preachers. The human tragedy is very real, but for us, brought up on a vision of Calvin as an emotionally desiccated model of forbidding austerity, it is this vision of him as a celebrity preacher and tourist attraction that is most revelatory. In fact, beneath the grating (and always somewhat forced) humility of Calvin's epistolary style, he had a very clear view of his self-worth, and an enhanced gift for the dramatic moment. Summoned back to Geneva in 1541, three years after his acrimonious departure, Calvin returned to the pulpit with no allusion to past events. He merely turned to the next verse in the interrupted sequence as if nothing untoward had occurred since his last sermon.[26] Nothing could more completely have captured Calvin's sense of the preacher's office.

Preachers and people

In the years that followed, the preaching of the great reformers would be a beacon and an inspiration, as well as a model of the new evangelical method of systematic exposition. From the moment that Luther published his *Sermon on Indulgences* in German in 1518, evangelical sermons were made available in numerous printed editions; they would be a staple of Reformation printing throughout the century and beyond. Nevertheless the evangelical movement could not have prevailed had it relied on the exclusive efforts of a tiny group of leading reformers. The Reformation became a movement only because the initiative of Wittenberg and Zurich was emulated in dozens of pulpits across central Europe.

In this respect it is highly significant that Luther's movement first began to make itself felt in many towns during the period 1521–2, when

---

[25] Florimond de Raemond, *Histoire*. Translated extract in Duke, Lewis and Pettegree, *Calvinism in Europe. Documents*, pp. 37–8.
[26] Parker, *Calvin's Preaching*, p. 60.

Luther was sequestered from public view in the protective custody of the Wartburg, after his condemnation at the Diet of Worms. In the anxious months when his fate was unknown, the cause was sustained almost entirely by brave men who carried the cause for reform into their own pulpits.

The impact of this preaching was profound and demonstrable. Within a matter of years or even months the preachers had gathered a popular following prepared to press an agenda of reform on an often reluctant city council. The precise nature of the reform agenda proclaimed from these pulpits remains, however, more elusive, to the extent that interpretation of this crucial moment of the Reformation breakthrough remains highly contested. Some years ago the German church historian Bernd Moeller argued that the Reformation achieved its unprecedented impact because the first generation of preachers recapitulated for their audiences a disciplined and coherent view of Luther's new doctrine of salvation. Examining printed sermon collections, Moeller found in particular a common emphasis on the core doctrine of justification by faith.[27]

Other commentators have been less convinced. Concentrating on a more specific geographical area, the towns and villages around Wittenberg in Saxony, Susan Karant-Nunn found a far less coherent and homogeneous pattern. To her the wide variety of teachings propounded by Luther's first clerical followers evoked the tradition of *Wildwuchs*, or wild evangelical growth, postulated by the earlier work of Franz Lau.[28] Recent scholarship, while not denying the influence of Luther's writings, has tended to support the main lines of Karant-Nunn's argument. It is justly observed that Moeller, by drawing his evidence from published (and largely Latinate) sermon collections, inevitably concentrates on the most educated priests from among the first generation of evangelicals (though of course, since these men were by and large speaking from the main city pulpits, their influence would have been disproportionately greater). And even if these men (at least in the subsequent published versions) did lay stress on Luther's core doctrine of salvation, is this necessarily what their audiences heard? Reporting on the public agitation that accompanied the sensation of Luther's progress across

[27] Bernd Moeller, 'Was wurde in der Frühzeit des Reformation in den deutschen Städten gepredigt?', *Archiv für Reformationsgeschichte*, 75 (1984), pp. 176–93. Now in English translation: 'What was Preached in German Towns in the Early Reformation?', in C. Scott Dixon (ed.), *The German Reformation* (Oxford, 1999), pp. 36–52.

[28] Susan Karant-Nunn, 'What was Preached in German Cities in the Early Years of the Reformation? *Wildwuchs* versus Lutheran Unity', in Philip N. Bebb and Sherrin Marshall, *The Process of Change in Early Modern Europe* (Athens, Ohio, 1988), pp. 81–96.

Germany to the Diet of Worms, the Imperial Legate Aleander made little attempt to hide from Charles V the high degree of enthusiasm evinced for the new celebrity. But the issue that had most seized the public imagination, aside from the drama of Luther's fate, was his evocation of the Scripture principle: *Rein Evangelium*, the 'Pure Gospel', was the slogan on everyone's lips.

This is powerful and important evidence, for it seems that those who promoted Luther's message were also aware of the charged and diverse implications of the evangelical appropriation of the call for 'Pure Gospel'. For this was at one and the same time an unexceptional statement of a generalized desire for Christian regeneration and a partisan slogan: impossible to gainsay if the first, highly inflammatory when the second. The potent ambiguity of the phrase was what gave it its extraordinary power, a power ruthlessly exploited by the city magistrates when they moved, usually after a passage of years, to institutionalize the Reformation. The decisive moment of defeat and repudiation for the Catholic clergy was often couched in terms of an order that henceforth only Pure Gospel was to be preached. The threadbare evocation of a non-partisan purpose was finally abandoned when these orders were followed by abolition of the Mass and expulsion of the remaining adherents of the old faith.

The protean versatility of the call for the 'Pure Gospel' was a large part of its appeal. Evangelical preachers could build around their pleas for an idealized vision of Christian purity a denunciation of corrupt local clergy, and the condemnation of any number of deplored practices and financial exactions. In many parts of Germany, as their auditors revelled in the almost daily sensations surrounding Luther's struggles, this proved an intoxicating brew. But for Luther's movement there was also a price to be paid. For, in Thomas Brady's masterful summation, the reformers could not always control the interpretations placed on their words. The evangelical leaders:

gained hearings largely because they offered answers to long-posed questions, and they sowed seed on long-prepared soil. Even when such answers and such seed were not, from the preachers' perspective, central to their Gospel, they hoped that by addressing such questions – usury, tithes, clerical immunities, clerical indiscipline – they would win a hearing for pure doctrine. Luther showed the way by trying to touch every sensitive nerve of his day, at the price of sowing unclarity about his message, though not about his person. Some of his partisans came to see the world through his message; others did not.[29]

---

[29] Thomas Brady, *Turning Swiss: Cities and Empire, 1450–1550* (Cambridge, 1985), p. 153.

This is well put. For the urban reformers the fruits of victory were always tainted by the need to rein in the expectations of those roused by their evocation of a world reformed and renewed. Necessary though those supporters were to their initial triumph, their expectations could be a long-term cause of volatility and political instability. In this new world the preachers would struggle to re-orientate the expectations of their congregations to the twin imperatives of true doctrine and worldly obedience. But this is to leap ahead. For the moment we need to re-enter the world of those who sought to bring Luther's message to life in their own communities.

The evangelical message made its first inroads, not surprisingly, in the towns and villages around Wittenberg. In Zwickau, Luther's cause was taken up, among others, by Johann Egranus, preacher in St Mary's church until 1521, when he moved on to Joachimstal. One of his auditors, Stephen Roth, took intermittent notes on his sermons, preached between 1519 and 1522, in both places. To judge by these notes Egranus offered a pot pourri of current issues and theological precepts. He criticized the Pope and the cult of saints; he affirmed the validity of only two sacraments, and declared that only Christ was man's true intercessor. None of this would have disturbed Luther, though Egranus never proclaimed a personal allegiance to the Wittenberg reformers.

'We should not', he suggested in a sermon of 1522, 'be divided into sects so that we say, "I am a Martinian, I am an Eckite, I am an Emserite, I am a Philippist, I am a Carlstadter, I am a Leipziger, I am a papist", and whatever more sects there may be. I will follow Saint Paul and say that I am of Jesus Christ. I preach the Gospel . . . In sum I am a follower of the Gospel and a Christian'.[30]

Luther would have been less troubled by this repudiation of party allegiance than by the fact that Thomas Müntzer was numbered among Egranus's colleagues at Zwickau. Müntzer was a robust and rousing preacher. His attacks on the mendicants found considerable resonance, not least because he was prepared to single out particular individuals for criticism. Interestingly, it was not the uproar that followed Müntzer's sermons that concerned the city council. Only when Müntzer turned his fire on his fellow minister Egranus did the council turn against him, and resolve to seek a replacement.

Events in Zwickau illustrate one important model of Reformation preaching: an established and prominent member of the local clergy proclaiming allegiance to the Gospel teaching and attempting to carry his congregation with him. This model, following the precept of Luther

---

[30] Karant-Nunn, 'What was Preached?', p. 84.

himself and Zwingli in Zurich, brought the Reformation some of its most valuable and influential adherents. Elsewhere, however, reformed preaching came to German and Swiss cities by a more complicated process. Sometimes the Gospel would be proclaimed by a daring newcomer, defying the established church hierarchy by appealing directly to the laity. Elsewhere the initiative for an appointment came from the congregation itself. In Worms in 1524 the parish of St Michael deposed its parish priest and appointed a former monk who had taken a wife. The inspiration for their actions came from the parish priest of St Magnus, who had taught for the last two years that every Christian community had the power to elect its own minister. In this early moment of evangelical fervour such teaching could create a powerful bond between preacher and people. In several places congregations fought an extended battle with a sceptical city council for the right to hear an evangelical minister. In Hamburg groups of engaged citizens in the city's four parishes first articulated the wish to appoint an evangelical minister in 1523, but three years would elapse before the council eventually gave way. Such a protracted struggle itself played an important role in shaping the Reformation movement, as the frustrated parishioners were obliged to articulate with ever greater force and clarity their reasons for judging their existing clergy inadequate. In this situation conflict itself played a pedagogic role, guided no doubt by advice received by leaders of the new movement both within and beyond the city gates.

The complex dynamic at work in the first Reformation movement can be effectively illustrated by the case of one of the leading cities of the Empire, Strasbourg.[31] In Strasbourg, the Reformation was initiated by Matthias Zell, preacher in the Chapel of St Laurence. In 1521 he was moved first to defend Luther against his enemies, and then to announce that he himself would preach the pure Gospel according to the new method. This was greeted with public enthusiasm. After Zell attempted to move his sermons to the main cathedral pulpit, only to find it locked against him, local carpenters constructed a portable pulpit that was taken into the body of the cathedral for each sermon, and then carefully stored by supportive citizens.

Public support made it impossible to silence Zell even when he turned his fire on the bishop. The year 1523 brought a new sensation when a leading member of the cathedral hierarchy, Wolfgang Capito, took to the pulpit to affirm the new movement. According to a contemporary chronicler, 'the people crowded round with wonder, that a provost should

---

[31] Miriam Usher Chrisman, *Strasbourg and the Reform. A Study in the Process of Change* (New Haven, Conn., 1967), pp. 81–130.

preach and concern himself with such trifles'. Capito's conversion was a major surprise, but it was the authorities' attempt to discipline a much humbler figure, the married priest Anton Firm, that provoked the decisive confrontation. A petition requesting the council to provide the parish churches with evangelical preachers was followed by an orchestrated attack on the Dominican monastery, and then a second petition making three main demands: the abolition of the Mass, the closure of the religious houses, and the removal of idols from the churches. The council found itself obliged to give way; an edict of Easter 1525 agreed that the Mass should be abolished.

Since the lay petition of 1525 proved decisive in the case of Strasbourg, it is interesting to compare its demands with the views articulated by the preachers in the preceding four years. Of these we are reasonably well informed, since notaries assigned by the cathedral had attended evangelical sermons to monitor the views expressed. According to these and other accounts, Zell had preached against the Mass, denied Purgatory, and censured the practice of tithing. Caspar Hedio had echoed the criticism of tithing, while Martin Bucer contributed a blistering attack on the local cult of St Aurelie. Capito was more conciliatory, and called for mutual understanding between the contending parties. What is interesting is that the lay petitioners should have distilled from these diverse and wide-ranging criticisms a pointed agenda that focused clearly on the essentials of a local programme of reform. Here one can only guess at the informal process of negotiation and recension from which emerged so coherent a manifesto.

For the evangelical clergy, this lay participation did not come without a price. Congregations energized by evangelical preaching had also been empowered. They felt, not surprisingly, greatly strengthened in their future relations with a clergy that they had fought so hard to install. Shorn of the sacramental powers that had bolstered even the most inadequate of the pre-Reformation clergy, the new ministerial cadre faced a demanding audience fully conscious of their role in shaping the new church. For the preacher in the pulpit this created an uneasy dynamic that the Reformation never entirely resolved.

Taming the prophet

In the first years of the Reformation, preaching often provided the decisive impetus for lay activism. Sometimes, as in the Strasbourg example, an orderly petition succeeded in ensuring the abrogation of the Mass, or the removal of images from the churches. But sometimes, where the authorities proved hesitant or recalcitrant, their hand might be forced by unauthorized action. Attacks on church buildings to remove the disapproved statues and pictures were a feature of each stage of the Reformation movement, and often such iconoclastic attacks followed directly after idols had been denounced from the pulpit. In the winter of 1521 Wittenberg experienced a wave of attacks on church property after Luther's colleague Karlstadt had spoken out against the images – Luther was forced to make a rapid return from the Wartburg to quell the uproar. These early stirs set a pattern that would be replicated again and again when members of the new evangelical churches wished to force the issue in the face of political opposition. In both France at the beginning of the Religious Wars, and in Scotland, critical incidents occurred directly after pulpit denunciations of idolatry. When John Knox preached in the parish church of Holy Trinity in St Andrews in June 1559, with the Scottish Reformation delicately poised and opposition forces marshalling against him, he chose as his text the Gospel story of the cleansing of the Temple. The conclusion of the service led directly to forcible and violent removal of all the images from the burgh's parish and cathedral churches – the reformers had seized a decisive, and it would prove irreversible, initiative. A similar moment of political catharsis followed the arrival of Pierre Viret in the southern French cities of Nîmes and Montpellier in 1562. Sometimes, in retrospect, the reformed leadership would attempt to distance themselves from direct responsibility for such actions, but the authorities were not deceived. Few really believed that bitter and incendiary denunciations of idols could be balanced by pious warnings to wait on the magistrate.

Iconoclasm represented the most spectacular collision between the competing imperatives of reformation: the renovation of the church and the preservation of social order. But it was not the first or only occasion on which the passions raised by Reformation preaching would trouble the new Protestant societies.

Luther shared absolutely the belief, prominent also among the charismatic preachers of the previous generation, that when the preacher mounted the pulpit God spoke through him. It was to him, and to many that followed in the new Protestant churches, an awesome responsibility. The English Protestant divine Richard Greenham experienced 'very sharp and trembling fears in the flesh' before preaching, which he attributed to the malevolent energy expended by Satan to stop his mouth.[32] It certainly could not have been unfamiliarity, since Greenham preached every day but one in the week and twice on a Sunday. The

---

[32] Kenneth L. Parker and Eric J. Carlson, *Practical Divinity: The Works and Life of Revd Richard Greenham* (Aldershot, St Andrews Studies in Reformation History, 1998), p. 62.

sense of the responsibility that came with charismatic authority was one that united many preachers through the Reformation century: the more so as it was so obvious that this responsibility could be abused.

From the first days of the evangelical movement Luther had felt his mission troubled, even imperilled, by the reckless enthusiasm of those who took on the burden of prophecy without qualification or calling. In Wittenberg his personal authority was sufficient to rein in Karlstadt, and to quell the Zwickau prophets, but others proved beyond even Luther's powers to restrain. The bitter quarrel with Thomas Müntzer, an early enthusiast whose radical eschatological fervour had led him to embrace a mystical doctrine of redemption through suffering, is a case in point. For Müntzer too, preaching was a means to call the people to repentance:

If our wretched, crude Christian people is to be saved . . . the first, and all-important step is to listen to an earnest preacher who, like John the baptiser, will cry out piteously and dolefully in the waste places of the mad, raging hearts of men, so that through God's work they may find the way to become receptive to God's word.[33]

Although Müntzer's social Gospel found its bloody nemesis in the Peasants' War, his radical interpretation of Luther's call for spiritual renewal had brought the evangelical enterprise close to shipwreck. The movement would face many such challenges during the years of church building. This was hardly a surprise. The Reformation had gained much of its early following by harnessing a visceral sense of the shortcomings of the pre-Reformation clergy. Luther's response was to strip the clergy of their vital intercessory power, postulating instead a direct, unmediated relationship between the Christian and his redeemer: a complex of ideas sometimes encapsulated in the clumsy formula, 'the priesthood of all believers'. But this was a potent phrase, with emotional resonance that went beyond the limited theological implications that Luther had in mind. His rather idealized vision of an empowered laity stopped well short of the gift of spiritual interpretation. In his view, only a lifetime of continuous study equipped one for the awesome responsibility of preaching.

The point at which the Reformation evolved from a movement of protest to building a new church therefore required a difficult process of adjustment. Each church faced an early challenge from enthusiasts who chafed at the limitations of institutional reform, and who scorned the dead letter of Scripture if it were not revivified by inspired prophetic

---

[33] Tom Scott, *Thomas Müntzer. Theology and Revolution in the German Reformation* (Basingstoke, 1989), p. 63.

interpretation. In Zurich disappointed early supporters of Zwingli found refuge in alternative communities led by men of little formal theological education: a common characteristic of the early Anabaptist movement. Anabaptism found its grim apotheosis in the fiasco of Münster, proclaimed the New Jerusalem in 1534 amidst wild enthusiasm from its radicalized population. For Protestants and Catholics alike this was a grim warning of the consequences of unrestrained prophecy. A less spectacular but stubbornly enduring problem was that posed by ministers, often former priests, who adhered to the new movement, but lacked either the theological discipline or the learning to serve it. In the new Lutheran churches of the German princely states the most obvious case was of former parish priests who transferred to the new church without any clear concept of how their new duties differed from those of the old Mass priests they had been. But even in the second generation, the Calvinist movements in France and the Netherlands were afflicted by many recruits of questionable ability. In France, the pace of growth of the Huguenot movement between 1560 and 1563 (from a mere handful to over one thousand churches) meant that it was simply impossible to keep close control over those who proposed themselves for ministerial office. The French national synods issued regular lists of expelled or disqualified ministers, warning churches to beware lest they attempt to intrude themselves elsewhere. Some of these descriptions read like an ecclesiastical wanted poster:

One Charlir or Charles, who says of himself that he was a Counsellor of Grenoble . . . a man of mean stature, his beard waxing grey, deposed from the ministry of Uzerche by the brethren of Limoges for lying, cheating, forgeries, roguish tricks, drunkenness, unchaste kissings, and at Pamier for dancing and contumacy against the church. This fellow intrudes himself into all places where he can get admittance to preach.

Simon du Plessis, going by the names of Mr Peter Grueill, La Mulle, Nevill, Grand-champo, La Jaunière, formerly a Franciscan friar, deposed at Orbec by the classis of Eureux, because without any call or ordination he had usurped the ministry of the Gospel, quitting and retaking at pleasure his friar's weeds.

Jean Clopet, alias Chald, a wretch full of heresies, a champion for the Mass asserting its goodness, in two points only excepted, viz. prayers unto the saints and the dead. Maintaining that the good and bad have equal privilege to communicate in the body of Christ . . . and that Calvin did very ill in writing of predestination. He is a man of mean stature, of yellowish beard and speaks somewhat thick.[34]

---

[34] The Sixth National Synod, Verteuil, 1 September 1567. Cited Duke, Lewis and Pettegree, *Calvinism in Europe. Documents*, p. 98.

The churches' response was to institute a regime of training, if necessary in-service, to ensure that those charged with the cure of souls could sustain their responsibilities with dignity. An early and influential model of training was the Zurich *Prophezei*. Initiated by Zurich in 1525, the *Prophezei* was a regular gathering of the city clergy, also attended by senior students of the Latin school, at which Bible texts would be systematically examined, both in the original languages and the vernacular. The *Prophezei* was part of a wholesale re-organization of the city's educational provision, and this was a general feature of the new Protestant polities, echoed in the foundation of the Genevan Academy, the new Protestant universities in Germany, and new Protestant colleges in Cambridge. The cornerstone of all these academic enterprises was knowledge of Scripture, conveyed by systematic lectures, and underpinned by technical training in the scholarly languages. In the second generation the new churches also began to place far more emphasis on the formal process of ordination, though this was normally performed by the church to which a minister was called, after examination of his gifts, rather than as part of a terminal examination in the educational institutions.

Geneva was unusual among the new reformed academies in the attention it gave to practical training. Promising students were often sent out into Geneva's dependent villages to serve an apprenticeship in the rural school of hard knocks before being trusted with a major city parish. Even so, there still remained tensions between the academic training available and the more human skills that characterized successful parish ministry. The issue was raised specifically in correspondence between Geneva and the church in Rouen, Normandy, in 1613, when the Rouen church questioned the aptitude of two men Geneva had proposed to serve them:

As for the second one, whom you say was born and raised in your church and whom you used for a while as a replacement preacher in an extraordinary assembly near the city, because we are not sure of the strength of his voice, we fear it will not be heard by the four to five thousand people who make up this church, a point which we raised specifically when we wrote to two of the members of your company. You do not mention this matter when describing this man, but only recommend his morals and learning.[35]

When Richard Greenham gave up his Fellowship at Pembroke College Cambridge to take on a parish charge at Dry Drayton it was to fulfil an urgent calling to the parochial ministry. But its geographical

[35] Karin Maag, *Seminary or University? The Genevan Academy and Reformed Higher Education, 1560–1620* (Aldershot, St Andrews Studies in Reformation History, 1995), p. 110.

proximity also allowed him to establish a sort of household seminary to assist eager young graduates gain practical experience before plunging into pastoral responsibilities. In other places energetic ministers banded together in informal combinations for mutual support and continuing biblical education. It was unfortunate that in England such combinations excited the disapproval of political leaders through their association with forward critics of the established church. But England was unusual in a number of respects, not least in instituting a separate tier of licensed preachers as an individually selected subset of the parish ministry. Elsewhere in Protestant Europe it was taken for granted that a properly called minister would be a preaching minister.

What then do we know of the quality and impact of this preaching, in the generations when the Protestant churches grew to maturity? As has already been the case, some of the best evidence for the practical divinity of the Protestant clergy comes from notes taken by those who sat in the congregation. Recently Margo Todd has undertaken an exhaustive survey of this surviving evidence for the case of Scotland, and her conclusions are worth citing in detail, for a vignette of what at least an important subset of literate auditors made of the preachers' performance:

What strikes modern readers . . . are the repetition of themes, so useful for oral transmission of complex ideas; the frequency of numbered lists of ideas, again a practical device to aid memory; the simplicity and vividness of the language; and the combination of rather dry exposition of text – purely a transmission of data and doctrine – with intensely emotional and evocative language in exhortation.[36]

If we take this as an accurate survey of the effective Protestant sermon, we discern here a shrewd blend of certain timeless features, standards of the preacher's craft since before the Reformation, with certain elements peculiar to Protestantism. The essential and necessarily somewhat dry Biblical exposition is balanced by the intense emotional engagement of the preacher, and the clear application of the Biblical precepts to the lives of the community. Scottish preachers generally followed the Reformation principle of preaching sequential sermons which moved steadily through a book of the Bible – sometimes when they had finished one book they would ask the advice of their kirk session as to what they should undertake next. All sermons were expected to proceed to a clear model or form, in three essential parts. An opening point by point recounting of the Biblical text would give way to a middle passage of

---

[36] Margo Todd, *The Culture of Protestantism in Early Modern Scotland* (New Haven, Conn., 2002), p. 50.

exegesis, before turning, in the final section, to the application or 'use'. In this final section preachers often moved quickly from imparting knowledge to vigorous denunciations of sin. It was important to maintain a balance of comfort and terror: some ministers kept checklists of doctrines appropriate to each purpose. But above all the congregations expected visible signs of emotion. The ability to transfer his own emotional intensity to the auditory was widely regarded as a sign of an effective preacher. The charismatic Edinburgh preacher Robert Rollock developed such a hold on his audience that he succeeded in persuading the city fathers to authorize a third Sunday sermon.

On the Sabbath morning at seven o'clock – a thing which had never been done in Edinburgh before – he began to preach, and that with such demonstration of the Spirit and of power, with such mighty force of sentiment, and such grave impressiveness of style, that the minds of the greater parts of his hearers were stirred up, and they were irresistibly impelled to admire the preacher. For he not only excited the ordinary class of hearers, but he affected men of learning.[37]

Such accounts could have been replicated all over Protestant Europe, though the sermon tradition did differ from place to place. In Lutheran Germany, evocations of the Devil played a much more prominent part in sermon culture than elsewhere – a protean doctrine of denunciation that could be turned against sin, the Turk, papist, or Calvinists. To the Englishman Richard Greenham, reflecting on the preacher's art, it was principally 'necessary that the Minister of God doe very sharply rebuke the people for their sinnes, and that he lay before them God's grievous judgements against sinners'.[38] So long as such structures were not directed against specific individuals, such caustic Jeremiads caused much less resentment than one might imagine. For the prophetic role was well understood, even seen as seemly and proper. In the endless competition to enter the narrow door that led to the kingdom of heaven, few expected to be congratulated that their place was assured.

All of this was clearly understood, so long as preachers kept within certain recognized limits. It was seldom wise to denounce specific individuals, especially people of influence. Nor could one risk too much generalized criticism of the forces of authority. In all of Europe magistrates kept a careful watch that the emotional display of pulpit oratory was kept in bounds; and particularly that criticism of immorality did not stray towards criticism of public authorities that failed to act to repress it. One preacher who clearly overstepped the boundaries of the permissible

---

[37] Ibid., p. 29.
[38] Parker and Carlson, *Practical Divinity*, p. 66.

was the famous Brother Cornelis of Bruges, a zealous and vehement opponent of the Reformation, who chose the politically sensitive moment of 1566 to embark on a remarkable tirade from the pulpit:

'You Flemings', he shouts while jumping up and down and bashing the pulpit, 'are the most rebellious of all Dutchmen. It's a flaw in your character, you have always revolted against your princes. You were the first ones to turn against the catholic religion and to preach all kinds of heresies. You are the initiators of Iconoclasm. Therefore I advise you to keep quiet and to shut up. Shit all over yourselves! All misfortunes, miseries, plagues will befall you. In short, you will be slaves for ever, you are finished and so are all your laws and privileges. From now on I don't want to pay any attention to you anymore. I shit on your rights, I wipe my ass with your privileges!'

Naturally this flow of vitriol left his audience stunned. But when Brother Cornelis began to invoke the massacre of the Innocents, fear turned to dismay.

Some people ran out of the church, looking back over their shoulders, others crossed themselves and shouted, 'God save us!' People cried, children screamed, because brother Cornelis himself was screaming, bashing the pulpit, stamping his feet, jumping up and down and thrashing around. People in the streets were telling each other, 'Brother Cornelis is as nutty as a fruitcake. God help him to regain his senses'.[39]

This was too sensitive a moment to allow a minister to further rouse the populace, and Brother Cornelis was soon deprived of his pulpit. In less troubled times the authorities were prepared to allow preachers a large degree of licence. The relationship between preachers and magistrates was mutually supportive, for all the day-to-day frustrations. In the Netherlands the reformed clergy resented the fact that the magistrates were not prepared to enforce strict measures to ensure church attendance and suppress competing sects, and often voiced these frustrations to their own congregations.[40] But the magistrates were slow to anger. They, after all, held the strongest hand, since they both owned the church buildings and paid ministerial salaries. For all their complaints, positions in the most prestigious city churches were keenly sought after, and preaching ability was the essential key to promotion. Young men of

---

[39] Karel Bostoen, 'Reformation, Counter-Reformation and Literary Propaganda in the Low Countries in the Sixteenth Century: The Case of Brother Cornelis', in N. Scott Amos, Andrew Pettegree and Henk van Nierop (eds.) *The Education of a Christian Society. Humanism and Reformation in Britain and the Netherlands* (Aldershot, St Andrews Studies in Reformation History, 1999), pp. 175–6.

[40] Andrew Pettegree, 'Coming to Terms with Victory: The Upbuilding of a Calvinist Church in Holland, 1572–1590', in Duke, Lewis and Pettegree, *Calvinism in Europe*, pp. 160–80.

ability chafed volubly if consigned to an unrewarding rural parish, but for those in the principal pulpits high standards were expected. Preaching was, above all, physically demanding. Delivering sermons for an hour or more to large congregations in the cavernous Dutch churches placed a heavy strain on stamina and lungpower.[41] Even in the smaller Scottish churches the demands of multiple Sunday and weekday sermons left many ministers exhausted.[42]

Relations between church and state were often tense, sometimes acrimonious, but essentially mutually supportive. Throughout Protestant Europe congregations laid out considerable funds in building the fabric of the new worship service, not least through the erection of fine new pulpits that by their imposing physical presence would properly reflect the new centrality of the sermon. In Germany, Scotland and the Netherlands such finely crafted works in stone or wood were a feature of many churches, new and old; in Norway the Lutheran wooden pulpits of the post-Reformation period are some of the most beautiful of all religious artefacts. In new buildings the internal architecture often reflected an elegant resolution of the competing claims to influence and rule that marked any early modern society. The new church at Burntisland, Fife (1613), was constructed to the most modern principles, with a fine ornate gallery and an imposing closed pew for the laird. It appears very lordly, until one mounts the pulpit. From here, directly in his line of sight and less than five yards away, the minister looked directly down upon the laird's pew: far from providing privileged privacy, every fidget, yawn or attempt at diversion would be directly under his eye.

The predicament of the laird of Burntisland offers an appropriate closing vignette with which to reflect on the powerful influence of the Reformation preaching tradition. There is little doubt that from the first days of the Reformation preaching played a formative role in shaping the new movement; and it would continue to play a vital part in shaping the new Protestant churches in the generations ahead. The sermon provided the ideal vehicle to express the bibliocentric core of Protestantism: in its turn it swiftly became the core of all Protestant worship. If sermons were an occasional, even somewhat exotic part of the pre-Reformation worship experience, this was never the case in any of the magisterial Protestant churches. The sermon became the central pivot around which Protestant worship was shaped. The new Protestant people lived

---

[41] One church in the Netherlands sadly had to reject an otherwise satisfactory minister purely on the grounds that his voice was not robust enough to carry.

[42] Todd, *Culture of Protestantism*, pp. 28–9.

on a diet of sermons: at every Sunday observance, and often through the week.

The role of preaching also tells us much about the culture of the new Protestant churches. This was intensely biblical. Sermons assumed a high level of interest in, if not always knowledge of, the text and meaning of Scripture. The expository method led congregations patiently through the books of the Bible, familiar and unfamiliar. The long regular hours of the expository sermon thus played an important catechismal function, even outside the formal catechism sermons set by many churches for Sunday afternoons. Most of all, sermons adopted a method and pattern entirely appropriate for illiterate and semi-literate populations: the purposeful use of lists, paired contrasts, repetition, summary and reiteration. It was the bedrock around which the churches harnessed other communication media.

3   Militant in song

A Catholic visitor to a Protestant worship service in sixteenth-century Europe would immediately have been struck by stark contrasts to the familiar tradition of his own upbringing. The scale of the physical alterations would obviously vary, depending on whether he had stumbled upon a church cleansed of all images for Calvinist worship, or a Lutheran church, in which the internal fabric might be largely untouched. But it is unlikely, one might surmise, that if the service were in progress, his mind would linger much on architecture and internal decoration: more arresting by far was the essential unfamiliarity of the worship service. For a start, there would only have been one service in progress; in this Protestant church he would not have observed one priest celebrating Mass at the High Altar, while others were engaged in duties in the side chapels. No priests would have been hearing confession; the familiar bustle and variety would have been missing. Rather the attention of the congregation gathered in the nave would have been focused on the pulpit, from which the minister would be conducting the service. If his arrival was unplanned, our Catholic visitor would in all likelihood have first heard the voice of the minister, leading the congregation in prayer, reading from Scripture or preaching. Preaching would obviously have occupied the longest time: probably an inordinate length for someone not inured by long practice. But if he persevered through the whole service he would ultimately observe the unfolding of a whole new ritual, utterly different in rhythm and focus from the Mass: the familiar rites replaced by a new order of prayer, Scripture, preaching and communal singing.

It was this last, communal singing, that, along with regular preaching, represented the most distinctive innovation of the new evangelical worship service. The singing of hymns and psalms, punctuating and framing the periods of exhortation and intercession, became a ubiquitous part of Protestant worship. For many people it was the part of the service they found most congenial, and it played a profound part in inculcating a sense of loyalty and identification with the new worship tradition. The reasons for this are not hard to fathom. The Protestant tradition of communal singing drew on a deep love of song in mediaeval sociability, and at the same time articulated one of the core principles of the Reformation: that the people should be animated by an active, living faith. The leading reformers eagerly embraced the practice of singing as a primary expression of a lively commitment to an active religion.

As usual, Martin Luther found words to express these aspirations. 'I intend', he wrote to Spalatin in 1523, 'to make vernacular psalms for the people, that is spiritual songs, so that the Word of God even by means of song may live among the people.'[1] A generation later Theodore de Bèze would echo these same sentiments with an almost exactly parallel psychological insight. 'In truth', he averred, 'we know by experience that singing has the power to enflame the hearts of men so that they praise God with an ever more vehement zeal.'[2]

These were large hopes and large claims. But they do suggest that the role of music as a pedagogic tool in the service of the Reformation deserves a systematic exposition. Music had the power to move, but not always in simple praise and worship. The music of the Reformation also played a large role when the movement moved from praise to destruction, from exhortation to confrontation and ridicule. This must also not be ignored.

If the reformers invested such hopes in music, it was partly because singing was such a ubiquitous part of pre-industrial society. In the homes, at work, in the fields and workshops, wherever people gathered, they sang. Mothers sang to their children, as parents still do; schoolteachers taught their students through mnemonic rhymes, as teachers of infants still do.[3] In and out of the work place, people sang to while away the hours of toil and waiting. Weavers had their work songs, sung to the rhythm of the loom; miners had their distinctive tunes, the *Bergmannslieder*. Shepherds sang (and played) while they tended their flocks. When inspiration flagged there were often travelling singers and entertainers to offer new songs, and even news songs. In inns and drinking houses, or even in the market place (in fact wherever people gathered) travelling ballad-singers hoped to earn a few coins through entertaining the throng. Singing was particularly associated with wandering. Sailors,

[1] Robin A. Leaver, *'Goostly psalmes and spirituall songes'. English and Dutch Metrical Psalms from Coverdale to Utenhove, 1535–1566* (Oxford, 1991), p. 3.
[2] *Les pseaumes mis en ryme françoise* (Lyon, Des Tournes, 1563), sig. A4r.
[3] Peter Burke, *Popular Culture in Early Modern Europe* (London, 1978). Adam Fox, *Oral and Literate Culture in England, 1500–1700* (Oxford, 2000).

soldiers, beggars and journeymen all had their particular songs that told of life on the road or at sea.

The tradition of popular song was by no means confined to the more humble social orders. The entertainment culture of noble and court society also revolved around singing: at the loom, during and after feasting, though here, of course, the popular chansons and ballads were often performed by professional singers and players. The higher reaches of urban society developed a hybrid tradition that reflected the influence of both the court and the streets; for skill in singing and playing was prized here as a social accomplishment, if not as a means of earning a living.[4]

Almost the only place one would not expect regularly to find music was in the parish church. This remark requires some qualification. The Mass would have been conducted by the presiding priest according to a plainsong chant, if one not always wholly audible to the congregation. This was a rite that required little active congregational participation. Parishioners might sing on festivals, in processions, or at special observances, and there was a wide repertoire of religious songs for such occasions (which often took place outside the church buildings).[5] But congregational singing played no necessary part in the regular Mass.

In the larger urban churches, cathedrals and aristocratic chapels the Mass would offer a more elaborate spectacle. Most of these churches maintained choirs capable of performing a full choral Mass: it was indeed the composition and performance of such Masses that offered a principal outlet for the talents of music professionals in the century before the Reformation. During this period musical composition enjoyed a period of exceptional fertility, centred mostly on the great courts of Europe. As in so much of the cultural flowering of the Renaissance, Italy led the way, though the Flemish/Burgundian tradition also provided a powerful source of invention and virtuosity.

The Protestant churches were the heirs to the totality of this tradition, though their relationship with the more ornate polyphonic compositions of the late fifteenth century was a complex one. In the new Protestant tradition a lack of ornamentation, expressed in simplicity of metre and clear articulation of meaning through a strict strophic structure, became a positive virtue, in conscious contra-distinction to the decorated

---

[4] By way of introduction, Iain Fenlon, *The Renaissance. From the 1470s to the End of the 16th Century* (Basingstoke, 1989).

[5] For England see now Beat Kümin, 'Masses, Morris and Metrical Psalms: Music in the English Parish, c. 1400–1600', in Fiona Kisby, *Music and Musicians in Renaissance Cities and Towns* (Cambridge, 2001), pp. 70–81.

elaboration of the choral Mass. Here, Luther and his followers attempted to define a musical manifestation of the core Scripture principles of the Reformation: the pure word of Scripture was made manifest in the new music. The Renaissance tradition, however, also left its mark in several more positive respects, quite apart from this polemical antithesis. The Renaissance flowering of polyphonic composition inspired both an imitative bourgeois tradition and considerable interest in musical theory. These twin impulses brought forth much learned and perceptive theorizing on how music moved and affected the emotions: in this respect the humanist rediscovery of the wisdom of the ancients was also influential. Finally the wealth of musical inventiveness, and the demand for performance scores for professional and domestic use, led to significant developments in print culture. The circulation of music in the market place called for specialist types for musical notation. By the time of the Reformation the technical problems connected with this musical type had been largely resolved.

The Wittenberg Nightingale

Martin Luther was a man of refined artistic sensibility, and music was a special passion. As a young boy at school he quickly discovered a talent for singing; as a young adult he mastered both the lute and the flute. Music continued to play an important part in his life throughout his career in Wittenberg; it was a subject on which he thought deeply and intelligently, and with a clear understanding of contemporary music theory. His musical experience was undoubtedly broadened during his trip to Rome, and through his experience of worship in the Wittenberg *Schlosskapelle*, where Frederick the Wise employed a large number of singers and instrumentalists.[6] The polyphonic repertoire sung here was extensive, and included works by Josquin, Isaac and Obrecht.

Throughout his life Luther never wavered in his belief in music as a power for good.[7] In his most extended comment on the subject, a preface to an anthology of short Latin motets published in 1538, he acknowledged the powerful psychological and moral force of music first articulated by Aristotle and Plato. There was one important corollary: the obligation to employ this divine gift to God's glory.

---

[6] Carl Schalk, *Luther on Music: Paradigms of Praise* (St Louis, Mo., 1988). Paul Nettl, *Luther and Music* (Philadelphia, 1948). Friedrich Blume, *Protestant Church Music: A History* (New York, 1974).

[7] Not least as a means of warding off the depression that plagued him for much of his life. See Rebecca Wagner Oettinger, *Music as Propaganda in the German Reformation* (Aldershot, St Andrews Studies in Reformation History, 2001), p. 43.

The gift of language combined with the gift of song was only given to man . . .
that he should praise God with both word and music, namely by proclaiming
[the Word of God] through music and by providing sweet melodies with words.[8]

In these circumstances it was hardly surprising that music should play
a part in Luther's conception of a reformed liturgy. In the *Formula missae*
of 1523 Luther's innate conservatism dictated the retention of the traditional structure of the Mass, even though the theological precepts were
radically reinterpreted. The most radical departure in terms of communal participation was mentioned almost as an afterthought. 'I also wish
that we had as many songs in the vernacular as possible which people
could sing during Mass, immediately after the gradual and also after the
Sanctus and Agnus Dei.'[9] This change was consolidated in the *Deutsche
Messe* of 1526. Music is fundamental to this service. The simplified
programme of the traditional Mass provided for frequent instances of
congregational singing: of thirty-nine pages of text, thirty-one incorpor-
ate musical notation. Luther himself played a large part in the work of
composition, along with colleagues such as Agricola, Hegenwalt and
others.

Luther's conception of the new evangelical Mass was not without its
critics. In Wittenberg Andreas Karlstadt was a very reluctant musical
communicator. In a letter to Thomas Müntzer in 1524 Karlstadt laid
bare his basic philosophical objections: 'I cannot at all believe that the
people could be inspired by holy songs. Rather it is a fact that excess in
these matters acts as a deterrent to divine things.'[10] As this comment
suggests, Müntzer was by this point already well advanced with his own
project of a German *Volksliturgie*, though this had led him in a radically
different direction to Luther. He believed that a purified vernacular
version of the Gregorian chant was the best means to prepare elect
Christians for Christ's incarnation in their hearts. But Luther was not
persuaded, and in his exchange with Müntzer he articulated a clear
programme for the role of music in the communication process. For
Luther, Müntzer's translation of the Gregorian rite was insufficient. To
communicate the word effectively there had to be an assimilation of
sacred music to the tunes people actually knew. These might be derived
from traditional religion or even profane tunes.

[8] *Luther's Works. American edition*, ed. Jarislav Pelikan (54 vols., Philadelphia, 1955–86),
    vol. LIII: *Liturgy and Hymns*, pp. 323–4.
[9] Ibid., vol. LIII, p. 36.
[10] Günther Franz (ed.), *Thomas Müntzer. Schriften und Briefe. Kritische Gesamtausgabe*
    (Gütersloh, 1968), p. 415. Quoted in Helga Robinson-Hammerstein, 'The Lutheran
    Reformation and its Music', in her *The Transmission of Ideas in the Lutheran Reformation*
    (Blackrock, Co. Dublin 1989), p. 147.

This merging of the traditions of sacred and secular music is rightly seen as the distinctive contribution of Lutheran hymnody. For texts, Luther often drew on the inspiration of the psalms; other hymns were based on Latin texts familiar from traditional religious practice. By 1524 there had accumulated a corpus of around forty Wittenberg hymns (around half written by Luther); these formed the basis of the first Wittenberg hymnal, the *Geystliches Gesangk Buchlein*.[11] At Luther's encouragement, the composer, the twenty-eight-year-old Johan Walter, had composed polyphonic choral settings for the hymns in four or five parts. As Luther asserted in his foreword to this volume, he hoped this challenging format would:

Give the young – who should at any rate be trained in music and other fine arts – something to wean them away from love ballads and carnal songs and to teach them something of value in their place, thus combining the good with the pleasing, as is proper for youth.[12]

In liturgical practice these polyphonic settings were presumably sung by a choir, quite possibly in alternation with the congregation and singing alternate stanzas in unison. If this was so, the enduring Lutheran tradition of combining simple congregational song with complex polyphonic music was established at an early date.

The first Lutheran hymns achieved a rapid popularity. It is thought that the first compositions circulated as broadsheets, though survivals in this format are rare. But there is definite evidence of a wide circulation, with printed copies published in Augsburg and Magdeburg as well as Wittenberg.[13] In 1524 an enterprising Nuremberg publisher collected a number of these hymns and issued them in a single volume, the *Achtliedebuch*. There were further small collections published in Erfurt this same year. Hymns also became part of the stock in trade of the street pedlar. The city chronicle of Magdeburg, a free imperial city 70 kilometres distant from Wittenberg, reported that on 6 May 1524 a poor old man stood in the market place and sang two of Luther's earliest hymns, 'Auf tiefer Not' and 'Es wollt uns Gott genädig sein', which he also offered for sale.[14]

In Wittenberg, Walther's *Geystliches Gesangk Buchlein* was followed in 1529 by a new congregational hymnal, the *Geistlicke lieder*, a work that went through at least eight further editions during Luther's lifetime.

---

[11] Markus Jenny, *Luthers geistliche Lieder und Kirchengesänge. Vollständige Neuedition in Ergänzung zu Band 35 der Weimarer Ausgabe* (Cologne, 1985).
[12] *Luther's Works*, vol. LIII, p. 316.
[13] Leaver, 'Goostly psalmes', p. 6.
[14] Gustav Hertel (ed.), *Die Chroniken des niedersächsischen Städte: Magdeburg* (Leipzig, 1899), vol. II, p. 143.

These works formed the cornerstone of a huge mass of published hymnals that continued throughout the century. If we count only those editions that have survived, the principal catalogues of sixteenth-century printed music list more than 2,000 hymn editions. Given the likelihood that many more have not survived, for this is a class of literature susceptible to a very high rate of attrition, we may confidently assert that as many as three to four million hymnals and song sheets were circulating in sixteenth-century Germany.[15]

The continuing popularity of the earliest hymns in the later editions also helped to keep alive the memory of the Reformation's most exultant, optimistic phase, in a period later in the century when other theological literature became increasingly complex and introspective. Of course Luther's hymnody also evolved. He included a number of important embellishments to his *Geistlicke lieder*, including a section of hymns based on the five main parts of the Short Catechism of 1529. From this point on the Lutheran hymn repertoire became a fundamental part of religious pedagogy. The typical school day cited by Gerald Strauss from a school ordinance of Oldenburg is packed with German hymns and psalms from morning prayer to the final blessing before departure home.[16] Educators recognized and were quick to exploit the mnemonic powers of verse set to recognizable tunes, and schoolchildren were expected to lead adults in singing during the service. When, later in the century, visitors observed a lacklustre performance by the congregation, they often prescribed increased singing in the schools. In this way the musical repertoire of Lutheran hymnody passed into the fabric of society, and from the churches out into the streets.

The liturgical experiments of Wittenberg quickly found their echo in other parts of Germany.[17] In Nuremberg the pioneering church order of 1525 established an extended place for congregational singing. The hymn texts inserted into the liturgies were usually those of Wittenberg, though Nuremberg also developed its own lively tradition of hymn composition: the work, in part, of the multi-talented artisan author Hans Sachs. To the north, centred on Rostock, a further distinctive tradition of hymnody developed, influenced particularly by the work of the local reformer, Joachim Slüter. His *Gantz schone unde seer nutte gesangk boek* contained fifty-four hymns, including hymns for Matins and Vespers.

---

[15] The estimate is adapted from the data presented by Christopher Boyd Brown, 'Singing the Gospel: Lutheran Hymns and the Success of the Reformation in Joachimsthal' (Harvard University, Ph.D. dissertation, 2001). A revised version of this dissertation is shortly to appear as a monograph with Harvard University Press.

[16] Strauss, *Luther's House of Learning*, p. 231.

[17] This paragraph follows Leaver, '*Goostly psalmes*', pp. 17 ff.

The influence of this Rostock tradition was also felt in Denmark and Sweden. But most important by far was the largely independent liturgical tradition crafted in the Rhineland city of Strasbourg. The liturgy as it emerged from the years leading to the abolition of the Mass allowed a central role for congregational singing. Martin Bucer, writing at a time when the church order was not yet finally fixed, described his intentions thus:

When the people gather on Sunday, the minister exhorts them to confess sins and to pray for mercy. He confesses to God for the congregation, prays for mercy, and proclaims remission of sins to the believers. The people then sing some short psalms or hymns of praise, after which the minister says a brief prayer and reads something from the epistles of the apostles, expounding it briefly. Hereafter the congregation sings the Decalogue or something else. The minister then reads the Gospel and delivers the sermon, whereafter the people sing the articles of faith.[18]

This striking level of communal participation, repeated through the service, betrays a clear theological purpose. The canon of the Mass had been eliminated and in its place stood the Word of God. But it was necessary for the congregation to verbalize its response, and for each individual to witness to his Christian commitment and to encourage others in theirs. This became the leitmotif of the Strasbourg Reformation. During 1524 at least six editions were published of this basic liturgy, and a further six between 1526 and 1537. With each the structure of the service was simplified, the sermon emphasized, and the role of psalmody enlarged. It would be the distinctive contribution of the Strasbourg Reformation.

The full potential of Lutheran hymnody in the mature church tradition has been demonstrated in a superb recent study of Joachimsthal by the American church historian Christopher Brown.[19] Joachimsthal was a new town in the German/Czech *Erzgebirge*, created after the discovery of rich silver deposits. By 1520 it was home to over 5,000 miners and at its peak in 1533 the inhabitants numbered more than 18,000. Luther's teaching entered Joachimsthal along with the influx of Saxon miners who dominated both the work force and the prosperous mine owners who held sway among the city elite. The wealth of the new town spawned a range of urban institutions, including a renowned Latin school, a girls' school and a hospital.

The musical culture of the town was shaped by two men: the composer Nicolas Herman, cantor in the Latin school, and Johan Mathesius,

---

[18] Quoted in Ibid., p. 25.   [19] Brown, 'Singing the Gospel'.

successively rector of the Latin school and senior pastor of the Joachimsthal church. Mathesius promoted the use of music in church and school with extraordinary zeal, both from the pulpit and in his steady support for Herman's work. Herman was responsible for several collections of more than two hundred hymns, intended to be sung in the school, in household devotions, and in the church.

True to the comparative conservatism of Lutheran liturgical prefer-ences, Herman and Mathesius preserved the essential shape of the Latin liturgy. The overwhelming enthusiasm of the congregation for hymn singing was accommodated partly within the service, but also by an hour of congregational singing before the service began. This was popular and well attended. A high standard of performance in the formal rite was assured by the systematic use of music in schools where the church choir was trained. The town government also supported music actively, both through its financial support of the school, and by funding a staff of professional musicians who helped supply the town's musical needs. The communal musical tradition of Joachimsthal must have been exception-ally rich, and certainly reached into every aspect of city life, symbolized by the practice of the choral students making a twice weekly perambu-lation of the town's streets, singing hymns. Mathesius also positively promoted the practice of hymn singing in a domestic context – indeed this flourishing of the domestic hymn tradition was one of the clearest manifestations of Lutheranism's popular success.

What was the impact of all this musical instruction? There is little doubt that the citizens of Joachimsthal revelled in their singing – but did it teach? This question is particularly pertinent when considered against the background of a recent historiographical tradition that has been distinctly sceptical about the ability of the new evangelical preachers to engage the masses at other than a superficial level. The case against the effectiveness of the new pedagogic culture can be distilled into three main charges. Firstly, that the reformers replaced one sort of eschato-logical despair with another. In this perception the fear of Hell stirred up by the teachings of the late mediaeval church was replaced by the hopelessness induced by a grim theology of man's powerlessness to influence salvation. Secondly, sceptics cite empirical data that appear to show that the reformers failed to impart even the most basic under-standing of the essentials of faith, even over the course of several gener-ations. Finally, it has been suggested that as the new evangelical churches became institutionalized, the close co-operation between a formally educated clergy and the state power caused an increasing distance to grow up between minister and laity in the parish.

Yet if we follow Christopher Brown in his sensitive evocation of the 'gentle pedagogy' of Lutheran hymnody, then we can see that the Lutheran hymn tradition offers a partial response to all of these concerns. It is clear, firstly, that in Joachimsthal at least church life was the joint creation of both clergy and laity. The evolution of the liturgical round represented a joint enterprise in which citizens and ministers had all invested heavily. Hymns played a pivotal part in this relationship. They were written by clergy, but were definitely regarded as a part of lay culture.

They could also play an important role in conveying the central messages of the new evangelical teachings. Luther and his colleagues provided hymns for each part of the catechismal cycle, and catechism hymns are arranged in hymnals for use in instruction. But congregational hymns also addressed quite directly core theological concerns such as justification by faith. The powerless of fallen man to fulfil the Law was of course axiomatic, and combined with the natural moralizing tendency of the pulpit, preaching could have a salutary but depressing effect. The hymn, in contrast, could present the heavenly paradox of evangelical theology, Law and Grace, in a much more positive light. To quote Brown: 'One of the greatest virtues of the hymns was that, whereas a sermon taken in isolation . . . might seem excessive in its emphasis on the law, the Lutheran hymns within their relatively small compass usually succeeded in presenting both law and the Gospel, using the contrast which Lutheran theology posited between these two doctrines to great dramatic and psychological effect.'[20]

Other hymns promote works of love and neighbourly service, and they are of course enacted in a context that epitomizes this sense of a living, active community. Here all the aspects of faith – emotional, psychological and rational – combined with physical activity to encapsulate the core teachings of the new church and its claim, so important to Luther, to create a new Christian people. This sense of the power of the sung word was distilled, as is so often the case, into parables of wonder-working miracles. One such was the tale of a possessed girl whose inner demons resisted all the powers of the clergy until she was brought by her despairing family into the church service. Here hymns sung by the congregation drove out the evil spirits.[21] The Christian people in song possessed their own power to heal and make whole.

[20] Ibid., p. 202.   [21] Ibid., p. 220.

The Power of the Word

Luther always intended that his hymns and spiritual songs should find a life outside the liturgical setting: in schools, but also in the streets and taverns. The Lutheran Reformation in fact spawned a remarkable range of musical settings, some for the worship service, others for less formal settings, though this is a distinction not always easy to maintain. The overlap between the two cultures is well illustrated by two of Luther's most famous hymns, *Ein neues Lied* and *Ein feste Berg*.[22] Luther composed *Ein neues Lied* to mark and celebrate the witness of two Augustinian monks executed in Brussels in 1523 for their refusal to recant their Lutheran beliefs. Luther was powerfully affected by their deaths, and the depth of his emotion is vividly evident in the twelve stanzas of the hymn composed after the executions. The text was obviously a new composition, and although it later found a place in congregational worship, it had not been written for liturgical purposes. In fact it owes more to the tradition of the news song, traditionally sung in the market places in the manner of the *Bänkelsänger*. The hymn *Ein feste Berg*, by contrast, was always clearly intended for liturgical use. Based on Psalm 46, it is the archetypal metrical psalm – the biblical text in the vernacular set in strophic form – a form that would become the most characteristic musical creation of Protestantism. But the overwhelming resonance with Lutheran congregations and the militant lyric of *Ein feste Berg* ensured it a life in and out of the church building. With its militaristic language it became a battle song, the 'Marseillaise of the Reformation'.[23] At the sensitive time of the Augsburg Interim, *Ein feste Berg* was actually banned from use in Nuremberg until a version less offensive to Catholics could be crafted. So the two forms – the liturgical hymn and the polemical song – were always to some extent interwoven.

Beyond this, however, there soon also emerged a tradition of overtly polemical literature that had little place in the church setting. These songs drew on the same sources of inspiration for their tunes. Like Luther's hymns they made much use of contrafacta, melodies taken from secular traditional or religious songs; indeed, the two repertoires showed a considerable degree of overlap. Many of the polemical songs addressed the burning theological and political issues of the day: the cult of saints, the abuse of Marian devotion, the expectation of the end-time. Others exulted in the confounding of Luther's enemies, the Pope and the

---

[22] See here Wagner Oettinger, *Music as Propaganda*, pp. 62–9. The following section is heavily indebted to this seminal study.

[23] Ibid., pp. 46–7.

Catholic clergy. Some had very specific targets. The anonymous
'Martinus ist nit geschwigen' contained an explicit attack on the
Catholic theologian Jerome Emser, under the guise of 'the Goat': 'Goat,
desist with your bleating!'[24] This reference points us to the mixed and
varied social appeal of these songs. Only those who had followed the ebb
and flow of Reformation polemic with some understanding could have
been familiar with this designation of Emser, a Leipzig opponent with
whom Luther had engaged in a furious pamphlet war over the canoniza-
tion of the local saint, Benno. Interestingly, Emser countered Luther's
Against the New Idol with a verse work of his own, 'Ach Benno, du vil
heiliger man'. This was published in broadsheet form on the press
maintained to publish Emser's work in Dresden: perhaps it was this
unwelcome appropriation of the popular medium by a Catholic opponent that inspired the contemptuous anonymous response above.[25] Although there is no evidence that Luther penned the verse attack on
Emser, he was not averse to extending his frequent *ad hominem* attacks
into verse. His two-stanza work, 'Ach du arger Heinze', attacks Heinrich
of Braunschweig for permitting the execution of Protestants. He follows
the song with the comment, 'When I complete this song I will also find a
verse to deal with the fellow in Mainz' – by which he meant Cardinal
Albrecht of Brandenburg.[26]

The most successful songs were those that addressed the core issues of
Reformation debate and encapsulated the essence of the new teaching.
Between 1523 and 1525 the Nuremberg shoemaker–poet Hans Sachs
contributed a range of Christian songs to the cause, alongside the
thirteen translations of the psalms he contributed to the German Mass.
Beneath their polished accessibility, these songs, which dwelt on core
evangelical themes such as   justification and right devotion, reveal a
considerable subtlety of compositional method. Sachs' overt purpose
was to effect a 'Christianly correction' of traditional songs. For this
reason he purposefully took as his model well-known songs of Marian
devotion. In this instance the contrafactum served a double purpose.
It not only made use of a familiar tune, so that the song was more
instantly memorable, but it performed a deeper theological act: sup-
planting traditional beliefs with those more fitting to evangelical sensibilities. This illustrates an important aspect of the success of Lutheran
polemical songs, known as intertextuality. The new text is overlaid on

[24] Transcribed, with translation, in Ibid., pp. 310–12.
[25] Frank Aurich, *Die Anfänge des Buchdrucks in Dresden. Die Emserpresse, 1524–1526*
(Dresden, 2000), pp. 54–5.
[26] Oettinger, *Music as Propaganda*, pp. 118–19.

the old words, but the memory of the original text resonates through the meaning. This applies whether the old text is inverted or transmuted (as with the traditional songs of Marian devotion 'cleansed' by Sachs) or whether the original enhanced the new version. The popular traditional German song, the *Judaslied*, continued to be sung well into the sixteenth century in its original version, as well as providing the melody for a host of Lutheran contrafacta. The resonance of the original, 'O wretched Judas, what have you done? You have betrayed my Lord', provided easy targets for modern enemies of the evangelical cause. Not surprisingly, polemical songs that used this tune enjoyed a particular resonance during the Augsburg Interim, with Maurice of Saxony the obvious, if not always stated, target.

The use of these familiar tunes was of utmost importance to their success. For both Luther and his successors it was a quite deliberate strategy, as they were happy to acknowledge. The authors of the dedicatory preface to the 1575 song book of the Bohemian Brethren commented: 'our singers took up [secular melodies] intentionally, in order that the people be attracted to a grasp of the truth more easily through familiar sounds'.[27] Familiar tunes made memorization that much simpler, and exploited the ubiquity of song in pre-literate societies. Their use also vitiated the need to print these songs with the expensive and complex musical type. Most often the song would be published in a text-only version, with a prefatory note, 'to be sung to the tune . . .' Of the 183 broadsheet songs that have survived in the precious Meusebach collection in Berlin, over two-thirds cite a well-known tune as melody in this way.[28] Most important of all, the reformers with their newly written spiritual songs had created a genre that worked with the grain of sixteenth-century society. Their importance can be gauged from the frequency with which Luther commented on the need to teach singing, and the theme was frequently evoked in the new German church orders.

The new spiritual songs quickly made their way into the general entertainment culture of the new Lutheran societies. The Spanish Carmelite Thomas à Jesu was surprised to find Luther's hymns being sung in private houses, workshops, market places, streets and fields; even, according to one more hostile report, in the bathhouses.[29] We should not be surprised. In contrast to the scepticism expressed in this book that a printed broadsheet image could be 'read', as is often asserted, it is relatively easy, in the case of song, to chart a path from

---

[27] Ibid., p. 5.   [28] Ibid., p. 26.
[29] Robinson-Hammerstein, 'Lutheran Reformation and its Music', p. 161.

print to oral culture. A literate person would be needed to read the new text and fit it to the (usually well-known) tune; thereafter there was a well-established tradition both of individual public singing and of group conviviality, by which it could be made known to, and swiftly learned by, a wider audience. Hans-Christoph Rublack has brilliantly demonstrated the process of dissemination in one particular instance, the case of a seditious song that circulated in the city of Nördlingen during the Peasants' War in 1525. The author of the song was a local weaver, Contz Anahans, and the interrogation of the local ringleaders of the revolt revealed much about how it spread around the city. It was sung at the inn of Balthasar Fend, one of the leaders of the revolt. Later, one Anton Forner asked the author to sing it in his house. After a third singing in another inn, within a month it was so well known that Hans Trumer could render it: it was his drunken performance of the song while meant to be on watch duty that alerted the magistrates to its seditious content. Trumer claimed to have heard it in Spangenberg's inn, where fifty citizens had been present, including the master of the Weavers' Guild.[30]

Popular song performed many important functions in sixteenth-century society. It provided an important artistic outlet for less-educated people, for virtually everyone can sing. Song is cheap and accessible, and requires no staging or training for enjoyment. Its potency as a tool of Reformation is obvious in an age where most opinion forming took place in a communal, rather than a private setting.

A powerful illustration of the potency of singing as a means of harnessing and channelling dissent even without the agency of print is provided by its role in the Hussite Revolution, a half-century before the advent of print. The songs born in the excitement of the Czech rebellion ran the full gamut of political and religious grievances.[31] They inveighed against the wealth of the church and the 'Judas clergy'; they pilloried the Council of Constance and the pitiless destruction of Hus:

> O you Council of Constance
> Who call yourself holy,
> How could you with such neglect
> And great lack of mercy
> Destroy a holy man?[32]

---

[30] Hans-Christoph Rublack, 'The Song of Contz Anahans: Communication and Revolt in Nördlingen, 1525', in R. Po-Chia Hsia (ed.), *The German People and the Reformation* (Ithaca, N.Y. 1988), p. 112.

[31] Thomas A Fudge, *The Magnificent Ride. The First Reformation in Hussite Bohemia* (Aldershot, St Andrews Studies in Reformation History, 1998), pp. 186–216.

[32] Ibid., p. 191.

The most famous of all Hussite songs was the battle song, 'You enemies of God'. Stunning Hussite victories inspired new songs, such as
'Faithful ones, rejoice in God'. According to the most systematic
modern study of this literature, the long daily sermons and popular
songs together characterize the dominant form of communication in
the movement.[33]

Despite Luther's initial sensitivity that his movement of reform
might be tarnished with the brush of Hussite heresy, there was little
doubt that sixteenth-century reformers learned much from the echoes of
the Bohemian controversies.[34] For modern scholars too the Hussite
agenda – their rhetoric of holy war, the faithfulness to God, the raucous
satirizing of the Catholics – certainly inspires obvious comparisons with
the boisterous public polemic of the Reformation century. This was all
the more obviously the case as the Reformation moved into the more
perilous age of religious conflict and warfare in the second half of the
century.

Psalms from Geneva

The Swiss reformers, in this as in so much else, took a more austere view
of the place of music in the worship service than the Wittenberg
tradition. Ulrich Zwingli, though himself an accomplished musician,
accorded music no divinely ordained role in worship; on the contrary,
he saw it as a hindrance to true worship.[35] The liturgical round
of reformed worship in Zurich became a service of prayer, reading
and preaching with no musical embellishment.[36] Fortunately for the
development of the reformed musical tradition, Calvin's perception
evolved in a different direction. In the first edition of the *Institutes*, Calvin

---

[33] Ibid., p. 192.

[34] The last Wittenberg hymn collection of Luther's lifetime, the *Bapstsche Gesangbuch*, in
fact took two hymns from the hymnal of the Bohemian Brethren. Leaver, '*Goostly
psalmes*', p. 15.

[35] Markus Jenny, *Zwinglis Stellung zur Musik im Gottesdienst* (Zurich, 1966). Charles
Garside, *Zwingli and the Arts* (New Haven, Conn., 1966).

[36] Though in fact the Zurich reformers strongly endorsed the value of the singing of
religious songs outside the worship service, and both Zwingli and Bullinger composed
texts (and in Zwingli's case also melodies) to be sung among the Christian community
at times of trial or rejoicing. H. Reimann, 'Zwingli – der Musiker', *Archiv für Musikwissenschaft*, 17 (1960), pp. 126–41. Markus Jenny, 'Reformierte Kirchenmusik?
Zwingli, Bullinger und die Folgen', in Heiko Oberman and Gotfried Locher
(eds.), *Refortiers Erbe. Festschrift für Gottfried W. Locher*, *Zwingliana*, 19 (1991–2),
pp. 187–205.

allowed a cautious place for congregational singing in the liturgy, specifically the singing of psalms before and after the Eucharist. In his first years in Geneva he recommended the use of the metrical psalms in a submission to the city council: 'the psalms can stimulate us to raise our hearts to God and arouse us to an ardour in invoking as well as in exalting with praises the glory of his name'.[37] But his real awakening to the full potential of the psalms in a liturgical setting came in the years of service in Martin Bucer's Strasbourg (1538–41). Calvin, bruised and humiliated after the brusque termination of his first Genevan ministry, was here put in charge of the small French exile church. He was able both to observe the mature Strasbourg church order and to apply its essential features to the worship of his congregation. Almost immediately, he began to prepare an edition of the metrical psalms in French. Some of the translations were his own; the rest were the work of the French court poet, Clément Marot.

Clément Marot was one of the most accomplished of sixteenth-century French poets, and a favourite at the court of Francis I. A protégé of the king's sister, Marguerite of Navarre, Marot had flirted with evangelism early in his career, but this was not evident when he began his work on the versification of the psalms in 1532. Perhaps ironically, in view of their later history, the psalm versifications were initially much praised by the king and his circle: Francis, his son Henry, and Catherine de' Medici were all said to have had their particular favourites.[38] The collection of the first thirty translations completed in 1539 was dedicated to the king. Their appropriation for the new evangelical liturgy in Strasbourg might well have been thoroughly unwelcome, and certainly it made it difficult for Marot to remain in Paris. In 1542 he left France for good. His verse translations were formally condemned by the Sorbonne in 1544, the year of his death.

The French metrical psalms obviously drew on the same scriptural canon as many of the Lutheran hymns; the Calvinist worship tradition as it emerged in Strasbourg and Geneva was, however, distinctive in a number of ways. Firstly, the singing of the psalms became the core congregational activity of a reformed service that had abandoned the traditional canon of the Mass. The psalms also represented the total corpus of Calvinist hymnody (along with a small number of versifications of other scriptural prayers and canticles). They were not, as was the case in the Lutheran tradition, part of an extended hymn repertoire. Because

[37] Leaver, 'Goostly psalmes', p. 41.
[38] Henri-Léonard Bordier, Le chansonnier Huguenot du XVIe siècle (reprint edn, Geneva, 1969), p. ix.

of the important part they played in his conception of reformed liturgical practice, it was vitally important to Calvin that the whole canon of the Psalter be available in the new metrical translations. Marot had completed fifty at the time of his death; the work hung fire for a number of years, before, at Calvin's urging, the task of completing Marot's work was undertaken by Theodore de Bèze.[39]

De Bèze completed his work in 1562, a momentous year for French Calvinism in more ways than one. In its mature form the Calvinist metrical Psalter exhibited one final element of striking originality: all the melodies were newly composed. This was an important, and quite conscious, choice on Calvin's part. In contrast to Luther, Calvin eschewed the use of contrafacta. He saw no place for secular or popular religious tunes in the worship service. Some of the new tunes were based on plainsong melodies, and all were chosen for the 'gravity and majesty' of their style. All had to be simple, dignified, modal and free from secular overtones.

This set a difficult standard. Because of the large variety in the metrical structure of the translated verse, there was little capacity for duplication in the use of tunes. The complete Psalter uses 128 different melodies, written in 110 different metrical patterns.[40] Initially this enormously complicated the whole project. The tunes had first to be composed (this was largely the work of an unsung hero of the enterprise, Louis Bourgeois). Then the tunes, and words, had to be learned. For this Genevan ministers enrolled the schoolchildren, who then assisted the congregation to familiarize themselves with the new repertoire.

The large range of melodies was one reason why the Genevan psalms were seldom published without musical notation. This again made for a much more complex and expensive publishing project. The printing of musical notation posed the industry special problems, which it had taken some time to resolve. Initially printers had sought to exploit the double impression method used for rubrication, or two-colour printing. The page would be printed first with the bare staves; then the text and notes would be added in a second pressing. But this process required extreme precision with every pull of the press; if a page was even marginally out of alignment the notes would be printed off key, with calamitous results. The solution, which became generalized throughout the industry

[39] Christian Meyer, 'Le psautier huguenot: notes à propos de quelques éditions antérieures à son achèvement (1554–1561)', *Bulletin de la Société d'Histoire du Protestantisme Français*, 130 (1984), pp. 87–95.

[40] Pierre Pidoux, *Le psautier huguenot du XVIe siècle. Mélodies et documents* (2 vols., Basle, 1962). Edith Weber, *La musique protestante de langue française* (Paris, 1979). Waldo Pratt, *The Music of the French Psalter of 1562* (New York, 1966).

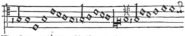

Ein Christenlichs lied Doctoris
Martini Luthers/die vnaußsprechliche
gnaden Gottes vnd des rechten
Glaubens begreyffendt.

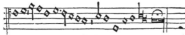

Nun frewt euch lieben Christen gmein.

Nun frewt euch lieben Christen gmein/Vnd laßt vns frö-
lich springen/Das wir getrost vnd all in ein/Mit lust vnd
liebe singen/Was got an vns gewendet hat/Vnd seine süsse
wunder that/Gar theür hat ers erworben.

Dem Teüffel ich gefangen lag/Im todt war ich verloren/
Mein sünd mich quellet nacht vn̄ tag/Darinn ich war ge-
boren/Ich viel auch ymmer tieffer drein/Es war kain güts
am leben mein/Die sünd hat mich besessen.

Mein güte werck die golten nicht/Es war mit jn verdor-
ben/Der frey wil hasset gots gericht/Er war zum gut er-
storben/Die angst mich zu verzweyffeln treyb/Das nichts
dann sterben bey mir bleyb/Zur hellen müst ich sincken.

Do jarmert Got in ewigkait/Mein elend vber maßen/Er
dacht an sein barmhertzigkait/Er wolt mir helffen laßen/
Er wandt zu mir das vater hertz/Es war bey jm fürwar
kain schertz/Er ließ sein Bestes kostes.

Er sprach zu seinem lieben son/Die zeyt ist hie zu erbarmen/
Far hyn meins hertzen werde kron/Vnd sey das hayl dem
armen/Vnd hilff jm auß der sünden not/Erwürge für jn
den bittern todt/Vnd laß jn mit dir leben.

Der sun dem vater gehorsam wardt/Er kam zu mir auff
erden/Von einer junckfraw rain vn̄ zart/Er solt mein Bru-
der werden/Gar haimlich fürt er sein gewalt/Er gieng in
meiner armen gestalt/Den Teüfel wolt er fangen.

Er sprach zu mir halt dich an mich/Es sol dir yzt gelin-
gen/Ich geb mich selber gantz für dich/Da wil ich für dich
ringen/Dañ ich bin dein vn̄ du bist mein/Vnd wo ich bleyb
soltu sein/Vns sol der feindt nicht schayden.

Vergiessen wirdt er mir mein plüt/Darzu mein leben rau-
ben/Das leyde ich alles dir zu gut/Das halt mit festem glau-
ben/Den todt verschlingt das leben mein/Mein vnschuldt
tregt die sünden dein/Da bistu selig worden.

Gen hymel zu dem vater mein/Far ich võ disem leben/Da
wil ich dein der maister dein/Den geyst wil ich dir gebē/Der
dich im trübtnup trösten sol/Vnd lernen mich erkennen wol/
Vnd in der warhait leytten.

De sa flambe, va consummant
Les chariotz, les abysmant.

Pourtant, faict à tous à sçauoir,
Qu'il est celuy, qui redoubté,
Doit estre, pour son grand pouuoir,
Et en tout le monde exalté.
Dieu des armees le Recteur,
Nous sera tousiours pour tuteur.
Le Dieu de Iacob, nous sera
Pour refuge, & nous gardera.

PSALME LI.

I se ricorde au paoure vici-

eux, Dieu tout puissant, par ta grande clemen-

effa cer mon faict perni cieux. Laue moy

Sire, & re la ue bien fort, De ma commissi-

niqui té mauluaise, Et du peché, qui m'a ren-

du si ord, Me nettoyer, d'eau de grace, te plaise.

Car de regret mon coeur vit en esmoy,
Congnoissant, las, ma grand' faulte presente:
Et touteffois, mon peché se presente,
Incessamment, noir & laid, deuant moy.
En ta presence, à toy seul, i'ay forfaict,
Si, qu'en donnant arrest, pour me deffaire,

Figure 3.1. The progressive sophistication of musical typography. From
the *Achtliederbuch* of 1524 to the French Reformed Psalter of 1563.

through the 1530s and 1540s, was to print all notes as separate charac-ters, each with a small portion of the five-bar stave. These could then be set up in lines of type as if they were conventional letter characters. It was an elegant and ultimately highly satisfactory resolution of a complex problem, but only if the publisher was prepared to go to the considerable expense of purchasing the special fonts of musical type.[41]

That the Genevan publishing industry was able to undertake the necessary investment was the consequence of two circumstances: the large injection of capital that followed the arrival in the city of established members of the well-founded Paris print fraternity, and the enormous popularity of the psalms themselves. From the time of Calvin's return to Geneva in 1541, the psalms became an essential part of church life.

Calvin's *Forme des prieres*, established soon after his return from Strasbourg, incorporated all of the Marot psalms then extant; an edition of 1543 used all of the fifty versifications completed before Marot's death. All of the early editions were published in small formats, often in parallel with editions of the *Catechisme* and *Forme des prieres ecclesias-tiques*. Booksellers took to binding the three books together, emphasizing their importance for private and congregational use. The responsibility to render the musical notation accurately and without variation was one that the printers took seriously, and that magistrates and ministers rigidly enforced. When one musically literate printer spied a note that had slid down from its stave and silently corrected the error for a new edition he was reported and imprisoned for twenty-four hours. The symbolic point was clear: not only the words of Scripture, but also the translation and the appointed melodies, were regarded as having near canonical status. In this way they were appropriated to the Gospel principle of the 'pure word of Scripture'. In fact, although new translations of Scripture did appear, there was little attempt to revise or vary the text of the psalms. They became, in this first and final form, a staple of French Calvinist culture.[42]

There is little reason to doubt the enormous and immediate popularity of the new metrical psalms. The new congregational singing had a profound resonance, both with the church community in Geneva, and among the embryonic congregations back in France. Editions of the psalms were a staple of the colporteur trade managed from Geneva

[41] Pierre Pidoux, 'Les origines de l'impression de musique à Genève', in J.-D. Candaux and B. Lescaze (eds.), *Cinq siècles d'imprimerie genevoise* (2 vols., Geneva, 1980), vol. I, pp. 97–108.
[42] The exception was Calvin's own early and rather clumsy versifications; these were quietly replaced by more accomplished translations by Théodore de Bèze.

by Laurent de Normandie, who supplied pedlars with the wares (often on credit) that they then carried over the mountains into France.[43] The explosion of public worship in France in the early 1560s brought a further surge of demand. Already by this point public psalm singing was identified as the defining activity of the new Calvinist congregations.

The expansion of the churches in France coincided with the completion by de Bèze of the Marot canon. This event was marked by one of the most extraordinarily coordinated publishing ventures of the sixteenth century. Anticipating the likely degree of public interest in the newly completed Psalter, the Genevan authorities organized a syndicate of printers in Geneva and France to bring it to the market. The enterprise was managed by the Lyon merchant Antoine Vincent, who licensed publication by some thirty printers in five different locations: Geneva, Lyon, Paris, Caen and Rouen. The intention was to ensure the availability of 35,000 copies of the work within a year.[44] This seems to have been comfortably accomplished, not least because in this brief interval the Psalter could be published without fear of reprisal. Although the 1561 Colloquy of Poissy had failed in its intention to promote reconciliation between the contending religious parties, Théodore de Bèze had taken advantage of the mood of conciliation to ask for a royal privilege for the Psalter. Incredibly, this was granted, a circumstance that explains the sudden enthusiastic involvement of so large a number of Parisian printers.[45]

The atmosphere of goodwill that fuelled the discussions of 1561 was quickly dispelled. With the outbreak of fighting in 1562, Parisian printers who had engaged with Protestant publishing found themselves badly exposed: most were swiftly ruined and driven out of the capital. But the psalms retained a tenacious hold on Protestant affections, even in this most Catholic of cities. When in 1571 the stock of the Protestant bookseller Richard Breton was seized and destroyed, more than half was comprised of editions of the psalms.[46]

---

[43] Heidi-Lucie Schlaepfer, 'Laurent de Normandie', in G. Berthoud (ed.), *Aspects de la propagande religieuse* (Geneva, 1957), pp. 176–230. Olson, *Calvin and Social Welfare*, pp. 51–2.

[44] Eugénie Droz, 'Antoine Vincent. La propagande protestante par le psautier', in Berthoud, *Aspects de la propagande religieuse*, pp. 276–93.

[45] Pidoux, *Le psautier Huguenot.*

[46] A further 10 per cent of the stock comprised combined editions of the New Testament and the Psalter. Barbara Diefendorf, *Beneath the Cross. Catholics and Huguenots in Sixteenth-Century Paris* (New York, 1991), pp. 132, 136.

How does one account for this extraordinary popularity? Of course, the metrical psalms could rely on the enthusiastic patronage of the ministers and consistories of churches that had grown with extraordinary speed in the last five years. But in France, too, the use of the metrical psalms quickly outgrew the confines of formal congregational worship. Psalm singing became the defining activity of the Protestant insurgency. Even in the years of persecution, condemned evangelicals walked to their execution with the psalms on their lips. The crowd often responded by singing with them in an embarrassing gesture of solidarity. Certainly the French authorities were discomforted: their response was to order that those condemned to die should have their tongues cut out to prevent such communal acts of defiance.[47] As the churches grew in size and confidence, psalm singing became successively a badge of identity and a symbol of militancy. In 1557 it was a vast public demonstration, accompanied by the singing of psalms, that alerted Henry II to the progress made by heresy in the capital. As events hurtled out of control clashes between rival gangs of religious enthusiasts in Bordeaux, Rouen and the cities of the south were invariably accompanied by rowdy psalm singing on the Protestant side.[48] In this context the sound of the familiar psalms, swelling from a nearby street or market, would be as public a signal as the ringing of the town bells, and citizens could either beat a hasty retreat or join the fray. But this use of the psalms for the insolent appropriation of public space undoubtedly played a large part in the rising sense of anger and frustration among the Catholic population – an anger that fuelled the extraordinary passions of the Religious Wars. So too did the violence that accompanied the psalm singing. At the famous Givry fair in 1561, the site of a notorious public preaching, gangs of Protestants rampaged among the stalls, singing psalms and overturning the wares of Catholic vendors. Iconoclastic attacks on churches and wayside shrines would invariably be accompanied by boisterous singing. To Catholics this double inversion of the religious purpose of Scripture – outdoors and part of a rite of violence and destruction – encapsulated their sense of alienation from a religion run riot – often quite literally.

---

[47] The French martyrologist Jean Crespin reported that, despite this, prisoners on occasion miraculously still retained the power of speech at the stake – an echo, no doubt conscious, of similar miraculous manifestations attending the deaths of the early Christian martyrs. *Histoire des vrays tesmoins de la verité de l'Evangile* (Geneva, 1570), ff. 79r, 163v, 290v. David Watson, 'The Martyrology of Jean Crespin and the Early French Evangelical Movement, 1523–1555' (University of St Andrews, Ph.D. dissertation, 1997), pp. 37, 62, 101.

[48] Philip Benedict, *Rouen during the Wars of Religion* (Cambridge, 1981), pp. 49–70. Philip Conner, *Huguenot Heartland. Montauban and Southern French Calvinism during the Wars of Religion* (Aldershot, St Andrews Studies in Reformation History, 2002).

How had the psalms assumed this potency as a badge of party allegiance? In part this owes much to the power singing has to forge bonds and connections that goes beyond the normal stratification of community life. In particular, song had the pedagogic power to unite different sorts of people in a way that cuts across divisions between the literate and the illiterate. The mnemonic power of song, drilled in the congregational worship service, was particularly enhanced in the case of the psalms. This circumstance was given added potency by certain compositional features of the psalms themselves. Because of the complex metrical structure of the original verse, there was little capacity to reuse melodies; most remained (in the French context at least) specific to a particular psalm. This left a large repertoire to be taught, but once it was known the potency of the text was enhanced by association with a particular melody. The most popular psalms soon built their own web of associations. Psalm 68 became the song of battle: 'Let God arise, may his enemies be scattered'. Victory achieved, the Huguenot host would sing Psalm 124: 'If it had not been the Lord who was on our side, now may Israel say . . '.[49]

In this context, one did not even need to hear the words to feel the well of association, constantly deepened and enriched by contemporary events: joyous, triumphant or tragic. The metrical psalms took a powerful part of the Scripture canon and shaped it to the needs of an evangelical movement. Singing expressed both the powerful urge to witness, and the power and strength of a communal moment.

The Huguenot movement in France soon lost the extraordinary vitality of this evangelical moment. But the affection for the psalms endured. Numerous witnesses, friendly and hostile, testify to the enduring popularity of the metrical psalms in the reformed communities. Catholics fretted that the French joy of singing made the poor particularly soft targets for the heretics. Some urged the poets (including the great Ronsard) to take up their pens to reclaim the psalms for true religion.[50] A poignant codicil is provided by an incident recently recovered from the records of the Spanish Inquisition. In 1557 or 1558 a group of around forty French Protestants left their homes in Normandy to resettle in Toledo.[51] Here they lived incognito, meeting together in secret to sing

---

[49] W. Stanford Reid, 'The Battle Hymns of the Lord. Calvinist Psalmody of the Sixteenth Century', in Carl S. Meyer (ed.), *Sixteenth Century Essays and Studies*, vol. II (St Louis, Mo., 1971), pp. 36–54.

[50] The task was taken up by Artus Desiré, who composed a volume of Catholic hymns specifically to make it unnecessary for Catholics to use the Protestant psalms. Artus Desiré, *Hymnes en François* (Paris, Ruelle, 1561).

[51] The case will be discussed at length in a forthcoming study by Clive Griffin.

psalms and reaffirm their faith, until they were discovered and denounced. Apparently a number of members of the group had been heard singing psalms as they went about their work. The practice had become so engrained that they could not help themselves.

The metrical psalms would be a signature part of the reformed tradition wherever it became established. The French experience exercised a particularly powerful influence in the Netherlands, where evangelicals shared a common experience of exile, and joined in the same joyous explosion of public worship in the 1560s. But the Dutch churches also developed their own independent tradition, incubated in the exile churches of London and Emden in the 1550s. The provision of metrical psalms for the London Dutch church was the achievement of Jan Utenhove, faithful collaborator of John a Lasco and later translator of the Bible. Utenhove, a patrician intellectual from a literary family in Ghent, drew on an eclectic range of sources. He had spent time in Strasbourg, and the Genevan French psalms would have been familiar from their use in the London French church. Utenhove also drew on the *Souterliedekens*, a song book published in Antwerp in 1539–40 that contained translations of all 150 of the psalms. Since the *Souterliedekens* made much use of familiar folk melodies, including drinking and hunting songs, in this way the popular repertoire infiltrated the Dutch metrical tradition.[52]

Utenhove's psalms acquired an instant popularity both in London and Emden, the north German town to which the congregation had been forced to move after the accession of Mary Tudor in 1553. In 1559, following the accession of Elizabeth, the Dutch church in London was re-established, and it was here that the work of adding to the psalm translations went forward. Utenhove died in 1563, so it was left to his London colleague Godfried van Winghen to supervise the completion of the project, finally published in 1566.[53]

With the outbreak of the Dutch Revolt in the same year this must have seemed as propitious a coincidence as that of the French publication in 1562; in fact, the influence of Utenhove's psalms would be far less enduring. Even before completion it was having to compete with independent rival ventures, most notably that of Pieter Dathenus. Dathenus identified two major deficiencies of the Utenhove psalms: a certain scholarly pedantry in the use of language, and the bewildering eclecticism of the melodies.[54] In contrast the psalms of Dathenus all closely follow the French models in structure and metre, so that the

[52] Leaver, '*Goostly psalmes*', pp. 92–8.
[53] Ibid., pp. 257–69.   [54] Ibid., pp. 269–71.

French melodies could be employed for the same psalms in the Dutch. This was a significant advantage in a culture like the Netherlands where connections between French and Dutch-speaking evangelicals were so close.

In these circumstances the version of Dathenus was bound to prevail, though not without some moments of comic farce when members of the new churches coming from different exile backgrounds struck up the psalm to competing melodies. The first Dutch synods, recognizing the problem, made a decision for Dathenus, and in 1571 even the London congregation fell into line. In the intervening years the metrical psalms had already taken their place at the centre of Dutch reformed worship. In the years of struggle they emerged, as in the French case, as a badge of identity. Condemned evangelicals went to their deaths singing the psalms; in 1565 a returning exile from Emden was fortunate to avoid the same fate when he arrived drunk in a Catholic service in Antwerp and started singing psalms during the Latin chants. When in the summer of 1566 the rising opposition brought thousands out into the fields to hear the returned exile preachers, enterprising printers in the Netherlands rushed out editions of the psalms to meet the new demand. Some even appropriated the familiar device of the Emden printer Gilles van der Erve, the principal publisher of Dutch Calvinist texts during the previous ten years. The Psalters were brought out into the fields and sold to the crowds for a stuiver, or less.[55] Here, too, Catholic observers had no doubt of the part played by communal singing in fostering the extraordinary growth of the evangelical churches during the Dutch *Wonderjaar*. When the inquisitive and thoughtful patrician diarist Marcus van Vaernewijck wandered out to observe the construction of the new Calvinist church in Ghent, he quickly discerned the importance of both the psalms and communal singing in the life of the new communities. The psalms, he observed, 'fostered a truly godly exhilaration, the more so because each understood the fine words of the Holy Scripture which he sang'.[56] With this simple comment Van Vaernewijck captured the true potency of the psalms as both a form of scriptural teaching and a tool of communal self-identification.

---

[55] Pettegree, *Emden and the Dutch Revolt Exile and the Development of Reformed Protestantism* (Oxford, 1992), p. 140. Howard Slenk, 'Jan Utenhove's Psalms in the Low Countries', *Nederlands Archief voor Kerkgeschiedenis*, 49 (1968–9), pp. 155–68.

[56] Quoted in Duke, Lewis and Pettegree, *Calvinism. Documents*, pp. 153, 155. According to Van Vaernewijck the community used to teach each other the psalms in the evenings, that is, outside of the worship service.

In Scotland and England the psalm tradition built on these continental beginnings in rather different ways. The Scottish tradition drew on the two streams of the Genevan Psalter and the Sternhold and Hopkins collection popular south of the border. As in Geneva, where John Knox had spent educational and profitable years, psalm singing became an integral part of the service. As in England, the local vernacular translations drew on a drastically reduced canon of melodies. The use of simplified melodies does not seem to have impeded their popularity – quite the contrary. Although the First Book of Discipline had cautiously regarded psalm singing as desirable but not strictly necessary, the congregations took to the psalms with enthusiasm.

Psalms were sung before and after each sermon; no doubt they provided welcome relief after the prolonged period of attentive listening to the preacher. The Scottish practice (as was also the case in the Netherlands) was for the psalms to be lined out by a precentor, the congregation then repeating back the line, an ideal method for committing the tune to memory. Naturally they were sung unaccompanied. This practice of alternation, between cantor and congregation, which is still practised in some parts of the Western Isles, could create a strong emotional impact. As a boy Andrew Melville found the singing of the blind precentor in Montrose so delighted him that he 'learned many of the psalms and tunes thereof in metre, which I have thought ever since a great blessing and comfort'.[57] By the end of the century the practice of psalm singing was so deeply engrained that congregations reacted very adversely to attempts to introduce a new version. 'The people', it was objected, 'has been so long acquainted with the old metre that some can sing all or at least many of the psalms without the book'.[58]

In England, the infiltration of the metrical psalms into the liturgical tradition was more complex. England had a more robust and independent tradition of vernacular hymn translation, reaching back into the first generation of reform, when Miles Coverdale published his *Goostly Psalms* (1535). The forty-one texts in this volume were drawn, in the main, from Luther's hymns. The practice of singing psalms in England was significantly developed during the reign of Edward VI, though here Coverdale's work was eclipsed by the new translations of Thomas Sternhold, a Gentleman of the Privy Chamber during the last years of Henry VIII. In the tradition of Clément Marot, Sternhold began writing psalms to sing at court, apparently to popular chanson tunes, but it was

---

[57] Todd, *Culture of Protestantism*, p. 72.   [58] Ibid.

only with the accession of Edward VI that the psalms gained a wider currency. These psalms had no immediate liturgical purpose, since the 1549 Prayer Book made no explicit provision for hymn singing. The popularity of the new Psalter, both Sternhold's version and a complete cycle published by Robert Crowley, suggests informal liturgical use.

English Protestants first became attuned to the full potential of psalmody during the years of exile under Mary. In Emden, Wesel, Frankfurt, Strasbourg and Geneva, the English congregations first observed then adopted a form of worship service in which congregational singing was integral.[59] The climax of this activity was the publication in 1556 of William Whittingham's *One and Fifty Psalmes of David*, the majority based on Sternhold's originals, though heavily revised. As was the case with the Dutch Psalter of Utenhove, the canon of translations was gradually completed after restoration of the English Protestant church under Elizabeth.

The English metrical psalms were immediately popular. The right to publication was for John Daye a profitable part of his vice-like grip on the staples of English congregational life, and repeated re-editions appeared very steadily from his press. According to the latest tabulation there were over 130 separate editions during the reign of Elizabeth, and a further 340 before the English Civil War. This popularity is all the more extraordinary when one considers that the liturgical function of the psalms in English worship rested on most insecure foundations. The royal injunctions of 1559 that permitted the performance, before or after Evening Prayer, of a 'hymn or such like song', may have covered the psalms, but the psalms were never specifically prescribed for worship. At the same time, the range of tunes in use actually diminished. Whereas the editions of the 1540s had used over forty tunes for the repertoire, by the end of the century this had so diminished that over half the psalms were appointed to be sung to just three tunes. This seems not to have diminished their popularity. By the time of the English Civil War there may have been as many as one million copies of these books in print, many in convenient small formats bound for personal use with catechisms and Bibles.

Militant in song

In England then, as in Scotland, France and the Netherlands, the psalms quickly became embedded in the culture of the new Protestantism.

---

[59] Leaver, '*Goostly psalmes*', pp. 175–237.

Their popularity and use spilled out from the worship service into the streets and private homes (in England, quite possibly the psalms made the reverse journey). Times of crisis accentuated and focused their purpose as a badge of identity and militant defiance, though in this respect the original text often required little embellishment. This point was made with some force in the uncomfortable proceedings conducted by the Genevan magistrates after the failure of the Conspiracy of Amboise in 1560, an ill-judged armed insurrection in which the Genevan ministers appeared to be implicated. Among the charges levied against Théodore de Bèze was the text of his translation of Psalm 40, a veritable hymn to violence:

> Who will rise up for me against the evil-doers?
> And he shall bring down upon them their own iniquity;
> And shall cut them off in their own wickedness;
> Yea, the Lord our God shall cut them off.[60]

On this occasion the council chose to believe de Bèze's denials. Two years later he would be in France, rallying support at the headquarters of the Duke of Condé, preaching with a sword at his belt.

In such circumstances few could deny the potential for incitement embedded in the text of Scripture. But, as in the Lutheran tradition, the clash of religious cultures also nurtured the growth of an explicitly polemical song tradition, often of a tone and virulence that made it wholly inappropriate for formal congregational worship. Once again, the French led the way. The first known examples of protest songs in France date from 1525; they emanate from the Meaux circle, and are expressive of the bitterness felt when Bishop Briçonnet abandoned his flirtation with diocesan reform. They survive not in print, but in a report from the lieutenant-general of the bailliage of Meaux registered in the records of the Parlement of Paris. The local officer had carefully transcribed the song, of which this gives a flavour. It warns the preacher, Michel d'Arende, a friend of the reformer, Guillaume Farel, of the dangers of dissent:

> Don't preach the truth, Master Michael!
> If you continue the Gospel way
> There is too great a danger
> Of landing in prison, in the Conciergerie.[61]

The tune was that of a popular song, *N'allez plus au bois jouer*.

[60] Quoted Donald R. Kelley, *François Hotman. A Revolutionary's Ordeal* (Princeton, N.J., 1973), p. 125.
[61] Bordier, *Chansonnier Huguenot*, pp. xiii–xxiii.

The first age of evangelical print also provided opportunities for the dissemination of satirical songs. In 1532 Pierre de Vingle published the *Chansons des dix commandements de Dieu* by Antoine Saulnier; three years later he published a first collection of anti-papal songs. In the first generation these satirical songs trained their fire almost exclusively on traditional targets: the corruptions of the Mass, the decadence of the Catholic clergy, the venality of the Pope. This sort of rhymed ridicule had at least the tacit support of the leaders of the new church. For all the scholarly authority of the *Institutes* and his biblical commentaries, in his early years Calvin had shown an unexpected talent for prose invective, a tradition in which his principal collaborators Farel and Viret also excelled. The chanson collections breathed the same defiant spirit, alternating invective with a more contemplative mood of patience in adversity. Many of the new songs were the work of Eustorg Beaulieu, whose *Chrestienne resjouissance* was published in Geneva in 1546. This formidable collection contained 160 songs, all original compositions, according to the author.[62]

There is plentiful evidence that these early collections circulated quite freely in France. In 1542 the Parlement of Toulouse published a list of forbidden books which contained two volumes of chansons, one of seventy-six and one of fourteen songs. In Paris, in 1549, the tailor Jacques Duval was sentenced to be burned alive with the book with which he had been apprehended, *Chansons spirituelles*. If he persevered in his defiance, his tongue was to be cut as he left the prison.[63]

With the crisis of government that ushered in the Religious Wars, verse satire took on a new intensity. It became simultaneously more pointed and more polemical. In 1559 Huguenot authors rushed to celebrate the sacrifice of the Huguenot magistrate Anne de Bourg, who paid the price for his dramatic defiance of Henry II at the Parlement of Paris. Other more overtly political satires impugned the good faith of the Catholic councillors who were seen to be the malign influence behind the new king, Francis II. One of these new compositions raised for the first time the spectre of political assassination, with the Cardinal of Lorraine the intended target:

> Garde toy Cardinal
> Que te ne sois traité
> A la minarde
> D'une Stuarde.[64]

---

[62] Ibid., pp. xxviii–xxix.   [63] Ibid., pp. xxvii–xxx.

[64] Jacques Pineaux, *La poésie des protestants de langue française du premier synode national jusqu'à la proclamation de l'édit de Nantes (1559–1598)* (Paris, 1971), p. 103.

The reference is to Robert Stuart, who in December 1559 had assassinated Antoine Minard, the judge who condemned Anne de Bourg to death.

In these new types of political verse we observe the convergence of two separate traditions, religious song and secular poetry. The sixteenth century in France was a period of considerable poetical energy, much of it written under the sponsorship of the great. Poets were accustomed to bending their talents to heaping praise on their patrons: in this they took their cue from figures like Ronsard and Marot, whose polished verses of congratulation and praise achieved notable feats of sophistication and sycophancy. It was a small step from encomia of noble virtues to praise of their patrons' valour in the field of battle; another small step to heaping derision on their religious enemies. Huguenot poets took up the challenge with vigour, in a polemical exchange that reached its first climax during the brief reign of Francis II, when the domination of government by the Guise made them a convenient target of criticism. But even this political verse had not entirely outgrown its connection with the previous generation of anticlerical and religious literature. The *Estreines au Cardinal* took both its rhythm and rhyme from Marot's version of Psalm 38.[65] Other verses lauded the leaders of the new movement. The *Hymne à Dieu* compared Condé, with inevitable hyperbole, to Moses.[66]

The poetical battle reached its climax with the onset of the first religious war. These were the years in which the Huguenot movement expanded most rapidly beyond the literate core of its earliest congregations; perhaps not coincidentally much of this newly minted polemic was in verse. Many of the works from this period are extremely topical, celebrating the short-lived Huguenot victories of 1562–3, or heaping scorn on the vanquished Catholics. A number explicitly exploit the new familiarity with the melodies of the metrical psalms. The *Cantique et action de Grace au Seigneur* gave thanks for the Protestant victory in Lyon in verses designed to be sung to the tune of Psalm 7. The Protestant princes were singled out for special praise for their part in the military success. Another military victory was celebrated in the *Ode hystoriale de la bataille de saincte Gile, sur le chant du pseaume huitante vn.*

[65] Ibid., p. 112.

[66] Jacques Pineaux, 'Poésie de cour et poésie de combat: l'admiral Gaspard de Coligny devant les poètes contemporains', *Bulletin de la Société d'Histoire du Protestantisme Français*, 118 (1972), pp. 32–54.

The end of the conflict brought forth the *Echo parlant a la paix . . . sur le chant de pseaume trente trois.*[67]

Most of this new polemical verse was published without music; from which we may infer that the melodies of the psalms were now so familiar that they could easily be turned to these new purposes. For a movement that had initially eschewed both the use of contrafacta and the use of violence this was a somewhat ironic turn of events, but from the point of view of the polemical conflict highly significant. Whereas an edition with musical notation would require the intervention of an established printing house, these new highly contemporary verses could be brought out at speed, by printers close to the events described. These little books are highly ephemeral, and seldom survive in more than one or two copies; some are only now coming to light. From typographical evidence it appears that, during the brief period when the Huguenots held sway, Lyon had become a major centre of production of this verse polemic. From composition to distribution in the streets could be a matter of a few days, if that. On one occasion an account of the Protestant coup advertised itself as having been ready for sale the same day as the events it describes.[68]

This literature is popular in the sense that it was intended for a wide and disparate audience. The internal evidence suggests, however, that the verses were penned by men of education, who expected their work to be enjoyed in the parlours of the bourgeoisie as much as in the taverns and on street corners. This verse then, in some senses, stands as a symbol of both the political and the social aspirations of the new movement: to vanquish the Catholic Mass, and build in its stead a community of all Christian people. These hopes would be dashed almost from the point when the Protestant *grands* accepted peace terms in 1563, which prefigured the slow death of the major urban churches, at least in the north. But for this brief moment of optimism, French Calvinism had been a genuinely mass movement.

In the Netherlands the outbreak of the Dutch Revolt unleashed a torrent of political songs. The ground was well prepared, since evangelicals had been using anticlerical verses to undermine the Catholic authorities since at least the 1550s. In some cities in Flanders subversive song became such a problem that the municipal authorities banned

---

[67] These works are discussed in Andrew Pettegree, 'Protestant Printing during the French Wars of Religion. The Lyon Press of Jean Saugrain', in Thomas A. Brady, Katherine G. Brady, Susan Karant-Nunn and James D. Tracy (eds.), *The Work of Heiko A. Oberman. Papers from the Symposium on his Seventieth Birthday* (Brill, 2003), pp. 109–29.

[68] *Cantique de la victoire pour l'Eglise de Lyon. A Lyon, le iour de la victoire, dernier du mois d'Auril. 1562* (Lyon, 1562). Copy in Aix, Bibliothèque Méjanes: Rec. D 9 (1358).

singing in the market square, and even attempted to prohibit any references to Scripture in song.[69] The first revolt of 1566 was speedily repressed; members of the congregations retired back into exile, to plan for another day, while the Duke of Alva arrived from Spain to restore obedience. Among those caught up in the clampdown on dissidence were a number of street vendors, including the seventeen-year-old pedlar Cornelis Peterz, arrested in Harlingen in December 1567 for singing scandalous songs. Since his stock was impounded as evidence, three examples of his wares actually survive with the papers deposited in the Kampen Stadsarchief. One is a thin strip printed in a simple black letter type, no doubt exceptionally cheap to produce. Peterz deposed that he received his songs from intermediaries, and when he sold out he had them reprinted in Steenwijk.[70]

It was the administration of Alva, and particularly his hated tax, the infamous Tenth Penny, which inspired the largest and most varied repertoire of opposition songs. Many of the literally hundreds of songs mentioned the tax by name, and Alva was a particular focus of patriotic and religious hatred. On 16 March 1572, days before the rebels landed back in Holland, the people of Ghent found their streets littered with copies of a parody of the Lord's Prayer, in 'the style of the rhetoricians', in honour of Alva:

> Hellish father who in Hell doth dwell
> Cursed be thy name in heaven and in hell
> Thy kingdom, which has lasted too long, be gone
> Thy will in heaven and earth be not done.[71]

The Beggar songs used a mixture of popular folk tunes and contrafacta of the by now well-known metrical psalms. Many of the psalm tunes were used over and over again, in a complex genealogy that piled layers of allusion on top of one another. In 1564, for instance, the execution of the Calvinist minister Christoffel Fabritius was commemorated with a newly composed song, 'Antwerpen rijck, O Keyserlicke Stede'. It was sung to the tune of Psalm 79. 'Antwerpen rijke' became a classic protest song of the movement, and the tune was used again and again for newly composed songs for over a hundred years.[72] Louis Peter

[69] Johann Decavele, De dageraad van de Reformatie in Vlaanderen, 1520–1565 (Brussels, 1975), pp. 220–9.
[70] Martine de Bruin, 'Geuzen- en antigeuzenliederen' in L. P. Grijp (ed.), Een muziekgeschiedenis der Nederlanden (Amsterdam, 2001) pp. 174–80.
[71] Geoffrey Parker, The Dutch Revolt (London, 1977), p. 127.
[72] Louis Peter Grijp, 'Van geuzenlied tot Gedenk-clanck', De Zeventiende Eeuw, 10 (1994), pp. 266–76.

Grijp has enumerated over twenty examples in a wide range of political and confessional contexts, including three further Beggar songs and five Calvinist religious tunes. The song was also appropriated by Roman Catholics, and by the Dutch Anabaptists on no fewer than twelve occasions. Here then is a complex web indeed: a song to commemorate a Calvinist martyr, based on a Calvinist psalm, that becomes a staple of the competing Anabaptist tradition.

Nothing illustrates the extraordinary richness and complexity of this tradition of polemical song better than the history of the *Wilhelmus*, now the Dutch national anthem.[73] The *Wilhelmus* was composed around 1568 as a song in exultation of William of Orange, newly emerged as the champion of Protestant resistance to Alva. The composer of the fifteen-verse lyric is thought to have been the statesman theologian Marnix de Ste Aldegonde, a close ally of Orange, but the tune was French. In fact it was taken from a contemporary Catholic political song, composed to celebrate the defeat of Condé at the battle of Chartres. Despite this mixed heritage, the *Wilhelmus* swiftly attained an extraordinary popularity, becoming the model for numerous contrafacta. The tune was used for over twenty different Beggar songs. But this did not prevent it being appropriated with equal frequency by both Anabaptists and Roman Catholics (or re-appropriated, in the latter case). A Catholic song lamenting the fate of the priests martyred at Gorcum (a notorious Protestant atrocity of 1574) was set to the *Wilhelmus* tune, and this began a tradition that extended well into the Dutch Golden Age.

The appropriation of an anthem for satirical, oppositional purposes is an obvious and deliberate provocation. Here the previously insurgent Dutch, now established as the rulers of the free north, were repaid in their own coin. Small wonder that in times of tension the rulers of the Netherlandish towns tried to restrict public singing of these highly inflammatory tunes.

For all its exceptional popularity, the *Wilhelmus* exhibits several features typical of the song repertoire of the age. Nothwithstanding its purpose as a rallying cry for a mass movement, and its extraordinary success in this regard, the lyrical composition was one of considerable complexity and sophistication. The fifteen eight-line verses are organized to reflect a compositional symmetry: verses 1 and 15 are paired in terms of subject material, as are 2 and 14, until they converge at verse 8. The first letters of the fifteen verses spell out the name Willem van Nassau. In this respect the *Wilhelmus* continues the arch, elegant

---

[73] Martine de Bruin, 'Het Wilhelmus tijdens de Republiek', in Louis Peter Grijp, *Nationale hymnen. Het Wilhelmus en zijn buren* (Nijmegen and Amsterdam, 1998), pp. 16–42.

compositional tradition of the *Rederijkers*, and the same could be said of much of the 'popular' music of the first Calvinist era.

Godly ballads

In England, the potential of verse had been consciously exploited by both proponents and opponents of religious change since the beginning of the Reformation. In his efforts to build support for the measures of Henry VIII, Thomas Cromwell proved an effective pioneer of the exploitation of verse for propaganda purposes. As later reported by the martyrologist John Foxe, he was the sponsor of many 'excellent ballads and books . . . contrived and set abroad concerning the suppression of the Pope and all Popish idolatry'.[74] Among his sponsored authors was William Gray, whose *Fantasie of Idolatry* denounced the false images, miracles and shrines of the saints. With compositions of this sort Cromwell and his creatures tapped skilfully into the complex web of gossip, rumour, news and libel that was the staple of village sociability. But such weapons could also be turned against the Reformation: soon Henry's minister was forced to confront a groundswell of damaging rumours and prophecies inspired by the unsettling effects of the assault on the Catholic church.

The conflict ebbed back and forth through the generations of mid-century religious change. The Edwardian Reformation stimulated a new wave of anti-Catholic ballads, including at least one title, *Mistress Mass*, that was still circulating in England during the reign of Mary. The Marian exile authors also did not neglect the culture of cheap print. The former bishop John Poynet was among those urging the historian John Bale not to immerse himself wholly in scholarly projects: 'Ballads, rhymes and short toys that be not dear and will easily be born away, do much good at home among the rude people'.[75]

Beyond such orchestrated campaigns, the English Reformation also developed a robust tradition of commercial ballad prints on religious subjects.[76] These 'godly ballads' were very much part of the general

---

[74] Quoted in Fox, *Oral and Literate Culture*, p. 383.

[75] Ibid., p. 386.

[76] For what follows see especially Tessa Watt, *Cheap Print and Popular Piety, 1550–1640* (Cambridge, 1991). Some of the interpretative conclusions of Watt's analysis of ballads have recently been challenged by Ian Green. See especially Ian Green, *Print and Protestantism in Early Modern England* (Oxford, 2000), pp. 445–72. See also now, Christopher Marsh, 'The Sound of Print in Early Modern England: The Broadside Ballad as Song', in Julia Crick and Alexandra Walsham (eds.), *The Uses of Script and Print, 1300–1700* (Cambridge, 2004), pp. 171–90.

entertainment culture of Elizabethan England, particularly in the first half of the reign. Their most recent historian, Tessa Watt, has offered a careful estimate of the total size of this market. Based on the titles registered in the records of the Stationers' Company, she reckons that as many of three or four million copies of these broadsheets may have been published in the eighty years before 1640.

These are staggering, but plausible, figures. The output is especially impressive when one considers that all of these publications had to radiate out from one centre of production, London. Of course it is possible that, in the particular case of England, the fact that publishing was wholly concentrated on the metropolis may actually have increased the appetite for these prints. In 1641 one print advertised itself with a bold claim: 'for a peny you may have all the Newes in England, of Murders, Flouds, Witches, Fires, Tempests, and what not, in one of Martin Parkers Ballads'.[77] That is precisely the point: the domination of the metropolis meant that only through London could one have 'all the news of England' – and incidentally much foreign news as well.[78]

Although the major commercial purpose was always titillation and entertainment, it is possible that at least at the beginning of Elizabeth's reign some godly preachers saw the penny ballads as a useful adjunct to the preaching of the church. It is easy to see why, when one considers the helpful topography of subject material supplied by Tessa Watt on the basis of her analysis of the records of the Stationers' registers. Many of the ballads addressed, even if in rather simplistic terms, some of the major issues confronting citizens of sixteenth-century Protestant societies in their devotional lives. Ballads focused attention on the ubiquity of sin, and the immorality of everyday living; on the uncertainties of salvation, and on fear of the afterlife. The concern for the hereafter was clearly an especially lively, nagging anxiety. This was reflected in a hugely popular style of ballad based on last dying words, some of pious citizens who had lived a good life, others of repentant sinners: in this case the very popular subgenre of the execution ballad was an especially important example. This provided a perfect example of the interweaving of the desire for sensation and titillation with a degree of sententious moralizing. Was this latter element merely a fig leaf of respectability, or did the drama of execution really turn the minds of witnesses to

---

[77] Watt, *Cheap Print*, p. 11.

[78] On the market for foreign news see below, chapter 8. On Elizabethan news pamphlets see also Sandra Clark, *The Elizabethan Pamphleteers. Popular Moralistic Pamphlets, 1580–1640* (London, 1983).

contemplation of sombre verities? If so, the execution ballad carried these concerns to a wider audience.

Despite the apparent eclipse of the godly ballads as the psalms tightened their hold on English parish life towards the end of the six-teenth century, some of them were sufficiently enduring to form part of the Stationers' stock until deep into the seventeenth century. Particularly popular were those that celebrated Protestant heroes, such as Anne Askew and the Marian exile, Katherine Brandon, Duchess of Suffolk. The complex interpretative difficulties of the ballads are well represented by a 1602 broadsheet of this evergreen tale of exile and adventure. On the one hand, the ballad makes much of the more theatrical elements of a tale that seems to have accrued additional comic elements with the passage of the years. In this respect the ballad has more in common with any number of tales of fortitude and adventure told with little moralizing purpose. On the other hand, as the opening of the ballad makes clear, there is no doubt who are the heroes, and who the villains:

> When God had taken, for our sinne
> That prudent prince, King Edward away,
> Then bloody Bonner did begin
> His raging malice to betway
> All those that did God's Work professe
> He persecuted more or less.[79]

The required name recognition is here, at the very end of Elizabeth's reign, especially interesting. Not only do we have invocation of Edward VI, the godly prince, but clearly the reference to Bishop Bonner, the pantomime villain of John Foxe's narrative of the Marian persecutions, is expected to raise a frisson of horror. Other popular ballads attacked popery, and called attention to the ceaseless struggle against the forces of international Catholicism, cruel, cunning and ubiquitous: a theme which dovetailed neatly with the pamphlets relating news of Protestant trials and triumphs in the continental wars, and indeed with the themes of much of the topical drama on the London stage.[80] Of course we have to consider that, even if not reprinted, many of these ballads may have continued to circulate in manuscript copies, by word of mouth, and as part of the repertoire of performance of travelling entertainers. In this way the ballads composed in the aftermath of the Elizabethan settlement could resurface to articulate the rumbling unease at the Romanizing tendencies of the Laudian agenda of the early seventeenth century.

---

[79] Watt, *Cheap Print*, p. 91. The broadsheet is illustrated on p. 92.
[80] Below, chapters 4, 8.

In recent years historians have begun to call attention to the interpretative paradox we have been offered in recent studies of the English Reformation, a narrative in which English people deeply loved the practices of the old church, resented its disruption, and accepted the new rites with passive incomprehension.[81] And yet within two or three generations they cared sufficiently about their new church to want to defend it, doggedly and passionately, against two generations of the Stuart monarchy. By the seventeenth century, for all that they might not understand precise points of doctrine, many people held their new church in great affection, and felt an equal and profound dislike of Catholicism.

Why this might be so is addressed more systematically in a later chapter, but one may already see how the singing traditions discussed in this chapter may have played their part in this process. Godly ballads and psalm singing should not in this respect be viewed as being in an antagonistic relationship. For the ballads, for all their simplicity of purpose and style, do sketch the basis of a coherent layman's theology. Their enduring popularity demonstrated that English parishioners were perfectly capable of absorbing their messages as part of a diverse entertainment culture.

It is a characteristic of the mature Protestant churches that as their clerical leaders developed a narrower view of the acceptable means to enlightenment, they spurned traditions that had effectively articulated some of the core doctrines and debates of the sixteenth-century religious struggle. This was true of song, in so far as they looked askance when the authorized congregational singing of psalms and hymns strayed into a more popular idiom. It was also true of the theatre.

---

[81] J. J. Scarisbrick, *The Reformation and the English People* (Oxford, 1984). Christopher Haigh, *English Reformations. Religion, Politics and Society under the Tudors* (Oxford, 1993). Eamon Duffy, *The Stripping of the Altars: Traditional Religion in England, c.1400–c.1580* (New Haven, Conn., 1992).

4   Reformers on stage

After preaching and song we turn to examine one further aspect of oral culture: drama. As with the other two media, drama had a rich and varied mediaeval heritage; the three modes of communication were in many respects closely connected, and each drew on the traditions and associations of the other. Popular theatricals made much use of song and the playing of musical instruments: drums, horns and pipes provided the steady backcloth to the other more dramatic special effects expected by a discerning and demanding audience. Mediaeval drama also shared much in common with the preaching tradition.[1] We have already laid some stress on the theatricality of the mediaeval sermon, and preaching certainly shared with the more overt theatrical performances the sense of a special event for which large and eager crowds would gather in the expectation of something rousing and unusual. The two events had much in common in terms of their unfolding rhythm and drama: the long period of anticipation, the gathering of large bodies of eager auditors, milling noisily in the city's public space; the carefully managed choreography of the performance, the skill of the performer to rouse emotion and build to a thrilling climax. Preachers were well aware of the weight of expectations that fell on their performance; if they failed to entertain and enthral, travelling players offered other free entertainments.

This does not imply, however, that the great preachers were necessarily opposed to drama, or resented the competition of dramatic presentations. On the contrary, attendance at great passion plays was positively encouraged, even by the grant of indulgences. Mediaeval play records suggest that playgoers received remission (the most common period was forty days) for performances in Lucerne, Mainz, Strasbourg, Vienna and

---

[1] Carla van Dauven-Knippenberg, 'Ein Anfang ohne Ende: Einführendes zur Frage nach dem Verhältnis zwischen Predigt und geistlichem Schauspiel des Mittelalters', in Ulrich Mehler and Anton H. Touber (eds.), *Mittelalterliches Schauspiel* (Amsterdam, 1994), pp. 143–60.

several other cities.[2] Plays or processions were also staged in connection with the sale of indulgences.[3] The skilful preacher could make effective use of the dramatic repertoire to connect with the lives of his auditors.

It must always be remembered that the mediaeval dramatic tradition was born and nurtured in the church; the first dramatic representations formed an integral part of the liturgical round. Although by the fourteenth and fifteenth centuries these performances had become an entirely separate social experience, even though plays had emerged from the church, they remained exclusively religious in subject material and themes. As the preacher wove his web of allegory and exhortation, he would know that a large part of the repertoire of biblical stories familiar to his auditors emerged from performance drama: the mediaeval mysteries, miracle plays and farces. The Reformation engaged this tradition with an awareness of both the opportunities and the perils of a performance medium that gave full rein to the dramatization of emotion, belief and the perils of immoral living. It was a subtle and constructive relationship, though not without its bruising aspects.

Miracles and mysteries

Mediaeval drama had much in common with the preaching tradition. It was ubiquitous, but occasional; it was also fundamentally an urban phenomenon. The distinguished scholar Lynette Muir has described the popular passion plays and Corpus Christi plays as one of the outstanding cultural monuments of mediaeval Europe – a claim which, as we have seen, has also been made for preaching.[4] Further, the geographical heartlands of drama and preaching show a high degree of convergence: France, Italy, Germany, England and the Low Countries were the chief strongholds of the mediaeval biblical play. This convergence was far from accidental. Plays found their primary location in the heartlands of commerce and the centres of population mobility that offered the greatest opportunity to gather a crowd. Their sponsors were often the city fathers themselves, for the staging of plays represented one aspect of a growing civic sense of self-awareness, much as these same magistrates might seek to attract the best and most celebrated preachers. The kinship of these two special events is a reminder that the gathering

---

[2] Bernd Neumann, *Geistliches Schauspiel in Zeugnis der Zeit. Zur Aufführung mittelalterlicher religiöser Dramen im deutschen Sprachgebiet* (2 vols., Munich, 1987), nos. 2106, 2258, 2660, 3024.

[3] Glenn Ehrstine, *Theater, Culture and Community in Reformation Bern, 1523–1555* (Leiden, 2002), p. 18.

[4] Lynette R. Muir, *The Biblical Drama of Mediaeval Europe* (Cambridge, 1995), p. 1.

of large crowds outdoors was not just an occasion for worrying disorder (though it could be this also), but an important part of communal self-expression.

Drama also represented a crucial area of popular engagement with biblical teaching. Most of the varied forms of mediaeval drama were intensely biblical in their essentials. In broad terms, mediaeval drama conformed to one of three main styles: the mystery play, the miracle play, and the morality play. The first of these clearly hewed closest to the biblical narrative, while the miracle play generally presented the life of an individual saint. The morality play was a rather separate outgrowth, though still with a clear spiritual intent: generally it presented the choices of the Christian life through allegorical representations that personified the virtues and vices. It is this form too from which develops the humanist drama that forms a further important part of the inherited dramatic heritage of the Reformation.

Of all these various dramatic manifestations it was the mystery play that had the longest heritage and the greatest popularity. The best known were the passion plays and the Corpus Christi plays, these last specifically associated with the great Eucharistic feast that achieved such dramatic popularity in the late mediaeval period.[5] Many of these Corpus Christi plays were interwoven with the great processions that accompanied celebration of the festival in many parts of Europe – a reminder that mediaeval drama was often not confined to a single fixed location even for a whole performance. The passion plays, which reached the high point of their popularity in the late fifteenth and early sixteenth centuries, were also often combined with processions and religious festivals. The towns of France and Germany witnessed the most intense engagement with these play cycles, though England too had a rich heritage of sacred play cycles, several of which survive in reasonably complete form. The passion plays were, as their name suggests, centred on the life of Jesus, though this became the framework for a vast sprawling narrative that mixed stories from the Old and New Testaments. France, it seems, had the longest plays in Europe. The Acts of the Apostles of Simon and Arnoul Greban extended to 60,000 lines, and there were many others of considerable size. As this suggests, the staging of such plays was a vast undertaking, including large numbers of players, props and special effects. By the fifteenth century responsibility for the expense involved was shouldered jointly by the local city magistrates and the civil guilds. The guilds often contributed scenes representative of

[5] Miri Rubin, *Corpus Christi. The Eucharist in Late Mediaeval Culture* (Cambridge, 1991), pp. 277–87.

their craft: well keepers were responsible for Noah and the Flood, bakers for the Last Supper; blacksmiths portrayed Christ in chains before Pilate.[6]

These vast and sprawling performances combined the serious treatment of biblical themes with a strong element of the farcical. The low comedy was provided by stock characters such as Judas, the Jews and the Devil, who, interestingly, is frequently represented as a stupid bungler – a prototype of the modern pantomime villain. Judas received his ill-gotten reward in bad coin (a common concern of urban commercial life). The burlesque elements undoubtedly increased the capacity for rowdiness and social disorder inherent in so large an interruption to the normal workaday regime, and by the sixteenth century this was giving increasing concern to urban authorities even in Catholic countries. In 1548 the Paris authorities ordered a ban on further performances by the previously privileged Confrérie de la Passion. But with the public the passion plays retained a robust popularity. A wide variety of play texts successfully made the transition from manuscript to print: one of the most successful, the Passion of Jean Michel, a large text of 30,000 lines, went through at least twenty editions.[7]

The hagiographical miracle plays had developed in parallel with the mystery play in the fourteenth and fifteenth centuries, though they do not seem to have achieved quite the same popularity. These works, which generally presented the main events in a saint's life, seem often to have been written to be performed on a saint's name day. As this would imply, they were more restrained and sober performances than the mysteries; they were also much shorter. They seem to have been most popular in Spain and Italy, as well as in France, where the title sometimes concealed a play text that left far more room for contemporary drama and social comment. The forty plays in the collection *Miracles de Notre Dame* performed in Paris in the fourteenth century were large texts, with a cast of characters that stretched to as many as fifty roles. The plots, which each build towards a miraculous intervention by the Virgin, allow the portrayal of a complex web of crime and deceit: these plays have drifted far from the pious mysticism of the southern tradition.[8]

More general in its appeal was the mediaeval morality play, a form that spawned a wide variety of inventive and popular entertainments in many European cultures. The morality play revolved around a cast of

[6] James Parente, 'Drama', in *The Oxford Encyclopedia of the Reformation* (4 vols., New York, 1996), vol. II, pp. 4–9. Ehrstine, *Theater, Culture and Community*, p. 35.

[7] Graham A. Runnalls, *Répertoire des mystères français imprimés (1486–1630)* (Edinburgh, 1997), pp. 26–31.

[8] John Fox, *A Literary History of France. The Middle Ages* (London, 1974), pp. 251–2.

characters representing the personification of abstractions such as Vice, Virtue, Conscience and Faith. Their interaction (often with an Everyman figure, representing humanity) allowed the working out of the play's didactic element. This form of drama would prove to have an enduring influence in many future literary genres: one thinks, for instance, of the Reformation dialogue, which made extensive use of representative personifications of this nature. The mediaeval morality play also influenced the development of the allegorical moral plays that were the stock in trade of the emerging urban dramatic societies: in France the *puys*, in the Netherlands the *Rederijkerkamers*. The afterlife of the morality play was equally strongly felt in the Tudor interlude, a short moralistic drama performed as a diversion in a longer work. Placing speeches in the mouths of allegorical abstractions also allowed a pungent criticism of contemporary morality, a potential extensively exploited during the Reformation era.

Morality plays had a serious purpose, but they also employed many of the burlesque features that enlivened scenes in the mysteries. The comic potential is obvious enough in a play like *Bien-avisé et Mal-avisé*, two characters who set out on a journey together before going their separate ways. Bien-avisé follows Reason, who leads him to Faith; the comedy arises mostly through the adventures of Mal-avisé with his various evil companions. In France the *moralité* also spawned a specific subgenre, the *sottie*, a satirical farce performed by urban drama societies. Here the actors wore fools' clothing, allowing the clown's defence of critical distance from the plays' satirical parodies of manners and political events. The *sottie* had something in common with the farce, a form of dramatic performance that had largely outgrown the religious origins of the dramatic medium. These plays flourished especially in Germany as the *Fastnachtspiel* or carnival play, building on the carnival tradition of Shrove Tuesday, the last day before the Lenten fast. The plots of these plays usually revolved around the adventures of clever peasants deceiving each other and their social betters: a social representation that appealed to the largely urban audiences on many levels. In France the farces engaged a wider range of social types, though the plots still involved peasant cunning and the hoodwinking of the credulous. In *Pathelin*, composed around 1470, the eponymous central character is a rascally lawyer. He plots with a corrupt shepherd to hoodwink a foolish draper, only to be cheated in his turn by the sly servant. In this way the farces combined broad slapstick humour with the potential for social criticism (of the lawyer) and broad-brush moralizing. This double potential would be fully embraced by the Reformation in several locations where the *Fastnachtspiel* tradition was particularly robust.

The final development of significance in the pre-Reformation period was the growth of humanist drama.[9] Humanist drama emerged to a position of some importance as part of the vast expansion of educational provision in northern Europe during the fifteenth and sixteenth centuries: to many educational reformers it was to be (with music) a mainstay of the curriculum of the new Latin schools. Humanist teachers recommended the study of ancient drama, with Terence as the model, as a means to an elegant Latin style, but the movement also spawned a significant quantity of new writing. An important pioneer in this field was Gulielmus Grapheus, the Dutch schoolmaster who successfully combined Roman comic language with a biblical subject in his drama of the Prodigal Son, *Acolastus* (1529). This work was a milestone in a developing genre that would receive the enthusiastic support of all the mainstream Protestant churches.

Reformation drama

The Reformation effected considerable change to the mediaeval dramatic tradition, though not initially from a viewpoint of ideological scepticism. The Wittenberg reformers strongly advocated drama as part of the process of exposition and inculcation of the new religious faith, particularly within the school curriculum. In this respect drama was encompassed in the relatively benign Lutheran evaluation of the visual media, sometimes explicitly: Luther regularly referred to plays as paintings (*Gemälde*), pictures (*Bild*), or even, following Cicero, as a mirror.[10]

Nevertheless, the Wittenberg reformers remained wary of embracing the pre-Reformation dramatic tradition too wholeheartedly. For all their recognition of the pedagogic potential, their first concern was to distance themselves from the mediaeval passion play, which, with its transcendent emotionalism, they regarded as something akin to the Mass. Luther's first explicit comment on drama, in his *Sermon von der Betrachtung des heyligen leydens Christi* (1518), was thus directed far more towards a sustained attack on the Catholic tradition than a positive evocation of the principles of a new evangelical drama. For these reasons it would be some years before Wittenberg embraced the sort of civic public performance characteristic of pre-Reformation drama in Germany. Initial energies were directed towards encouraging drama in the school

---

[9] James A. Parente, *Religious Drama and the Humanist Tradition: Christian Theater in Germany and the Netherlands, 1500–1680* (Leiden, 1987).

[10] Ehrstine, *Theater, Culture and Community*, pp. 216–17. For a compendium of Luther's statements on drama see Thomas I. Bacon, *Martin Luther and the Drama* (Amsterdam, 1976).

curriculum, of which Luther and Melanchthon were enthusiastic proponents. This was a particular enthusiasm of Philip Melanchthon. Even before his arrival in Wittenberg, he had in 1516, at the precociously early age of nineteen, published an edition of six plays by the Latin dramatist Terence: this was one of his first published works.[11] Melanchthon's enthusiasm for Terence would find its echo in the new German church orders where the re-organized school regime frequently made provision for dramatic performance.

This positive but qualified endorsement of drama meant that while plays were to be performed in the schools, they did not, in Wittenberg at least, form part of the agitation for evangelical change. To the extent that reformers recognized the polemical potential of drama, this would have to be realized elsewhere. Here, Protestants seized on the convivial format of the carnival play, the established vehicle for much ribaldry and social satire; this was now turned in a much more systematic way on the old church. An early instance occurred in the north German city of Danzig in 1522, where Michael Schmarz (apparently a former pupil of Albrecht Dürer) directed an anti-papal carnival play, which enacted Luther's struggle against Rome until his disappearance following the Diet of Worms. The most significant flowering of the evangelical carnival play is found in two contrasting cities in Germany and Switzerland, Nuremberg and Bern. In Nuremberg the Protestant carnival plays formed part of the vast and varied output of the work of Hans Sachs.

We have already met Hans Sachs in connection with his hymns and poetical works publishing in the service of the Reformation, and these were indeed the genres that dominated the bulk of his astonishing output of some 1,700 original compositions. But Sachs also wrote over two hundred plays, in addition to the important group of religious dialogues published in support of the Reformation in 1524, a pivotal moment of decision for the Nuremberg Reformation.[12] Sachs contributed copiously to both the major genres of German Reformation drama, the carnival play and the biblical drama, but his output also shows definite patterns, hinting at a clear hierarchy of seriousness of purpose in the mind of the author. Sachs wrote his first carnival plays in 1517, too early to be influenced by the Reformation. There is then a gap of more than a

[11] Parente, *Religious Drama and the humanist Tradition*, pp. 20 ff.
[12] Paul A. Russell, *Lay Theology in the Reformation. Popular Pamphleteers in Southwest Germany, 1521–1525* (Cambridge, 1986), pp. 165–80. Philip Broadhead, 'The Contribution of Hans Sachs to the Debate on the Reformation in Nuremberg: A Study of the Religious Dialogues of 1524', in Robert Aylett and Peter Skrine (eds.), *Hans Sachs and Folk Theatre in the Late Middle Ages* (Lewiston, N.Y., 1995), pp. 43–62.

the duty of theology to teach piety and the true worship of God and to [cre]ate a lifestyle that pleases God and works that are good and consequently [reb]uke impiety, incorrect worship of God and depraved behaviour, all of these [thing]s are also in our tragedies, and in a certain way they are taught more [l]ively there; for as Horace says, 'things heard incite the mind much less [than] those things our trusting eyes see.'[16]

[T]his is an important statement, representing as it does a fundamen-[tall]y positive re-evaluation of what might be perceived through the eyes. [Th]e dramatists proposed nothing less than a synergy of the senses to do [Go]d's work.

This was an agenda that was embraced with particular enthusiasm by [Ha]ns von Rüte, author of a sequence of biblical dramas staged in Bern. [It] might legitimately be asked why Bern, a city of some 5,000 inhabitants [so]me way from Europe's main trade routes, spawned such a rich [d]ramatic tradition. The most recent study of this drama tradition sug-[g]ests that the lack of a local printing press until a comparatively late date [m]ay have played its part: certainly these biblical dramas were an import-[a]nt means of communal communication and enabled the forging of a shared religious identity.[17] Von Rüte composed five major plays over a period of seventeen years, all focused on a major heroic figure from the Bible narrative: from *Joseph* (1538) to *Goliath* (1555). This reflected a central theme of almost all Protestant dramas, the path of the individual towards salvation, though the performance of these plays continued to require a heroic application of effort to deploy the vast casts required for the successful staging of these extended dramas.

Von Rüte's compositions in Bern were accompanied by a considerable flowering of biblical drama throughout Lutheran Germany. This may partly have been stimulated by Martin Luther's more explicit praise of 'comedies blessed to God' in his 1534 commentaries on Tobit and Judith. That Luther's comments were influential is suggested by the fact that one Lutheran author, Paul Rebhun, actually reprinted Luther's remarks as an afterword to his new biblical play, *Susanna* (1535).[18] In 1538 the Dessau schoolmaster Joachim Greff even conceived of presenting the passion narrative as the central focus of a verse drama, thus raising the spectre of the dramatic representation of Christ, unknown in the Protestant tradition since their suppression of the medi-aeval passion play. The controversy raised by Greff's proposal in-duced him to reshape his proposed play to focus on the resurrection rather than the passion. When the local ministers continued to express

[16] Ibid., p. 217.   [17] Ibid., p. 59.   [18] Ibid., p. 21.

decade before he returns to the genre, a period filled by his hymns, poems, and the Reformation dialogues. Many of the carnival plays were published in a great burst of creative energy in the early 1550s, when many other authors had turned to more earnest biblical drama. That said, the best of Sachs' plays effectively combine the twin goals of entertainment and edification as well as any of the lighter dramatic performances of the Reformation. One gets a taste from a funny, rumbustious piece called *The Inquisitor with Many Cauldrons of Soup*. Simon Wirdt is sentenced to listen to the monks' sermons, when he is puzzled by the message that what people give in this life they will receive back a hundredfold in the next. Given that the monks give three caul-drons of soup a day to the poor from their leftovers, in the next life they will be drowned in soup – 109,500 cauldrons a year! This calculation so enrages the Inquisitor that he dismisses Simon, who would prefer to be at home reading his Bible in any case.[13]

The exploration of Hans Sachs' multi-faceted literary achievement in the service of the Reformation points the way to one particular problem of interpreting the dramatic oeuvres: the relationship between dramatic pieces intended to be performed, and the dialogue. So many of the early polemical writings of the Reformation were written in the form of a dialogue, with two or a larger cast of characters. Not all of these were intended to be performed; some were so stylized that they would have been totally unsuitable for performance.

Some distinguished studies of German literature deal with this con-undrum by effectively ignoring it: treating dialogues and dramas as if they are essentially one and the same. For our purposes this is clearly inadequate. One can certainly imagine that readers of the pamphlet dialogues had their reading enriched by the mental associations with performed drama; perhaps they even enacted dialogues with friends (though this required availability of more than one copy). But the reach of a dialogue that was read but not performed is quite different from the impact of a performed play: less extensive in terms of its social range, broader geographically. The play performed and the printed text also impact on their readers and auditors in different ways. Playgoers may come away with broad impressions that may focus on the central message, but could equally be of a spectacular piece of staging, or a comic episode that has little to do with the main plot. Readers may study

[13] This plot is described in John E. Tailby, 'Sachs and the Nuremberg *Fastnachtspiel* Tradition of the Fifteenth Century', in Aylett and Skrine, *Hans Sachs and Folk Theatre*, pp. 187–95.

a pamphlet at leisure, but they miss the reinforcement and impact of a communally staged event; and of course they must be readers.

Most effective of all would be if a play were both performed and printed, in which case it would profit from the mutually reinforcing strengths of both media. This is certainly the case with the plays of Hans Sachs, and with the second major source of Reformation play texts, the Swiss city of Bern.

The flowering of evangelical drama in Bern was in the first instance the achievement of another Reformation polymath, the painter and poet Niklaus Manuel. Manuel, an early convert to the Reformation, had by 1522 turned his back on his painting; instead his talents were poured out in a series of evangelical carnival plays that set a new standard for evangelical drama. Manuel's work influenced two of the most famous early dramatic creations of the Reformation: *Of the Pope and his Priesthood* (1523) and *The Indulgence Pedlar* (1525). It is noteworthy that these brilliant and excoriating denunciations of the stage villains of the Old church should have been performed before Bern had officially adopted the Reformation (in 1528). But although the Bern patriciate remained cautious on reform, Manuel was able to capitalize on the tidal wave of anti-papal feeling created by the recent alliance between Leo X and Charles V. This unlikely reconciliation between the ancient Habsburg foe of Swiss liberties and a traditional ally violated all the norms of Swiss politics, and sent a tremor of anxiety through the Swiss city states; in this context Manuel found eager auditors for his pageant denouncing the cynical abuse of clerical power. *Of the Pope and his Priesthood* is in fact a more subtle work than this may suggest. While the Pope's initial appearance with a parade of ecclesiastical officials establishes the play's general theme of ecclesiastical corruption, the lower echelons of priests, monks and nuns lament their growing impoverishment.[14] There are also explicit references to Bern's immediate political situation; Manuel was a well-connected member of the city's politically active citizenry, and well placed to reflect the feelings of political insecurity in the wake of the Swiss defeat at the battle of Bicocca.

Manuel's carnival plays were thus a highly contemporary as well as politically charged adaptation of the long-established tradition of the carnival play. We know from their staging that they could only have been performed with the explicit support of the city magistrates. The plays took place in one of the city's most prominent central locations, and the actors were drawn from among the younger male members of the

[14] Ehrstine, *Theater, Culture and Community*, pp. 94–5.

---

leading families of the city. Of course the p
entertain, and Manuel's play also made use o
ters whose boorish behaviour was a staple of th
This takes a more sinister turn in *The Ind*
inhabitants of the village set upon the eponym
they discover how his tricks have abused their n
is bound and hoisted up until he confesses to his a
and the worthlessness of his indulgences. The th
sympathy of the audience, but the enactment of pe
an untimely warning of the danger of unlicensed
abuses of clerical tradition – although the play wa
and subsequently circulated in manuscript among
was never published.

The carnival play captured a particular moment
agenda, and the boisterous undiscriminating anticleric
so powerful a component of the early urban reform mc
sober times its free-ranging satire might seem less appr
final triumph of the Reformation in Bern brought an
flourishing of the evangelical *Fastnachtspiel*. Elsewhere to
theologians embarked on a wholesale renovation of the wo
of the church, they also turned a more sceptical eye on ca
tions, which were condemned both as a relic of Catholic
an occasion for licentious behaviour. Encouraged to look
models of dramatic performance, Protestants found them
humanist drama, to which even the Wittenberg reformers had
unstinting support. Humanist principles permitted the elucid
new theory of dramatic performance that moved beyond th
satire of the carnival plays to a more constructive engagement
theological agenda of the evangelical movement. This was predi
a fundamentally different understanding of the interaction
audiences and religious imagery: one that fostered intellectual c
hension rather than an emotional response. These new principle
laid out with some clarity by the influential Reformation dra
Thomas Kirchmeyer (Naogeorgus), a Saxon pastor and the autho
series of important biblical dramas, as well as a number of more
ventional satires against the Roman church. It was the biblical pl
however, that pointed the way towards the future of German Protest
drama. In the preface to his *Judas Iscariot* (1538) Kirchmeyer laid out t
ideological motivation of his dramatic writing:

[15] Ibid., pp. 107–13.

misgivings, the matter was referred to Wittenberg, where both Luther and Melanchthon emphatically supported the dramatist.[19]

The shaking off of this last taboo was a dramatic demonstration of the extent to which Protestant theologians were comfortable in their reshaping of the mediaeval dramatic tradition. Most Protestant drama, it must be said, continued to find its main themes from the historical books of the Old Testament and the Apocrypha. But the tradition was popular and enduring, winning the support of reformers in all mainstream Protestant churches. Martin Bucer included a warm endorsement of drama in his last great work, *De Regno Christi*, and biblical drama also found its place in the French reformed culture, partly through translations of German authors such as Thomas Kirchmeyer. An especially popular work among the French Huguenots was the *Abraham sacrifiant* by Théodore de Bèze, a play that represents the perfect fusion of the humanist educational tradition and the new evangelical biblical drama.[20]

The Protestant tradition of biblical drama drew together several themes of importance for this study. Firstly, drama was conceived and orchestrated primarily as a pedagogic tool, exploiting and reshaping an important part of mediaeval entertainment culture to this purpose. It is important to recognize the extent to which this play tradition was appropriated and choreographed by the leaders of the new Protestant societies. Almost without exception, the authors of the plays were pastors, schoolmasters or members of the local patriciate. The staging of a performance could only be accomplished with the full co-operation of the city magistrates for, like mediaeval civic dramas, these were public occasions to which all members of the community would be freely admitted. The expense was undertaken because they both offered entertainment and forwarded the ideological agenda of the new Protestant establishment.

Drama was promoted because it also offered a particularly effective synergy of different modes of communication. Recent studies of Protestant theatre have drawn attention to the shared iconography between theatre and Protestant visual culture. The *Fair and Pleasant Play* (1538) by the Magdeburg playright Valten Voith was an attempt to adapt to the stage Lucas Cranach's artistic motif of the Law and the Gospel, and this was far from being the first example of such a synergy of image and

---

[19] Ibid., pp. 1–5.

[20] Théodore de Bèze, *Abraham sacrifiant. Tragedie françoise* (Geneva, 1550). Critical edition with introduction and notes by K. Cameron, K. M. Hall and F. M. Higman (Geneva, 1967).

drama.[21] Niklaus Manuel's second play of 1523, *Von Papst und Christi Gegensatz*, was a dramatic reworking of Cranach's seminar piece of visual polemic, *The Antitheses of Christ and the Pope*, a series of paired woodcuts designed jointly by Cranach and Philip Melanchthon.[22] The play adopts the same antithetical imagery in a series of tableaux that follow Cranach's designs closely; in the printed text of 1524 elaborate stage directions are provided to ensure visual clarity, with the Pope on one side of the stage and the attributes of the Gospel on the other.

This is 'the theatre as broadsheet'; but in many ways, to anticipate an argument laid out in chapter 5, it is superior to the broadsheet, because here one can observe text and image being brought harmoniously together. Later performances of biblical drama in Bern were also accompanied by the extensive use of singing, both choruses marked in the text and in interludes. What makes this particularly striking is that Bern had only recently begun to deviate from the strict ban on singing in congregational worship promoted by Zurich. With this, the impact of drama could approach the perfect encapsulation of the Reformation teaching, with all the arts and senses bent to the praise and promotion of a rational understanding of faith. This sense of the capacity of drama was perfectly captured by the Bern printer Samuel Apiarus in his foreword to von Rüte's *Goliath*:

For truly, God speaks to us now in many ways, extending to us his holy word not only in sermons, but also in books, in writings, in psalms and religious songs, and in elegant plays, through which the more prominent stories are taken from Holy Scripture, repeated, refreshed, and portrayed as if they were alive before people's eyes, so that we may well say that the wisdom of God shouts and cries in the street.[23]

The drama of dissent

Thus far our investigation of Reformation drama has focused exclusively on lands in which drama was employed as an adjunct to official policy in support of evangelical reform. The cities and states of Protestant Germany and the Swiss Confederation were in this respect heirs to the mediaeval tradition of the civic sponsorship of drama, though the entertainments were infused with a new and remarkably clear-minded ideological purpose. Several of the leading reformers tried their hands as dramatists. *Abraham sacrifiant* by Théodore de Bèze has already been

[21] Ehrstine, *Theater, Culture and Community*, p. 219.   [22] See chapter 2.
[23] Ehrstine, *Theater, Culture and Community*, p. 201.

mentioned, and Heinrich Bullinger also penned a youthful work of drama, his little-known *Lucretia and Brutus*. The play, written while Bullinger was still in Kappel, is a robust defence of the constitution of the Swiss Confederation through the medium of a story made familiar by the great Roman historian Livy. It was performed to great applause in both Basle and Aarau, and then revived again by the students of Zurich in 1939 at the outbreak of the Second World War, when its contemporary significance must again have been very obvious.[24]

Such plays, written for audiences ready to be both entertained and edified, had an obvious role as a communal expression of shared political and theological values. It remains to be seen whether drama could play a role in promoting the Reformation agenda in places where it did not enjoy official sponsorship. Such was the situation in the first half of the century in the largest states of western Europe, where advocates of the reform agenda faced formidable opposition; in this context, where advocacy of evangelical doctrine became too dangerous, drama might become the vehicle for more subtle messages of change. England, France and the Netherlands all developed a coded drama of dissent, reflecting in part the separate dramatic heritage of the different lands, but also the common interest in the new humanist drama. In this respect it was significant that precisely those educated intellectuals drawn to experimentation in new dramatic form also manifested a degree of commitment to the wider humanist agenda, with its sceptical examination of existing church institutions.

In the first half of the sixteenth century England was already exhibiting the trend towards the highly individual dramatic tradition that would become evident in the Elizabethan theatre. Whereas playmaking in Europe remained largely the preserve of non-professionals, England already had its first professional companies, normally bands of players associated with a noble household. Between 1530 and 1580 some fifty noblemen's troupes have been recorded.[25] These companies mostly performed in private to a privileged audience; but in times of political turbulence even such restricted performances could play an influential part in framing the religious debate.

It was in the fluid and complex politics of the reign of Henry VIII that the potential of drama for religious polemic was first systematically

[24] Emidio Campi, 'Bullinger's Early Political and Theological Thought: *Brutus Tigurinus*', in Bruce Gordon and Emidio Campi (eds.), *Architect of Reformation. An Introduction to Heinrich Bullinger, 1504–1575* (Grand Rapids, Mich., 2004), pp. 181–99.
[25] Paul Whitfield White, *Theatre and Reformation. Protestantism, Patronage and Playing in Tudor England* (Cambridge, 1993), p. 12.

exploited. In the brief period of Henry's active patronage of a reform agenda, plays were consciously employed to promote support for royal policies. This campaign reached its apogee in the co-operation between the king's minister, Thomas Cromwell, and the Protestant author, John Bale. Bale's involvement with drama seems to have pre-dated his association with Cromwell. In 1534 he wrote fourteen plays for the Earl of Oxford, a Privy Councillor and early exponent of reform. From 1537 Bale also enjoyed Cromwell's direct patronage. By this time Bale had his own troupe, 'Bale and his fellows', which performed in a variety of locations, at court and elsewhere. Between 1537 and Cromwell's fall in 1540, Bale's players toured extensively around England, in a series of annual expeditions that took them as far afield as Shrewsbury, York and Norwich. For many of these places the performances must have been the first visible sign of the new ideological wind blowing from court.

Bale played a critical role as both theatrical entrepreneur and author. The surviving texts reveal his wholehearted engagement with Cromwell's reform programme. Both *King Johne*, his best-known play, and the less-regarded *Three Laws* are viciously anticlerical in temper, presenting the Catholic clergy as 'the contemporary manifestation of a timeless spiritual evil corrupting God's laws through the ages'.[26] With *The Knaveries of Thomas Becket*, one of Bale's many plays for which only the title survives, we can presume that the text pursued a similar political agenda to that of *King Johne*, while at the same time endorsing the government attack on images and shrines. Bale's plays are not to be compared to the great civic dramas of Protestant Germany. Written for a much more modest troupe of players, they could be staged with much less ceremony in a wide variety of settings, public or private. But they seem to have hit their mark. John Alforde, a young man who attended a performance of *King Johne* in Canterbury in 1538, came away believing 'that it ys petie that the Bisshop of Rome should reigne any lenger, for if he should, the said Bisshop wold do with our King as he did with King John'.[27]

Such overtly political drama was inevitably wholly dependent on the protection of an influential patron. The fall of Cromwell brought an end to Bale's touring company, and the Act for the Advancement of True Religion in 1543 specifically prohibited interludes and printed matter meddling 'with interpretacions of Scripture, contrary to the doctrine set forth or to be set forth by the kynges maieste'. The emergence of a Protestant regime in 1547 brought the repeal of this statute and an immediate revival of anti-Catholic drama. Even the young king

---

[26] Ibid., p. 27.   [27] Ibid., p. 29.

apparently contributed: Bale's catalogue of books by British authors included an anti-papal interlude entitled *The Whore of Babylon*, which he attributes to Edward VI.[28] Outside the confines of the court, drama played an important role in promoting the new evangelical agenda. As in Germany, leading clerical supporters of the regime played a prominent role as authors: Bale, Becon, Foxe, Udall and Baldwin all wrote plays.[29] The brief opportunity of Edward's reign in fact witnessed the convergence of the two strands of German Protestant drama: the anticlerical satire of the carnival play and the biblical drama. The English authors also borrowed generously from the continental tradition, both in their choice of themes and styles, and in straightforward translations.

The sheer range and vitality of the dramatic tradition in England at this time is a fitting prologue to the more celebrated dramas of the later Elizabethan period, though later playwrights would never again match the ideological coherence of the Edwardian era. John Foxe would have no hesitation in evoking drama in his famous trilogy of conduits of the Reformation, 'players, printers and preachers'. The Marian regime seems to have concurred, taking immediate steps to suppress the playing of unauthorized interludes within months of the queen's accession in 1553.

In France, evangelicals would never enjoy the luxury of such an extended opportunity to develop an independent dramatic tradition. For all that, dramatic performances had a long history of venting political dissent, and supporters of evangelical reform would make extensive use of this tradition in the first half of the sixteenth century. A convenient vehicle for the expression of coded criticism was provided by the *sotties* or *farces*, satirical entertainments often performed by local drama societies. Not all were critical of the established powers. The *Jeu de Princes* by Pierre Gringore in 1512 provided generous praise of Louis XII. Gringore, who earned his living partly as an organizer of mysteries and farces, was also an important religious author and an early opponent of Luther. *The Three Pilgrims* of 1521 was more daring, risking an attack on the king's mother, Louise of Savoye. In this drama three pilgrims emerge from retreat and find society much changed: the women govern and men think only of pleasure. They retreat back to their cells.

This was sailing close to the wind, and plays that attacked stock popular targets in the clergy became increasingly divisive. A sceptical voice was maintained in two contrasting locations: at court in the circle

[28] John Bale, *Scriptorium illustrium* (Basle, 1557), vol. I, p. 674.
[29] John N. King, *English Reformation Literature. The Tudor Origins of the Protestant Tradition* (Princeton, N. J., 1982), pp. 271–318.

of humanist intellectuals around Marguerite of Navarre, and in the municipal Latin schools. Marguerite, the king's sister, was herself the distinguished author of devotional poetry and the *Heptameron*, a collection of moral tales modelled on Boccaccio's *Decameron*. But while many of those protected by Marguerite were clearly reformist in inclination, their influence was limited by discretion and caution. A more public manifestation of evangelical energy was permitted by the rise of the municipal Latin schools.[30] France, in common with many parts of Europe, witnessed an extraordinary explosion of educational provision during the sixteenth century. Many towns seized the opportunity to found or reorder a Latin school, inspired by the fashionable humanist educational agenda. City magistrates vied for the most celebrated teachers, many of whom later gave trouble by their advanced views. As in Germany, drama played an important part in the school curriculum, but in many locations the students clearly preferred more controversial fare than the Terence prescribed.

A recent study of Bordeaux demonstrates how drama could come to play a central role in the clash of ideologies that would lead ultimately to the French Religious Wars.[31] The grammar school in Bordeaux, the Collège du Guyenne, was a typically bold municipal venture, founded in 1532 with a substantial endowment of 500 livres. Strongly supported by the city fathers, it also quickly became a hotbed of evangelical agitation. Matters were complicated by the fact that only two groups were permitted to stage dramatic entertainments on the streets of Bordeaux: the students of the college, and members of the *basoche*, the local confraternity of St Yves. The contrasting dramatic entertainments became the focal point for two competing worldviews. The *basoche* preferred the Catholic voice with ostentatious celebration of traditional public ceremonies; these were frequently derided by the scholars of the college, who took to attacking local ceremonies and processions. In 1556 the scholars organized themselves into military-style local companies. The magistrates were caught in between, miserable and impotent. They tried to restore peace by banning either side from performing 'aucunes pieces concernant la religion ou foi chrétienne, la veneration des saintes et les institutions de l'Eglise', but this had little effect. By 1559 both sides had taken to patrolling the streets of Bordeaux in rival gangs.

---

[30] George Huppert, *Public Schools in Renaissance France* (Chicago, 1984).

[31] Kevin Gould, '"Vivre et mourir en la religion ancienne, romaine et catholique". Catholic Activism in South-West France' (University of Warwick, Ph.D. dissertation, 2003). I am grateful to Dr Gould for permission to read and cite his dissertation in advance of its publication.

This transformation from dramatic society to vigilante mob may seem to us extreme, but it captures the potency of plays as a public expression of shared social values. When these values were shared, this was a source of strength; when they became contested, the dramatic tradition became very disruptive. This remained the case even when, as in the Netherlands, the principal focus for dramatic performance was in ostensibly closed drama societies such as the Chambers of Rhetoric (*Rederijkerkamers*).

The chambers were a peculiarly Netherlandish institution.[32] They have some echoes in the French *puys*, but nowhere did they attain the social significance of their place in the culture of the Low Countries. In this educated, highly literate urban society the chambers were a ubiquitous presence: in the Dutch-speaking provinces alone there were close to two hundred.

The Chambers of Rhetoric arose in the fifteenth century within the strongly artisanal culture of the merchant towns of Flanders, Holland and Brabant. They had much in common with religious confraternities, not least a strong occupational base and an interest in social conviviality. They also shared a strongly religious function, expressed often by the founding of an altar in honour of the chamber's patron saint. But their principal purpose was the performing of the serious allegorical plays (*Spelen van Zinne*) written specially for them. The *Spelen*, which had a strongly moralistic quality, might be performed at private gatherings of members, or in public. The public plays were sometimes sponsored by the civil authorities to accompany religious holidays or other special occasions; sometimes chambers from different cities would meet together for competitions, as in the famous and ultimately notorious national competition of 1539, the *Landjuweel*.

With respect to their membership the chambers attracted a good section of the wealthier artisans and professional and merchant elements of society. The themes of their plays were often overtly religious. In 1496 Antwerp's Gillyflower chamber hosted a contest involving twenty-eight chambers where the question assigned for debate was: 'What is the greatest mystery or grace ordained by God for the blessedness of humanity?'[33] As this example indicates, for competitions of this nature the host chamber established the theme and set the question.

Yet in a society such as the Netherlands it is hard to see how the chambers could have avoided engagement with the rising religious

[32] Gary K. Waite, *Reformers on Stage. Popular Religious Drama and Religious Propaganda in the Low Countries of Charles V, 1515–1556* (Toronto, 2000).
[33] Ibid., p. 42.

controversies of the sixteenth century. The contrast between the pietistic theme of the 1496 competition and the same Antwerp chamber's entry for the *Landjuweel* of 1539 is instructive. In the later competition the theme for discussion was, 'What is the greatest comfort for a dying man?' The Antwerp entry begins with a verbal battle between two allegorical figures, Examination of the Scriptures and False Meaning. Examination routs False Meaning with his affirmation that the soul's consolation is found in the pure untainted Word of God. The central character, Dying Man, then enters and approaches several further allegorical figures in an attempt to solve the mystery. Neither Reason nor Law can provide the answer: the solution is revealed when Preacher of the Word presents Dying Man with Luther's teaching on salvation.[34] The Antwerp chamber's presentation was bold, but not exceptional. At the 1539 *Landjuweel* only three of the nineteen plays could be described as orthodox.

At Ghent, the *Rederijkers* had overreached themselves; the *Landjuweel* caused a public scandal, and in the wake of the Ghent revolt (which broke out only weeks after this competition) Charles V ordered new measures to curb the chambers. Individuals do not, however, seem to have been punished. The members of the Antwerp chamber enjoyed the protection of the city magistrates, to whom they were well connected. It was very different in Amsterdam where the marginalization of the city's *rederijker* culture by the town regents had led the local chamber into much more dangerous paths, including a flirtation with Anabaptism in the mid-1530s. The more radical engagement with reform seems to have been a product of social alienation from a city elite who held themselves aloof from *rederijker* festivities. But when in 1535 the props of one of the Amsterdam chambers were used in an attempted Anabaptist coup, the rhetoricians were inevitably swept up in the subsequent retribution.

On the whole the more cautious and less provocative approach of the Antwerp chamber was the more typical. Despite the scandal of the 1539 *Landjuweel*, the Chambers of Rhetoric continued to provide an outlet for criticism of orthodox religion, albeit with greater subtlety and concealment. What is striking is how few plays ever mount a trenchant defence of orthodoxy. According to Gary Waite:

Even Catholic playwrights constructed their plays in ways that defended a traditional understanding of salvation and sacramental faith without unduly alienating reform-minded members of an audience. This could be done by

---

[34] Ibid., p. 68.

virtually ignoring contentious theological issues, and/or by so highlighting a criticism of clerical abuses that reform-minded viewers could still appreciate the play.[35]

Catholic authors also criticized materialistic piety and clerical abuses, revealing the extent to which impatience with the clergy and scepticism of the capacity of the organized church to lead reform spread across the religious spectrum. Perhaps this was not surprising. The plays of the Chambers of Rhetoric catered to the tastes and exposed the prejudices of a self-confident and assertive social class that was both politically powerful and numerous in the unusually urbanized society of the Netherlands.

For all this, it must be recognized that the Catholic church remained securely established, and largely unreformed, in the Netherlands until the onset of the mid-century agitation that led ultimately to the outbreak of the Dutch Revolt. Our judgement of the effectiveness of the dissenting voices expressed in the *rederijker* plays depends partly on how far we think such criticism may have prepared the ground for the more fundamental assault of Calvinism in the second half of the century. Without diminishing in any way the interest and literary quality of much of the rhetorician drama, one may doubt whether the causal connection was close. In the last resort drama functioned more effectively in reinforcing than in challenging communal values. This seems to have been the case in Germany, and even in Bordeaux, where traditional drama acted as a rallying point for conservatives outraged at evangelical attacks on cherished institutions. In the Netherlands, *rederijker* drama was essentially the exclusive preserve of polite society. The rhetoricians were by and large men who wished to signal a critical distance from some elements of traditional church life without fundamentally undermining the church (which was essentially the position of Erasmus).

The fate of *rederijker* drama points up the paradox of drama as dissent. Because it allows the participants the luxury of identifying themselves with fashionable criticism without the necessity of commitment, it may have done more to act as a safety valve than to focus energies towards a truly oppositional stance. In this respect it joined other forms of dramatic performance that provided a measure of social catharsis, while leaving essential social hierarchies intact, or even strengthened: this was the essential function of carnival. In this context the Antwerp city fathers showed some wisdom in regarding such performances with a benign eye. They posed no real threat to the religious status quo.

[35] Ibid., p. 203.

Throughout Europe, drama would make its most effective contribution to the evangelical cause in places where the Reformation had already been introduced, articulating shared values in a communal setting. It could contribute to this process even when theatregoers looked for less ostensibly religious subject material than the satires and biblical plays of the first Lutheran generation.

The theatrical city

In the first generation after the Reformation, drama pursued an overtly didactic purpose. Protestant reformers were persuaded of the value of drama; secular (particularly classical) plays were also approved and integrated into the school curriculum. Reformers were less supportive of drama that sought merely to entertain.

In the second half of the sixteenth century overtly biblical drama lost some of its appeal. This was a double-edged process. On the one hand the playgoing public desired plays with a wider repertoire of themes and styles: comedies and histories as well as improving moral tales. Meanwhile, the preachers seem to have lost some of their initial confidence in the beneficial consequences of playgoing. No doubt the two were connected. But the result was a realignment of the place of performance drama in Protestant culture.

Nowhere was this change more profound than in England. We have already called attention to the individuality of the English dramatic tradition, and this continued through the more spectacular developments of the Elizabethan era. The rapid evolution of the English dramatic tradition continued apace after the accession of Elizabeth. In the 1560s and 1570s provincial towns seem to have witnessed a significant decline in the number of civic and parish productions: repudiating their traditional mystery and miracle plays, they relied more and more for theatrical entertainments on visiting troupes of professionals.[36] London, meanwhile, experienced a contrary trend. Within the first two decades of Elizabeth's reign public playing was transformed from intermittent recreation, performed in taverns or, in a continuation of the amateur tradition, in the Inns of Court, to a regular scheduled event in permanently established playhouses. Between 1576, when James Burbage, leader of the Earl of Leicester's troupe, built The Theatre near Shoreditch, and 1598, when The Globe was opened, as many as nine of these theatres were constructed, though some were relatively

---

[36] Patrick Collinson, *The Birthpangs of Protestant England. Religious and Cultural Change in the Sixteenth and Seventeenth Centuries* (London, 1988), pp. 102–3.

short-lived. In their heyday they were a distinctive and influential part of metropolitan life.[37]

The era of the great outdoor London theatres lasted only eighty years, but in this time the culture of playgoing was changed utterly. The theatre became commercialized. Players were full-time professionals, but so too were playwrights, superseding the earlier generation of clerics and schoolmasters who, in England and elsewhere, had furnished the vast majority of texts in the first evangelical generation. Most of all, those who frequented the playhouses were customers who came, paying a penny to stand or threepence for the better seats, expecting diversion and entertainment. They came, too, in very large numbers. The larger playhouses could accommodate a considerable audience, perhaps up to three thousand. Even allowing for the fact that they did not always play to a full house, Andrew Gurr has suggested that in the 1590s the two main companies were visited by 15,000 people a week – 7–10 per cent of the population of the city.[38]

The development of the London play scene was unmatched elsewhere in Europe, and it is not altogether easy to see why it should have occurred in this way, at this time, and in England. The early development of the professional companies and the great outpouring of dramatic energy during the reign of Edward VI provided a solid foundation, but that does not entirely explain why the English tradition slipped its moorings in this way, with the precocious development of a commercial secular theatre. The stimulus may have been, paradoxically, the growing disapproval of theatricals in various official and church circles. In 1572 the travelling companies were severely compromised by the Act for the Punishment of Vagabonds, which specifically mentioned vagrant players among its intended targets. Two years later the City of London moved to rein in plays performed in inn yards; the following decade further criticism following a fatal accident at a bearbaiting induced Walsingham to lend his support to efforts to organize the London players into a single company under the patronage of the queen's name. With this clear evidence that the leading courtiers had not abandoned their tradition of theatrical patronage, the disapproval of the city fathers was not enough to kill off the theatre. Instead the theatres were built in the old liberties outside the city walls, in Shoreditch, Blackfriars, and across the river in Southwark.

---

[37] Jean Wilson, *The Archaeology of Shakespeare* (Stroud, 1995). Andrew Gurr, *The Shakespearean Stage, 1574–1642* (Cambridge, 1970).
[38] Gurr, *The Shakespearean Stage*, p. 140.

The shift in dramatic matter performed on the stage was also the result of a twofold change. On the one side, the great expansion of grammar school education produced a glut of talented men seeking appropriate employment. At the same time the homiletic clerical playwrights of the first Reformation era laid down their pens. Again, this loss of confidence in the power of drama seems to have been peculiarly English. There was no similar movement in Lutheran Germany, though in the seventeenth century Dutch Calvinists would also denounce the theatre. Some expressed a fear of large disorderly crowds, and this was where the views of the preachers and the London corporation most obviously converged. But the root ideological cause seems to have been a sense that the Word of God should not be defiled with the sort of bawdy, scurrilous language typical of the comic dramas likely to pique the interest of a playgoing public. The Word of God could only be preached. The use of actors to impart the Word of God was considered by some an intolerable affront to the Gospel. This perspective was elegantly encapsulated by Anthony Munday in his *Second and Third Blast*:

> When I see the word of truth proceeding from the hart, and uttered by the mouth of the revered preachers, to be received of the most part into the ear, and but of a few rooted in the hart: I cannot by anie means believe that the wordes proceeding from a prophane plaier, and uttered in scorning sort, interlaced with filthie, lewde and ungodly speeches, have greater force to moove men unto virtue, than the wordes of truth uttered by the Godly.[39]

Hostility to the theatre was not universally shared amongst the godly: to some extent it cut across other ideological alignments. Anthony Munday is a particularly interesting instance in this respect, since despite such trenchantly expressed sentiments he himself numbered stage plays among his numerous published works. He also wrote ballads and translated into English several popular romances, including *Amadis de Gaule*, a text much disapproved of in Geneva.[40] And audiences at the playhouse, though they might not include the especially righteous, were certainly respectable. When in 1602 the Privy Council ordered the clearing of 'places of resort of idle persons' so that they could be pressed for the army, the City authorities decided to start with the playhouses. But there they found:

> not only . . . Gentlemen, and servingmen, but Lawyers, Clarkes, country men that had lawe cawses, aye the Quens men, knightes, and as it was creditably reported one Earle.[41]

---

[39] White, *Theatre and Reformation*, p. 168.
[40] Helen Moore (ed.), *Amadis de Gaule, Translated by Anthony Munday* (Aldershot, 2004).
[41] Gurr, *The Shakespearean Stage*, p. 141. See also now Andrew Gurr, *Playgoing in Shakespeare's London* (Cambridge, 1987).

The attitude of these respected London citizens who attended the plays seems, on the whole, more measured than those pamphleteers who inveighed against the theatre. For although the London play tradition had moved away from the earlier taste for biblical drama, the new secular plays still provided plentiful opportunities to reinforce the values of a Protestant society. Perhaps it was more successful in this task because the proselytizing was largely unconscious.

We may explore this suggestion by considering a pair of plays performed to great applause on the Elizabethan stage in the last years of Elizabeth's reign, Marlowe's *The Massacre of Paris* and *The Shoemaker's Holiday* by Thomas Dekker. Marlowe was no Protestant, but he still scored a major success with his comic book representation of the French Wars of Religion, first performed, it must be remembered, at a time when English troops were in service in France in support of Henry IV. Critics are severe on *The Massacre of Paris* which, to be sure, wins no plaudits for sophistication of plot or character development. The main characters are little more than caricatures: the evil Guise, the plotting Catherine, the noble Henry. But for London's playgoers this seems to have been enough; certainly they flocked to see the play in droves.[42] For Marlowe's *Massacre* caught the mood of the moment. It crystallized a perception of French politics that Londoners would have been imbibing from many different sources: pamphlets with news of the French campaigns, at turns urgent and exultant; returning soldiers; the city preachers.[43] Here the play helped galvanize a population engaged in a struggle for national survival against ominously powerful enemies, a struggle in which the French played the unfamiliar role of allies.

The other allies in the wars of the 1590s were the Dutch, long the butts of unkind jokes on the London stage. Their new status as fellow warriors in the Protestant cause may account for their notably more favourable treatment in Dekker's *The Shoemaker's Holiday*.[44] In this play the plot revolves around a deception in which the hero Lacy, hoping to secure the hand of the lovely Rose, takes employment with the rich shoemaker Simon Eyre disguised as a Dutchman. This is a scenario

---

[42] Takings on the first night were £3 14s: an audience of around 900 if they all paid the basic entry rate.

[43] Lisa Ferraro Parmelee, *Good newes from Fraunce: French Anti-League Propaganda in Late Elizabethan England* (Rochester, N.Y., 1996).

[44] Paul S. Seaver, 'The Artisanal World' and David Bevington, 'Theatre as Holiday', in David L. Smith, Richard Strier and David Bevington (eds.), *The Theatrical City. Culture, Theatre and Politics in London, 1576–1649* (Cambridge, 1995).

charged with conflicting emotions for the curious beholder. The playgoing audience would have included many who were only too aware of the threat posed to native workmen by immigrant craftsmen. It was actually forbidden by law to employ an alien in the way Eyre does in the play, and the issue still caused rumblings of anger. In 1592–3 the Master of the Revels had been forced to insist that a representation of the life of Sir Thomas More could only proceed if the scenes depicting the anti-Dutch riot of Evil May Day were first excised.[45] Yet the Dutch were not only now allies but prosperous fellow citizens. Playgoers would have walked to the theatre through the streets of Southwark, the most Dutch part of London.

To these layers of complexity Dekker adds layers of biblical allegory. The scheming villain of *The Shoemaker's Holiday* is Hamon, the frustrated suitor of Rose. A scripturally educated audience would have known Hamon from the Old Testament Book of Esther. Hamon is the evil councillor who plots the destruction of the Jews living in exile under the Persian king Ahasuerus. The threat is averted only by the just and faithful actions of Esther and Mordecai, the king's Jewish councillor. This was a tale of great significance for the Dutch, adopted as an allegorical origin myth during their years of rebellion against Spain. Hamon was seen as the prefiguration of the Spanish Duke of Alva, and Mordecai was an allegorized version of William of Orange. The scene of Mordecai's vindication and Hamon's condemnation was frequently represented in seventeenth-century Dutch art.[46] Seen through this prism, *The Shoemaker's Holiday* becomes a testimony to the bonds that united Protestants in the struggle against evil; in the words of a recent commentator, 'an argument in favour of the extension of the borders of the spiritual community'.[47]

If the godly had no time for the play, the playwrights certainly reserved a space for God. Naming always had significance in Reformation literature, whether in the dialogues of the 1520s or the play. This was understood. Only an audience suffused with Scripture would have made sense of Dekker, an ambitious playwright who seized this

---

[45] Virginia Gildersleeve, *Government Regulation of the Elizabethan Drama* (New York, 1908), p. 95.

[46] Jacqueline Boonen, 'Verhalen van Israëls Ballingschap en Vrijheidsstrijd', in Christian Tümpel (ed.), *Het Oude Testament in de Schilderkunst van de Gouden Eeuw* (Amsterdam, 1991) pp.106–21.

[47] Jane Pettegree, 'Shoemakers and Dutchmen: Brothers under the Skin. *The Shoemaker's Holiday* and Thomas Dekker's Vision of Protestant International Brotherhood' (unpublished manuscript, St Andrews Reformation Studies Institute, 2003).

patriotic moment to offer the London audience a notably sympathetic presentation of the Dutch Protestant ally in the struggle against international Catholicism.

By the end of the sixteenth century Protestantism in England was pragmatic, patriotic and popular. One could also say that it was popular because it was pragmatic and patriotic. To achieve this, it had to have found a holistic role in national culture. This would have been far less likely had the more austere views of the preachers who railed against the drama prevailed.

5   The visual image

With preaching, music and drama we have investigated three different aspects of the collective culture of sixteenth-century society. Clearly the three impacted on the consciousness of the Christian people in different ways; whereas dramatic performances were occasional, special events in most contexts, by the second generation of the Reformation Protestant peoples would have heard sermons very regularly. Singing, meanwhile, was an engrained part of both their public worship culture and their private entertainments.

All helped ensure that the challenge of the new evangelical movement would touch all members of society, both those who had access to the new Protestant teachings through reading – the literate – and those who had not. That there should be no gulf in understanding between these two groups was of course a huge concern to contemporary churchmen, aware as they were of the bookish and cerebral tendency of the theological debate inspired by Luther, and the difficulties of teaching even the barest essentials of the new Christian principles to the population at large: a concern to which the great outpouring of pedagogic literature inspired by the Reformation bears eloquent testimony.

The question of how cognizance of the new Christian teachings could be inculcated among the broad mass of the population is also one that has preoccupied historians, though the context of the discussion has been rather different from that proposed in the first half of this book. In explaining how the evangelical teaching impacted on the population at large historians have postulated a special role for visual images, especially, in the context of Germany in the first evangelical generation, for the woodcut. There are very good reasons why woodcuts should have so captured the imagination of twentieth-century scholarship. It was one of the great and enduring glories of the Reformation that the first dawn of the evangelical movement should have coincided with one of the great ages of German art. This was the age of Dürer, Cranach and Hans Holbein; of Altdorfer, Breu and a host of other less-distinguished, but still reputable practitioners. From the middle of the fifteenth century the

wealth of the German city states had nurtured and inspired the development of an artistic tradition of unparalleled richness. It was a period,
too, when the German tradition had developed its own distinctive
independent style.

The German artists of this era excelled in a wide variety of media. The
outstanding achievements in religious art and portraiture are perhaps
now the most eye-catching, but at the time many artists were remarkable
for their extraordinary versatility. While a number gained a particular
reputation for their work with woodcarving or in glass, many artists
worked across a variety of media: in painting, engraving, or in the
woodcut.[1] This was, in particular, a great age for the development of
the woodcut. In the fifteenth century it was a relatively new technology –
woodblocks were used for playing cards and other small independent
objects from the end of the fourteenth century, and the technology seems
to have become widely known in the next fifty years.[2] But the real
explosion of interest in woodcut art came in the second half of the
fifteenth century, coincident with the emergence of the printed book.
The two technologies, in fact, marched closely in step, though woodcuts
were also from an early date conceived of as independent artefacts, for
devotional or recreational purposes. It was, however, to provide illustrations for printed books that woodcut artists would find their largest
and most reliable market. By the beginning of the sixteenth century
woodcuts were widely known, both as a means of beautification for
printed books, or as an independent art form – a form particularly
exploited by the young Albrecht Dürer, with his remarkable and highly
successful series on the passion and life of Mary.[3]

With the onset of the evangelical movement the woodcut found a new
and fertile field for the creation of new visual themes. The first generation of the Reformation witnessed an enormous outpouring of woodcut
art. Printers and publishers developed rich new genres to tempt the
buying public, including, from the first years of the evangelical movement, a range of flattering and somewhat idealized portraits of Luther
the reformer. The desire to get a clearer sense of the man of the hour was
clearly very widespread and a range of portrait woodcuts appeared
both in books and as single-leaf images.[4] As the movement developed

[1] Michael Baxandall, *The Limewood Sculptors of Renaissance Germany* (New Haven, Conn.,
1980). Andrew Morrall, *Jörg Breu the Elder. Art, Culture and Belief in Reformation
Augsburg* (Aldershot, 2001), for work in glass.
[2] Arthur M. Hinds, *An Introduction to a History of Woodcut* (2 vols., New York, 1935).
[3] Erwin Panofsky, *The Life and Art of Albrecht Dürer* (1943; rev. edn, Princeton, N.J.,
1971).
[4] Martin Warnke, *Cranachs Luther. Entwürfe für ein Image* (Frankfurt, 1984).

publishers essayed more complex representations. Some, again, were included in books, and therefore adjusted to the upright portrait form of the printed page. Others were published as single sheets, the woodcut either filling the printed page or leaving room for explanatory text. This outpouring of visual images certainly caught the attention of those charged with monitoring the perplexing explosion of public interest in Luther and his quarrels. Magistrates and agents of the Emperor all noted the unprecedented nature of the pamphlet campaign, and the particular presence of these seditious broadsheet woodcuts. The quantities generated were certainly very large – and for this we do not have to rely on the assiduous collecting of later scholars.[5] In 1522 the authorities in Leipzig seized 1,500 copies of a broadsheet attacking the local Catholic champion Johannes Emser (presumably the whole of the edition).[6] In this case we do not know for sure that this broadsheet was illustrated – it could have been text only or even verse – but there is no doubting the strong contemporary sense that the illustrative woodcut was an important component of the public agitation that accompanied the first stage of the Reformation. This is an interpretative insight that has been eagerly adopted by modern scholarship.

In 1981 the late Robert Scribner published an authoritative analysis of the polemical woodcut that has never since been equalled.[7] *For the Sake of Simple Folk* has been, without doubt, one of the most influential single works ever published on our subject. Subsequent scholars have been virtually unanimous in adopting Scribner's contention that woodcuts form a vital link in the process by which the German Reformation became a mass movement. Scribner's intentions and basic interpretative purpose is set out with characteristic clarity at the beginning of his work: 'Its argument is that through a study of visual propaganda we may gain a wider understanding of how the Reformation appealed to common folk.'[8] Prints were the books of the unlearned:

Printing made possible the exactly repeatable literary statement, but the print created the exactly repeatable visual statement. It thus fulfilled the same communication function for the illiterate and the semi-literate that printing fulfilled for those able to read in the narrow sense.[9]

---

[5] See here especially, Max Geisberg, *The German Single-Leaf Woodcut, 1500–1550*, rev. and ed. Walter L. Strauss (New York, 1974).

[6] *D. Martin Luthers Werke. Kritische Gesamtausgabe* (68 vols., Weimar, 1883–1978), Briefwechsel, vol. II, p. 268.

[7] R.W. Scribner, *For the Sake of Simple Folk. Popular Propaganda for the German Reformation* (Cambridge, 1981).

[8] Ibid., p. 1.   [9] Ibid., p. 5.

Given the importance of this thesis to the present study, it is important at the outset to acknowledge the brilliance of Scribner's analysis. His reading of the woodcuts is clear, authoritative and subtle. His analysis of different categories of woodcut – the hagiographical images of the reformer, woodcuts that ridicule the Pope and clergy, and more positive pedagogic images – has never been bettered. Scribner also brilliantly evokes the subtle interweaving of these visual motifs with the wider traditions of popular culture.[10] Our understanding of the appeal of popular culture has moved on, but for many of the scholars who have subsequently concerned themselves with German woodcut tradition, Scribner's basic categories of analysis have remained essentially intact. Our purpose here is not to deny the richness of this German woodcut tradition but to test whether woodcuts could, as is claimed, play such a vital role in helping the evangelical message to cross the crucial divide between an educated core and the broader mass of the population. The role of the woodcut in securing this wider public engagement has been far more often assumed than critically examined, still less demonstrated. Thus Christiane Andersson's confident statement that 'woodcuts manifestly played a crucial role in the spread of Lutheran ideas' sets the tone for the manner in which Scribner's work has been absorbed into the general literature, and most scholars are content to leave the matter there.[11]

Yet in fairness to Scribner, even in the original presentation of his case he never attempted to claim that woodcuts played a *necessary* role in this regard. On the contrary, he suggests that the woodcut moment was extremely brief, predicating 'the long term triumph of printing over the print as a major form of mass communication, a fact of which there could be no doubt by the middle of the sixteenth century'.[12] Although our sense of the process of Reformation has shifted since Scribner wrote these words – we would not necessarily regard the second half of the sixteenth century as part of the 'long term' – he is certainly correct in his essential point. The new Calvinist evangelism of the mid-sixteenth century certainly spawned a mass movement. Thousands were caught up in a rapid, dramatic movement of church building that challenged the Catholic ascendancy in France and the Netherlands. But these churches

---

[10] On this point see also Christiane Andersson, 'Popular Imagery in German Reformation Broadsheets', in Gerald P. Tyson and Sylvia S. Wagonheim, *Print and Culture in the Renaissance. Essays on the Advent of Printing in Europe* (Newark, N. J., 1986), pp. 120–50.

[11] Ibid., p. 121. For an example, among any number, of the universal and largely uncritical acceptance of the Scribner thesis, Peter Matheson, *The Rhetoric of the Reformation* (Edinburgh, 1998), p. 37: 'The visual images projected by broadsheets, woodcuts, portraits, medallions were also of incalculable importance.'

[12] Scribner, *For the Sake of Simple Folk*, p. 7.

engaged the enthusiasm of broad swathes of the population without the help of illustrative woodcuts. The French Huguenot movement produced virtually no woodcut images that had a broad contemporary popular appeal. The famous Torterell album, familiar from many dust-jacket illustrations, was essentially a set of high-quality narrative images for the bourgeois drawing room: this was not cheap print.[13] And the pamphlet literature of the movement made no use of illustration whatsoever. The conscious lack of adornment was indeed part of its polemical agenda. It sought to engage the intellect, not the senses.

In the Netherlands the tradition of the polemical woodcut began only with the outbreak of the Dutch Revolt in 1566, and then it concentrated almost exclusively on the obvious political targets, Alva and the Spanish, rather than on religious issues.[14] The dissident religious publishing that had so concerned the authorities for at least a decade was, again, wholly unillustrated.[15] Yet the French and Dutch churches certainly won, and with extraordinary rapidity, wide popular support for their challenge to traditional authority. In these cases at least, one must certainly look elsewhere to understand how the evangelical teaching inspired a mass movement. The woodcut image is simply not available as an explanation.

The recognition of this very different experience of the visual media in the second generation should at least encourage a sceptical re-examination of the role of the polemical woodcut in the German Reformation. The first generation of the German evangelical movement certainly produced a range of arresting images. But for whose benefit? And what precisely did they convey to those who possessed them? The presumption that woodcuts opened the complexities of the Reformation message to a wider public has become so ingrained that the question of how this could occur is scarcely ever asked. Yet if we undertake such an enquiry, we see that the assertion of the superior legibility of image over text is based on a layer of tiered assumptions that are scarcely ever tested. They may be summarized thus: that images could be seen, and therefore read, with clarity; that those who saw them could decipher their messages; and that, when this was not the case, the meaning could be conveyed to the visually illiterate by informed 'readers'.

---

[13] Philip Benedict, 'Of Marmites and Martyrs. Images and Polemics in the Wars of Religion', in *The French Renaissance in Prints from the Bibliothèque Nationale de France* (Los Angeles, 1995), pp. 108–37.

[14] Daniel Horst, *Die opstad in Zwart-wit* (2 vols., University of Amsterdam, Ph.D. dissertation 2000) discusses all extant prints surviving from the period 1566 to 1584, overwhelmingly political propaganda.

[15] Pettegree, *Emden and the Dutch Revolt*, chapter 4.

Only if these conditions were met could visual images function as the bridge between the message and the masses. However, all rest on largely untested assumptions; all, when tested, turn out to be highly questionable.

The world through blunted sight

In modern western society we are fortunate to be able to assume that most of us enjoy perfect, or at least perfectly corrected, sight. Access to corrective eyeglasses or lenses is routine, and those who do not enjoy this great blessing are, at least until extreme old age, a tiny minority of the population. Our fear of blindness reflects in part this assumption of clear-sightedness; in part too an understanding that in a society where so much essential information is conveyed through precise visual signals poor eyesight must be a considerable handicap.

Sixteenth-century society had a very different frame of reference. Poor eyesight was, as was the case for physical conditions and illness of all sorts, simply a condition that had to be endured. It is no means certain, however, that the absence of clear sight would have been so keenly felt. Certainly few cultural historians have considered at any great length the possible implications of this for the visual environment, and more specifically for the perception of works of art.

By far the most insightful and perceptive treatment of this question is the classic study by Patrick Trevor-Roper, *The World through Blunted Sight*.[16] Trevor-Roper, a distinguished ophthalmologist, was principally concerned to determine how eye defects in the great painters may have affected the composition of their works: whether long-sightedness in old age caused the loss of detail in the later work of Leonardo, Rembrandt and Titian; whether Constable's fondness for autumnal tints was due to colour blindness. Our concern, of course, is rather different: that is, to examine whether deficiencies in eyesight might have drastically affected the perception of works of art. But Trevor-Roper's treatment of the chronic problem of impaired vision makes a useful starting point for this present investigation.

The great majority of those whose sight is poor have had their vision blunted because of some optical imperfection in their eyeballs, so that they cannot receive a clearly focused image on their retinas, although the eyes are otherwise perfectly sound. Such optical anomalies can usually be neutralized by spectacles; but until the present century these were a luxury, usually chosen by trial and error from an itinerant vendor's tray.[17]

---

[16] Patrick Trevor-Roper, *The World through Blunted Sight* (revised edn, London, 1988).
[17] Ibid., p. 17.

The statistical extent of the problem is difficult to establish. Today, as many as three in ten of the population under forty may need corrective eyeglasses, though this is not necessarily a reliable guide to incidence of poor eyesight in the past. It might, for instance, be hypothesized that the use we make of our eyes today could have contributed to this epidemic of poor-sightedness. Although we are no doubt right to be wary of over-straining our eyes, the science does not in fact support such an explanation. The most common cause of impaired vision in the younger population is myopia, or nearsightedness: a sixth of the population is myopic. Myopia is the result of an eyeball that is too long, so that parallel rays of light come to a focus in front of the retina. It often presents in the low teens, because the eye has not grown at the same rate as the body. It is, by and large, a genetic condition, not caused by reading or inappropriate use of the eyes. Besides myopia, about 15 per cent of those in need of eyeglasses have astigmatism, a condition that causes distortion, rather than blurring, of the image: a round object will appear to be oval. This is a condition that one is born with.

There is nothing in the science to suggest that incidence of poor vision would have been lower in pre-industrial society. If anything, the reverse is likely to have been the case. The major environmental cause of eye damage is poor diet or malnourishment. In particular, damage can occur to the retina through vitamin A deficiency. Today we gain our major source of vitamin A through fresh food, especially vegetables. Our sixteenth-century forebears, however, suffered from a notably unbalanced diet. Lack of fresh vegetables was a particular problem for city dwellers, our target consumers of woodcuts.

It is certainly the case that this world of blunted sight was little commented on in the contemporary literature. There again, sixteenth-century peoples accepted a wealth of health problems as part of the unalterable burden of human existence; poor vision was by no means the greatest affliction that might have to be patiently borne over a long course of years. It is also the case that pre-industrial society had far less call for what we might call precision distance seeing (of, for instance, road signs or advertising hoardings). That said, it does appear that the rise of reading and writing (not least the invention of the printed book) sensitized society to the impediment of weak eyesight. Here we can cite one of the first recorded references to the impact of the Gutenberg Bible in the market place, when in 1455 the Italian humanist Aeneas Silvius Piccolomini recorded having met at the Diet of Frankfurt a 'wonderful man' who had been able to supply a Bible that might be read without spectacles and in 158 or 180 identical copies.[18] This reference, quite apart from its interest to scholars of printing, does indicate that, at least among the better off, eyeglasses were familiar enough among the cultural elite. Spectacles make their first appearance in the records towards the end of the thirteenth century. They appear first in Italy, and are mostly shown in pictures being worn, or held, by mature subjects. This is itself significant, for the first lenses were convex, and corrected farsightedness, a condition much more common in older people. By the mid-fifteenth century spectacle makers were making concave glasses to correct 'the weak vision of the young', that is, myopia. But it was far more difficult to grind and polish highly curved concave glasses: difficult and expensive. These were luxury items for the rich, such as Leo X, Luther's famous – and famously myopic – adversary.

In the century that followed, the use of spectacles spread from Italy to northern Europe. In England a spectacle makers' Company was formed in 1629. By the end of the sixteenth century potential purchasers could try their luck with travelling spectacle vendors in the market place. But it remained a remedy of desperation, confined to prosperous citizens (and usually those of riper years) with an occupational need to read to de-cipher papers. Most of the population still had to muddle through without.

The practical consequences for sixteenth-century society of this world of blunted sight have never really been fully explored. But from the perspective of this present investigation one consequence must have been that the visual culture of the period was not always perceived with precision. This applied to the world of fine art as much as to the printed woodcut. Paintings, one may surmise, achieved their impact as much from their rich colour as from a particular precision of line (colour blindness is much less common than other forms of visual impair-ment).[19] This was an age in which much art, particularly religious art, was highly tactile and highly coloured. The impact of public occasions designed to impress – such as religious or civic processions – was achieved partly through rich and lavish use of colour: on banners or on clothing. This was a more tactile age, an age sensitive to smell and touch. One must not assume that our own hierarchy of the senses, which gives such prominence to visual perception, is that of our forebears. Most particularly one must not assume that sixteenth-century citizens had that eye for detail that is an absolute staple of interpretation of art, or indeed of the satirical woodcut.

[18] Quoted by John Flood, 'Martin Luther's Bible Translation in its German and Inter-national Context', in Richard Griffiths (ed.), *The Bible in the Renaissance* (Aldershot, St Andrews Studies in Reformation History, 2001), p. 45.

[19] Males are more commonly afflicted by colour blindness than females: roughly 4 men in 200 are colour blind, compared to 1 of every 200 women.

Figure 5.1. The scholar as bespectacled fool.

Reading pictures

Those who served the first generation of evangelists clearly believed that images could aid their cause. The first decade of evangelical excitement produced a whole range of memorable images, not least images of Martin Luther himself. Luther's person excited great curiosity to those, on both sides of the debate, amazed that his criticisms had sparked such a public ferment. His physical features were made known through a series of woodcut portraits that followed a clear, and extremely effective, iconographic scheme: Luther was characteristically represented as monk, teacher and professor.[20] The simplicity of his garb spoke as a parable of the simplicity of the Gospel message, and the nobility of his stand against the overwhelming forces of the church hierarchy. Often he holds open the book of Scripture, validating his claim, as doctor and professor, to teach the pure Gospel.

These images were effective partly because of their clarity and apparently simplicity: though in truth they were also layered images drawing on a web of helpful cultural associations to bolster Luther's image. They were also, however, images capable of misinterpretation: many represented Luther accompanied either by a dove of peace or the nimbus of sainthood – associations that the new movement of reform could not sanction. There was without doubt, concedes Scribner, an extension of late mediaeval veneration of the saints to Luther: 'Luther was well on the way to becoming the object of a new cult, what both he and Erasmus called a "sect" when applied to the followers of mediaeval saints'.[21] The woodcut image of Luther with the nimbus of sainthood was specifically prohibited by the city council in Nuremberg in 1522.

Even these apparently simple images were therefore capable of complex interpretation – and misreading. If this was the case even for these graphically relatively simple designs, the more complex narrative and polemical images certainly required a high degree of interpretative sophistication. The early Lutheran Reformation certainly generated an unusual range and richness of such visual images – indeed, it was these that have largely excited the interest of Reformation historians. The Pope and his clerical minions were excoriated in a series of witty, bawdy portraits that poured scorn on the masters of the church for their exploitation of their power over a credulous people. They were shown as cynical, luxurious and gross: a marked contrast to the honest citizenry whose wealth they so recklessly appropriated. This was the negative

---

[20] Scribner, *For the Sake of Simple Folk*, pp. 14–36. Warnke, *Cranachs Luther.*
[21] Scribner, *For the Sake of Simple Folk*, p. 23.

imagery that accompanied the vicious pamphlet and sermon denunciations of clerical corruption; it made use also of a range of animal associations drawn from popular culture and prophecy. The church was peopled not only by rogues, but also by monsters. Other woodcut images attempted to portray not only the sins of the old church, but the contrasting vision of the new. These represented perhaps the most complex layer of the woodcut polemical agenda, articulating a vision of the reforming programme of pure Gospel, redemption and salvation.

These are the images that must ultimately bear the freight of interpretation for those who believe that the visual image played a major role in the dissemination of the Gospel message. Often the more complex images were accompanied by explanatory text, and this has been seized on as a further crucial stage in the dissemination process. According to Scribner:

> Pictorial representation can be a crude and effective means of communication, but it can never escape the danger of ambiguity. The addition of the printed word enabled it to spell out its message unambiguously. It thus served as a meeting point between the illiterate, the semi-literate and the literate. For those unable to read, the message of a popular broadsheet could be read from the visual images alone. More effectively, its printed text could be read out by someone who could read, creating a situation of oral interchange which was probably the most powerful means of spreading the Reformation.[22]

Leaving aside the final casual recognition of the primacy of oral dissemination in this quotation, this important statement does embody certain assumptions that are absolutely central to our present investigation. Firstly we note the assertion, without further discussion, that the visual image is inherently more comprehensible than text: 'For those unable to read, the message of a popular broadsheet could be read from the visual images alone'. Complex images were made more comprehensible by combination with text; these more complex images then crossed the barrier of literacy by being expounded by the literate. The first of these assumptions seems in fact highly questionable, based more on modernistic assumptions about the superior accessibility of visual culture than on a real understanding of pre-industrial society. The second – that texts were read out and thus complex images explained – is equally difficult to substantiate.

How was a visual image 'read'? Let us examine in more detail two of the most famous images of the day. The first, known as 'The Divine Mill', is a richly symbolic evocation of co-operation between Luther and Erasmus in bringing the pure word of the Gospel to the people

[22] Ibid., p. 6.

Figure 5.2. The Divine Mill. Luther and Erasmus distribute the harvest of the Gospel while the peasant Karsthans threatens the sceptical dignitaries of the church. Used with permission of Lois Scribner.

(Figure 5.2). At the top Christ pours grain, in the symbolic form of the four evangelists, into the hopper. The flour emerges as Faith, Hope, Charity and the church, indicated by small scrolls which Erasmus is ladling into his sack. Behind him Luther is distributing the baked bread as the Word of God to representatives of the old church, who allow it to fall to the ground unregarded. They face retribution for this disregard in the figure of the peasant Karsthans, who raises his flail to smite them.[23]

There is little doubting the genius of this composition, shaping a many-faceted narrative into a remarkably economic space. But was this really for the common man? The fact that the key elements of the story are identified by script suggests not. To appreciate the full resonance one would also have needed to know the history of the Host Mill, a pictorial evocation of the Catholic doctrine of transubstantiation especially popular in central Europe in the century before the Reformation. Here this popular Catholic pictorial tradition is transmogrified and cleansed, rather as the Gospel was cleansed – a process of transformation that the reformers would make familiar in their musical work as contrafactum, using an old, known tune as the basis of a new spiritual song.[24] This, then, was not simply a brilliantly evoked narrative of the Reformation drama, but a complex, layered piece of pictorial transmutation.

Our second image, Luther leading the faithful out of darkness, has a similarly bold narrative flow (Figure 5.3). On the left Luther emerges from a cave, pointing the people towards the figure of Christ crucified. The grateful people huddle around the base of the cross; but in the depths of the cave, among those turned away from Luther and avoiding his lead, are the figures of an emperor and a king. Above the cave are a series of clerical figures and Catholic opponents of Luther, who speak out and attempt to obstruct Luther's teaching. In the accompanying text the faithful cry out to Luther to pity them, so blinded are they by human Law that they cannot recognize Christ the redeemer.

It is hard to see what sense the viewer could have made of this particular print without the accompanying texts. Many of these opponents are represented with animal heads – the key which accompanies their speeches identifies them as the stage army of Luther's most notorious foes: Murner the cat, Emser the goat, Eck the sow. To understand and appreciate these references one would have to have known the epithets being hurled between the controversialists in their pamphlets: these are in-jokes for the literate. Nor is the central theological message, of salvation through faith alone, uncomplicated. In this case one must surmise that the true reading of this image was accessible first, and primarily, through the accompanying text.

If this is the case, we are being led to a new understanding of this visual polemic: that it functioned as a form of stimulation and additional edification (or entertainment) for those who already had access to this complex world of image and association through text. This certainly

---

[23] Ibid., pp. 104–5   [24] Chapter 3, above.

Figure 5.3. Luther leading the faithful out of darkness. At the back of the cave the princes ostentatiously turn their backs, while Luther's opponents, identified by their animal heads, are arrayed above. Used with permission of Lois Scribner.

conforms far more to how we know the world of the visual image functioned in polite society. Even before the developed tradition of the Emblem book became a cornerstone of literary society in the sixteenth century, the pleasure of visual imagery lay in its complexity: the layers of allusion to which only the educated would have access.[25]

This point is well made by Richard Cole, a perceptive commentator on visual imagery, when he calls attention to Henry Estienne's influential text, *L'art de faire les devices*.[26] Estienne, like others who promoted the language of the emblem, believed that emblems acted as a mirror, a visual epitome of morality and the rules of life. Materials from both

---

[25] Alison Adams and Anthony J. Harper (eds.), *The Emblem in Renaissance and Baroque Europe* (Leiden, 1992); Alison Saunders, *The Sixteenth-Century French Emblem Book. A Decorative and Useful Genre* (Geneva, 1988).

[26] Richard G. Cole, 'Pamphlet Woodcuts in the Communication Process of Reformation Germany', in Kyle C. Sessions and Philip N. Bebb (eds.), *Pietas et Societas. New trends in Reformation Social History* (Kirksville, Mo., 1985), pp. 103–21.

the New Testament and Egyptian hieroglyphics were useful to convey hidden meaning:

We see the Holy Ghost denoted by the Pellican, both the Pellican and Christ shed their precious blood for their young or loved ones. God is also presented by the Sun, Rocks and Lilley.[27]

It is highly significant that all of these symbols, particularly the pelican, sun and rock, were at different times adopted as printers' devices, where they functioned indifferently on both sides of the confessional divide. Here one sees how effectively apparently simple images could live a layered existence. An educated reader would understand the complex classical associations of the pelican. More straightforwardly, the printer's device functioned as an easy code of recognition: a logo, brand mark or livery. As printing shops developed a particular reputation, specialism or confessional orientation, such devices became a convenient and recognizable code for potential purchasers: a new layer of associations quite separate from the allusive purpose for which they had first been chosen.

At both these levels, of course, devices or emblems acted as symbols of belonging. To potential purchasers the device became a visual code or shorthand for what the books might contain: a guarantee of quality, or clue to genre or confessional orientation. To those with the knowledge to understand the more layered classical or liturgical associations of the device itself, their perception of this reaffirmed their place in the world of the educated. In this respect Scribner has a point when he compares some of the most straightforward print images with the pre-Reformation pilgrims' tokens. For these prints were accessible and easily obtained badges of belonging, a tangible symbol of identification with the new movement – just as the pilgrims' badges had been souvenirs of attainment. The point in both cases was that they were owned, not that they were 'read'.

The more complex evangelical images were by no means so accessible, in either sense of the word: they were not readily comprehensible, and they were not always placed in contexts to which the common folk would readily have access. 'The Divine Mill', discussed above, appeared on the title-page of a pamphlet, not as a broadsheet; other of the most famous images of the Reformation were also buried deep in the printed page. The famous Cranach images of the Apocalypse, discussed at some length by Scribner, were designed to adorn Luther's New Testament in 1522. This included the famous image of the whore of Babylon in the papal tiara, a feature that Cranach removed for later editions after

---

[27] Quoted in ibid., p. 106.

protests from the local authorities: it is a powerful and famous polemical image, but it is not the literature of the streets. The September
Testament was a costly book and a prized possession. This particular
image would have been available only to the relatively prosperous. One
wonders, indeed, whether these were not the natural target audience of
even many of the images printed as broadsheets.

Reading aloud

We must accept then that many Reformation woodcuts were not
instantly accessible, nor more obviously readable than a printed text.
This was clearly recognized by contemporaries, to the extent that the
most complex narrative images invariably combined image and script:
either as script scrolls in the picture itself, or in an accompanying text.
These texts clearly cannot be read by the illiterate. If these pictures are to
be made comprehensible to the masses, then they need to be mediated
by the literate, through a process of oral communication: reading aloud.

This is to many scholars a key aspect of the Reformation culture of
persuasion, and it obviously has a far wider application than merely to
the visual media. We have already quoted Scribner's affirmation of such
a scenario for the process by which a pictorial image might be explained,
and a similar process has often been affirmed for the dissemination of
messages contained in the texts of pamphlet literature. Thus Alexandra
Walsham, in her discussion of the doctrine of providence in early
modern England: 'First generation literates might share and show off
their mastery of this esoteric art by reading aloud to friends, family, and
neighbours at home or in local centres of sociability'.[28]

It is a pleasing and alluring prospect, and it is given some plausibility
by the fact that the reformers themselves explicitly recommended such a
method of disseminating the messages of their pamphlets. One of the
most famous of all the Reformation pamphlets, *Karsthans*, imagines
precisely such a scene: a literate evangelical son converts his farmer
father with the use of a pamphlet he has brought with him. So it is no
disrespect to Dr Walsham or any of the other myriad scholars who have
affirmed such a process – usually with reference to work by Scribner –
that there is very little contemporary evidence that books were ever read
in this way.

It is instructive in this respect to re-examine the evidence cited by
Dr Scribner in his most extended consideration of the issue: his article

---

[28] Alexandra Walsham, *Providence in Early Modern England* (Oxford, 1999), p. 36.

on oral culture and the diffusion of Reformation culture.[29] He cites a number of apparent instances of public reading, which, on closer examination, all tell a slightly different story. The most colourful examples come from the pamphlets themselves, where authors imagined a process of group reading and discussion, but Scribner acknowledges that there is no evidence that such hopes were ever realized. One well-known example, where an evangelical uses a pamphlet he has to hand to convert a Jew, Scribner acknowledges 'is probably a literary fiction'.[30] Instances he cites of occasions where it can be attested from contemporary evidence that a book was read aloud to a company all relate to Bible reading: some in a family setting, some to groups of evangelicals (groups which a decade later would be called conventicles). Such meetings played an important role in the growth of the Reformation movement, but they do not help explain the appeal of either pamphlets or woodcut images.

There may indeed be evidence that literate friends, workmates or employers read to their illiterate friends or employees. But if there is, it has so far eluded those who confidently assert this as an essential component of the process of oral dissemination.

In the two centuries before the Reformation, reading was often a communal event. Reading played an important part in the entertainment culture of aristocratic society, like storytelling or singing. What was read tended to reflect this social milieu. The text chosen would often be a romance or a chivalric tale, a genre that was highly successful and extremely popular both in the manuscript era and in the first century of print.[31] Noble households and princely courts were often read to in this way: this indeed, is the best-documented location of public reading outside of monastic communities.[32]

The essential point, however, is that in this setting reading would be performed by clerks or household servants: men who were the social inferiors of those they read to. Listening to such performances was much enjoyed, much in the way that noble households also enjoyed singing, tumbling or clowning. But in this context – much as in the monastic

[29] R.W. Scribner, 'Oral Culture and the Diffusion of Reformation Culture', in his *Popular Culture and Popular Movements in Reformation Germany* (London, 1987), pp. 49–69. Cf. his 'Flugblatt und Analphabetentum. Wie kam der gemeine Mann zu reformatorischen Ideen?' in *Flugschriften als Massenmedium der Reformationszeit* (Stuttgart, 1981), pp. 65–76.

[30] Scribner, 'Oral Culture', p. 57.

[31] On the chivalric romance see, for instance, the multi-lingual success of *Amadis de Gaule*, a text that enjoyed enduring popularity in Spain, France, and latterly England. John O'Connor, *Amadis de Gaule and its Influence on Elizabethan Literature* (New Brunswick, N.J., 1970).

[32] Joyce Coleman, *Public Reading and the Reading Public in Late Mediaeval England and France* (Cambridge, 1996).

house – the act of public reading implies little about the reading ability of those being read to. The evidence suggests, indeed, that many of those who listened would themselves have been readers. This might be less true of the women than the men, though it is now thought that literacy was quite widespread among women of high status by the end of the fifteenth century. Of Marguerite of Navarre, a distinguished author as well as reader and consumer of diverse texts, it was said:

When she was alone in her room, one saw her holding in her hands a book instead of a distaff, a pen instead of a spindle, and the stylet of her writing tablet instead of her needlework. And if she applied herself either to tapestry, or some other needlework (which was a most enjoyable pastime for her) she had by her someone who read to her from a historian, or a poet or another notable and useful author, or else she dictated to him some thoughts for him to write down.[33]

The imagined scenario of the Reformation pamphlets requires the reverse of this social norm: that those of higher social status should read to their social inferiors. This is, in sixteenth-century terms, truly the world turned upside down, and there is little evidence that such reading actually played any substantial part in the dissemination of text. What indeed would be its social context: that a master craftsman should break off from his work to read to his apprentices? It is in this social milieu that status was most highly prized, and it is hard to see it being compromised in this way. I have come across only one example, dating from the 1560s, when the Norman gentleman de Gouberville records in his diary his practice of reading to his family and household servants. The text, however, was not a Reformation pamphlet, but that staple of courtly entertainment culture, *Amadis de Gaule*.[34]

It is also the case that in social milieux where reading ability was far from universal, it was a prized and costly skill, and to some extent a commodity. Those who could read and write would not expect that this skill be freely dispensed, even in the service of the Gospel. This is the context in which we must understand the occasions on which pamphlets were read aloud in the market place, occasionally cited by Scribner and others. Here, what we see is the pamphlet seller advertising his wares,

---

[33] Charles de Sainte-Marthe, *Oraison funèbre de l'incomparable Marguerite* (Paris, 1550), p. 68. Quoted in Susan Broomhall, *Women and the Book Trade in Sixteenth-Century France* (Aldershot, 2002), p. 20.

[34] *Le Journal du sire de Gouberville* (4 vols., Bricqueboscq, 1993–4). Katherine Fedden, *Manor Life in Old France* (New York, 1933), p. 75. On *Amadis* see above, n. 31. In the fictional counterpoint to this documented occasion created by Noël du Fail in his *Propos Rustiques*, it is again largely romantic fiction with which the village reader entertains his audience. See Louis Raymond Lefèvre (ed.), *Propos rustiques de Noël du Fail* (Paris, 1928), pp. 14–15.

much as a ballad-singer might sing to achieve a sale.[35] The intention is to tantalize and lure the purchasers rather than engage in painstaking explanation. The one consistent exception we see to this pattern is group reading of the Bible, for which there is rich and varied evidence.[36] This apart, there appears to be little tangible evidence that the polemical messages of pamphlets and woodcuts were disseminated by being read aloud by readers to those who could not read.

To sum up: with respect to the visual propaganda of the Reformation, our investigation thus far casts considerable doubt on any easy assumptions regarding its place in the process of dissemination. We cannot assume that such pictures were seen with any clarity; those who appreciated their messages were likely to be overwhelmingly those who could also read; and it is almost impossible to imagine a scenario in which these literate 'readers' of woodcuts would share their understanding with social inferiors who could not read. In the light of these reflections the perception of the woodcut as a popular medium of communication begins to disintegrate. We are forced, in consequence, to attempt a more measured assessment of the place of the woodcut in the literature and information culture of the day.

Placing the woodcut

The illustrative woodcut, as an artistic genre, grew to maturity with the printed book. This engagement reached back to the first generation of print and long pre-dated the Reformation. The woodcut had a long and rich tradition as illustrative material in the pre-Reformation book world, in both a religious and a secular context.

The buoyant market in religious books inevitably provided one of the most fertile areas for exponents of the new craft. Books of Hours were always heavily illustrated; in the most lavish editions the central panel would be further embellished by intricately patterned borders, also made up of woodcut blocks. Although these illustrations revolved around a limited repertoire of themes, they often achieved considerable heights of artistic accomplishment. Their simplicity of line was a conscious choice, intended to permit hand colouring.[37] In this way the printed Books of Hours preserved an intimate connection with the manuscript tradition. Other popular pre-Reformation religious texts, such as vernacular Bibles, were also lavishly illustrated. The Bibles demanded their own

---

[35] Scribner, 'Oral Culture', pp. 60–1. Chapter 4, below.

[36] Chapter 7, below.

[37] Marie Berthail, *Les premiers graveurs français. Un art naissant: l'illustration du livre* (Nantes, 1986).

narrative cycles for the Old Testament books, and for the book of Revelation, though they sometimes also made use of generic designs first created for use in other devotional texts.[38] Once publishers had made the costly investment required to have a set of woodblocks cut, it made evident sense to exploit their versatility.

Two features of this early illustrative tradition should be stressed. Illustrations tended to be reserved for the most expensive books; they were, in turn, one of the most expensive features of these books. It is therefore little surprise that when the illustrative tradition began to spread from religious books to more secular projects, it was books aimed at more leisured aristocratic purchasers that were more likely to contain these illustrations. Examples include editions of the lighter literary classics (Ovid and Virgil), chronicles and historical works, and the ever popular chivalric romances.[39] The main exception to this pattern was the use of illustration to adorn the title-pages (though not generally the text) of early news books: officially sponsored publications advertising a notable victory, or justifying a decision to go to war.[40] In this respect these short pamphlets (often in the quarto format so characteristic of the German *Flugschriften*) are the most direct precursor of the Reformation appropriation of illustration for small books.

Given that the woodcut had established so significant a role in book culture, the impact of the Reformation was always likely to be profound. The German evangelical movement certainly found a function for new classes of polemical illustration; but at the same time it also called into question certain other categories of religious literature. Books of Hours were obviously no longer in demand in Protestant cultures, and production fell off sharply. Sometimes the accumulated stock of woodblocks could be used in other books. Often, though, they simply joined the lumber of the print shop, their value heavily discounted.[41] For artisan specialists of the woodcut trade these events presented a considerable challenge. Many diverted energies into purely secular forms of illustration, such as the peasant revels and carnival prints so prominent in the pages of the volumes of the *Single-Leaf Woodcut*. There is no evidence,

---

[38] Bart A. Rosier, *The Bible in Print. Netherlandish Bible Illustration in the Sixteenth Century* (2 vols., Leiden, 1997), vol. I, pp. 17–19.

[39] For examples, Berthail, *Les premiers graveurs français*; Hinds, *Introduction to a History of Woodcut*.

[40] Jean-Pierre Seguin, 'L'information à la fin du XVe siècle en France. Pièces d'actualité imprimées sous le règne de Charles VIII', *Arts et Traditions Populaires*, (1956), pp. 309–30; (1957), pp. 46–74.

[41] Graham A. Runnalls, 'La vie, la mort et les livres de l'imprimeur-libraire parisien Jean Janot d'après son inventaire après décès (17 février 1522 [n.s.])', *Revue Belge de Philosophie et d'Histoire*, 78 (2000), pp. 797–850, here pp. 806, 818.

however, that such plebian subjects were intended to appeal to purchasers from the social milieu they depicted. Rather, such prints were part of the entertainment culture of the same social groups who might purchase other prints, such as costume series or battle scenes.[42]

With the passage of years this crisis of purpose only intensified for artisans in the woodcut trade. The second generation of reformers was far less relaxed than Luther in its attitudes to the visual media.[43] His perception that all the senses played a legitimate role in the religious aesthetic was replaced by a far more rigid hierarchy of instruction. For Calvin and Bullinger nothing was permitted to impinge on the primacy of the Word. With this, the illustrative tradition largely receded from religious books, at least in Protestant centres. The Bible proved a partial exception, in at least a limited way. The narrative cycles used to adorn the Old Testament books (particularly the popular stories in Genesis and Exodus) retained their popularity, but the influential Geneva Bible would ultimately permit only maps, diagrams of the furniture of the Temple, and 'Godly Tables', charting the process of salvation.[44]

This represented, in truth, a crisis for the illustrative woodcut tradition. Salvation lay in the development of new genres of book that relied, indeed depended upon, the execution of high-quality woodcuts of very specific design. Such books included books of architecture; manuals of mining and military science; scientific diagrams; illustrations of costumes, plants and animals in works of anthropology and botany; medical handbooks and works of astrology and astronomy. These were, by and large, books published in folio, often in Latin, for technical, professional readers. Once again the woodcut had found its natural home in expensive books.

To the extent that the woodcut continued to play a role in cheap print, this was maintained by a stock of unambitious and rather crude illustrations that decorated the popular genre of sensation books: news of floods, comets, miraculous births, crimes, and the perils of Turkish conquest. These illustrations show little imagination or originality, and indeed were frequently reused from one book to another. The main

---

[42] Keith Moxey, 'Festive Peasants and Social Order', in his *Peasants, Warriors and Wives. Popular Imagery in the Reformation* (Chicago, 1989), pp. 35–66.

[43] For the Calvinist attitude to images, Eire, *The War Against the Idols*, and Sergiusz Michalski, *The Reformation and the Visual Arts. The Protestant Image Question in Western and Eastern Europe* (London, 1993). On Zurich, Lee Palmer Wandel, *Voracious Idols and Violent Hands. Iconoclasm in Reformation Zurich* (Cambridge, 1995).

[44] Catherine Delano-Smith and Elizabeth Morley Ingram, *Maps in Bibles, 1500–1600. An Illustrated Catalogue* (Geneva, 1991).

exception, and it is an important one, is the adoption of a woodcut printer's device in all classes of literature. We have already discussed the function of such a printer's device as a badge of identification, and it is clear that potential purchasers came to associate particular images with specific places of publication or classes of literature. This form of visual identification was particularly important in the second half of the sixteenth century, when Protestantism was making headway in countries where open affirmation of the evangelical doctrines was strictly forbidden. The printer's device here represented a visual trigger through which the purchaser could be led to a potentially interesting work without the addition of the incriminating place of publication or printer's name (Figure 5.4). In this respect a book of this sort was not truly anonymous: the printer sought a delicate balance, allowing the purchaser to recognize a potentially alluring text, without provoking the local authorities into necessary police action. This hybrid semi-anonymous text was characteristic of a certain stage of the Reformation, where controls on book publication had been loosened, without Protestant publication having been formally authorized.[45]

This apart, by mid-century the woodcut image had certainly receded from its heady prominence in the first evangelical decade. It found its natural milieu back where the woodcut had begun, as an adornment of books for a leisured, moneyed readership. This brief survey must reinforce our sense that when we search for explanations of why the Reformation became a Mass movement the woodcut offers us no explanatory key. The woodcut illustrations of the Reformation era provide us with some memorable images, which have become a staple of modern illustrated studies of the period (which contributes in no small part to the rather overheated perception of their contemporary importance). But at the time their enjoyment was largely confined to those who were already partisans of the new movement, and who were educated enough to enjoy and appreciate their references and allusions. Woodcuts were a refined rather than a plebian pleasure.

Art and the Reformation

Most of what has been said with respect to woodcut art must apply if we briefly consider the role of other visual media in the promotion of the

[45] I discuss this concept of different levels of anonymity in my 'Protestantism, Publication and the French Wars of Religion. The Case of Caen', in Robert J. Bast and Andrew C. Gow, *Continuity and Change. The Harvest of Late-Mediaeval and Reformation History* (Brill, 2000), pp. 163–79.

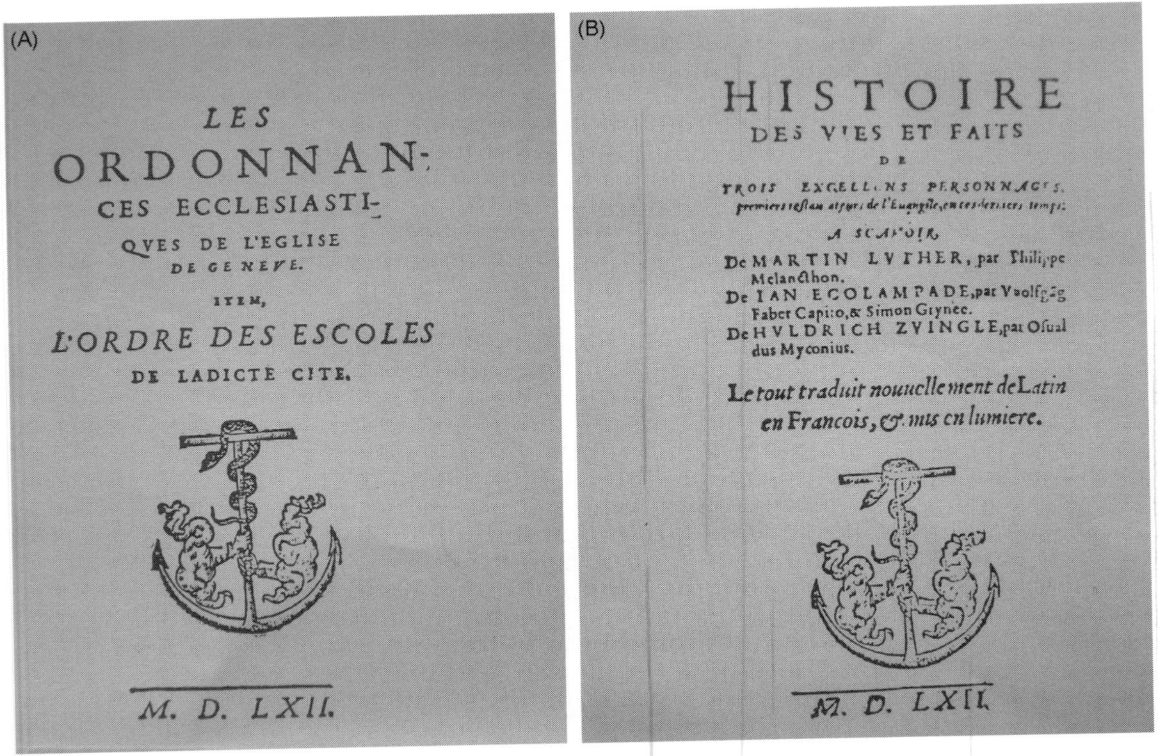

(A)

LES
ORDONNAN-
CES ECCLESIASTI-
QVES DE L'EGLISE
DE GENEVE.

ITEM,

L'ORDRE DES ESCOLES
DE LADICTE CITE.

M. D. LXII.

(B)

HISTOIRE
DES VIES ET FAITS
DE

TROIS EXCELLENS PERSONNAGES,
premierement assez de l'Euangile en ces derniers temps:

A SCAVOIR

De MARTIN LVTHER, par Philippe
Melanchthon.
De IAN ECOLAMPADE, par Vuolfg-
Faber Capito, & Simon Grynée.
De HVLDRICH ZVINGLE, par Osual
dus Myconius.

Le tout traduit nouuellement de Latin
en Francois, & mis en lumiere.

M. D. LXII.

Figure 5.4. Protestant branding. The printer's device was the famous snake and anchor of the Geneva printer Jean Crespin, though the publications were the work of a less-established printer in Normandy: a piece of commercial opportunism even for this godly purpose.

Reformation message. The Reformation certainly retained a place for art; indeed, the German Reformation movement brought forth some of the great, original artistic work of the early modern period.[46] But this too found its natural home among the familiar patrons of art, the nobility and the urban patriciate.

It is interesting to speculate whether this would still have been the case had Germany at this time not enjoyed so rich an artistic tradition; and if one of the premier artists, Lucas Cranach, had not been an intimate member of Luther's inner circle. Cranach's recruitment to Wittenberg had been the most tangible symbol of Frederick the Wise's determination to create a cultural capital worthy of his Electoral dignity.[47] His early work, as one would have expected, consisted mostly of conventional religious images, most memorably the extended series of woodcuts created to illustrate a catalogue of Frederick's enormous relic collection.[48] But Cranach was also captivated by Luther, and with the onset of the evangelical controversies the output of his formidable workshop was adjusted seamlessly to serve the new movement. The most evident (and arguably most enduring) product of this new engagement was the superb sequence of portrait images of Luther, from the visionary monk (the model for many of the woodcut portraits) through to the picture of the dead Luther peacefully at rest in 1546.[49] The Cranach portraits were undoubtedly a crucial polemical tool of the Reformation, and they were produced in considerable numbers, for Cranach had established in his workshops one of the earliest authenticated systems of artistic mass production. Cranach's workshop practice is extensively documented, and although we do not have such evidence for one of the Luther portraits, we know that in 1532 Cranach undertook a contract for sixty pairs of small matching portraits of Frederick the Wise and his successor, John the Constant.[50] One assumes these were to be distributed, whether as gifts or purchased, among the leading houses of Saxony and princely allies around Germany. For noble or bourgeois families a Luther portrait

[46] Carl C. Christensen, *Art and the Reformation in Germany* (Athens, Ohio, 1979). Otto Benesch, *German Painting from Dürer to Holbein* (Geneva, 1966).

[47] Max J. Friedländer and Jakob Rosenberg, *Lucas Cranach* (New York, 1978). Werner Schade, *Cranach: A Family of Master Painters* (New York, 1980).

[48] Dieter Koepplin and Tilman Falk, *Lukas Cranach. Gemälde – Zeichnungen – Druckgraphik* (2 vols., Basle, 1974), vol. I, nos. 97–101.

[49] For the earliest images see Ibid., nos. 32–5. The last image of Luther on his deathbed is in the Landesmuseum Hannover. For this iconic image of the dead reformer at peace Cranach may have been working from a sketch made at the bedside by Lucas Fortnagel. This portrait is reproduced in Heiko Oberman, *Luther. Man between God and the Devil* (New Haven, Conn., 1989), p. 7.

[50] Carl C. Christensen, *Princes and Propaganda: Electoral Saxon Art of the Reformation* (Kirksville, Mo., 1992), p. 39.

was a similar totem of allegiance. The two most popular images were the paired portrait of Luther and his wife, Katharina von Bora, the archetypal Protestant clerical family, and the portrait of Luther the mature reformer painted in 1528.[51] Paired portraits of Luther and Melanchthon have also survived.[52] Judging how many examples can be found of the most common workshop designs, these pictures must have found their place on the walls of countless burgher households.

The painters' workshops of the Protestant cities, in Wittenberg and elsewhere, also gave considerable attention to pictorial themes that converged theologically with the evangelical doctrines. Popular themes included Christ with the children, Christ the Good Shepherd, and of course the crucifixion. Protestant artists also gave much thought to art for the church, particularly the principal picture that adorned the high altar. Although Luther and his colleagues deplored iconoclasm and would not contemplate the wanton destruction of existing religious art, they gave discreet encouragement to the creation of new thematic schemes that would create a new tradition of the Protestant altarpiece. The two best-known examples, both from the Cranach workshop, adorn the churches of Weimar and Wittenberg. The Weimar altarpiece gives pride of place to a Protestant reordering of the crucifixion scene. Here the blood from the wound in Christ's side irrigates the text of the Bible held by Luther. The side panels replace the traditional saints with the ruling Saxon ducal family: truly the supports of the Reformation church.[53] In the Wittenberg altarpiece a still more radical reconception gives pride of place to the Last Supper, with side panels illustrating baptism and the Power of the Keys. The predella shows Doctor Martin preaching.

There is evidence that the reformers were intimately involved in creating at least some of these new designs. Cranach's famous and influential polemical woodcut series, *The Passion of Christ and Antichrist*, was published with texts provided by Melanchthon, who seems also to have been involved in the emergence of Cranach's great narrative antithesis, the Law and the Gospel.[54] This evocation of the Protestant

---

[51] Koepplin and Falk, *Cranach*, vol. I, pp. 177–81. Friedländer and Rosenberg, *Cranach*, pp. 187–90, 312–13.

[52] Koepplin and Falk, *Cranach*, vol. II, pp. 354–5. Friedländer and Rosenberg, *Cranach*, pp. 312–13.

[53] The Weimar altarpiece is illustrated in Friedländer and Rosenberg, *Cranach*, no. 434.

[54] *Gesetz und Genade. Cranach, Luther und die Bilder* (Torgau, 1994). All twenty-six woodcuts of the *Passional Christi und Antichristi* are illustrated in Gerald Fleming, 'On the Origins of the Passional Christi und Antichristi and Lucas Cranach the Elder's Contribution to Reformation Polemics in the Iconography of the Passional', *Gutenberg Jahrbuch* (1973), pp. 351–68.

doctrine of salvation emerged from the Cranach workshop between 1526 and 1530. There is an ink sketch of 1526 in Cranach's hand, followed by two divergent panel paintings, before the design takes its mature form.[55] Its most enduring expression is as a title-page frame, reworked to express the narrative flow in the necessary vertical format, and to make space in the blank central panel for the title text. In this manifestation the Law and the Gospel motif would have an extended life in Protestant print in several parts of Europe.[56]

The impact of Lutheran art was profound, though any sense of its social reach must be carefully qualified. Church art like the Wittenberg altarpiece would have been accessible to the public, though viewers may have been struck more by the novelty of the apostles represented by contemporary citizens of Wittenberg (with Luther as Junker Jörg) than by its theological originality. Designs like the Law and the Gospel lived a double life as panel paintings and in books. Some popular themes, such as Christ in the Vineyard, are found both in satirical woodcuts and in the new genre of the Lutheran epitaph picture. Yet even here one must proceed with caution. Artistic motifs like the Law and the Gospel that found their way into printed books through title-page designs still tended to appear only in the more expensive books, such as Bibles or biblical commentaries.[57] They are less evident in the realm of cheap print. Our appreciation of Reformation art may increase our understanding of the range of visual edification available for members of the new church to articulate their new identity. It is hard to see it as a primary instrument of conversion.

---

[55] The sketch of 1526 is illustrated in Friedländer and Rosenberg, *Lucas Cranach*, p. 24. For the panels, *Gesetz und Genade*.

[56] Andrew Pettegree, ' "The Law and the Gospel". The Evolution of an Evangelical Pictorial Theme in the Bibles of the Reformation', in Orlaith O'Sullivan (ed.), *The Bible as Book. The Reformation* (London, 2000), pp. 123–35.

[57] Ibid., plates 13, 17, 18.

6   Industry and intellect

We come, at last, to the book. For many who have addressed this subject, this is indeed to come to the heart of the question, for the book looms large in all explanations of the appeal of the evangelical cause: a view shared, it must be said, by the reformers themselves. To the extent that Protestantism was the religion of the word, the word was made print. Luther and his colleagues rejoiced; the reading public devoured the new literature. There can be little doubt that the book did much to shape the Reformation; it must also be acknowledged that the Reformation did much to reshape the book.

Our purpose here must be to acknowledge this role, but also to place it in context. As must by now be clear, the book did not function as anautonomous agency, but within the context created by the intermingling of a whole range of communication media. The world of oral communication impacted on print, just as print presented new possibilities for the development of preaching, drama and song. Print culture also brought its own particular dynamic. The Reformation erupted when the book was already a mature technology, tried and tested after seventy years of experimentation and refinement. Nevertheless this was still a developing industry. The full potential of print as a medium of communication had emerged only gradually as authors and publishers tested its relevance to the world of education, scholarship and government. The industry and associated trades of the print world had responded to these challenges in very particular ways. In the years before the Reformation the world of print had created both a pan-European network of commerce and exchange, and a series of very particular local markets, each organized in quite different ways. These evolving local markets – with different patterns of production, sales and regulation – also created quite different contexts for the emergence of the Reformation.

The European book world

In the first era of the printed book, those who dabbled in the world of print experienced all the excitement, risk and heartbreak of a dynamic, but experimental technology. Late mediaeval society was already a world full of books, and they were no longer the exclusive monopoly of churchmen and scholars. This was a rich and highly textured world, served by a highly developed commercial copying trade. Most towns of any size, particularly those that supported universities, cathedrals or centres of government, had commercial copy shops: the largest centres, such as Paris, had evolved systems that came close to pre-industrial mass production.[1] In a world where books were in such heavy demand the potential of the new production method, the technology of moveable type, was immediately clear. Large fortunes were laid out in the search for solutions to the most intractable problems (such as the development of an ink of sufficient viscosity to adhere to the paper, but not to blotch or run). Print benefited from the obsession of its first advocates, but also from the fact that it so quickly captured the imagination of the rich and influential. Print was seen as a prestige venture, with which those used to the exercise of cultural patronage would want to be associated. As news of the new technology spread, and presses were established in more parts of Europe, many of the first print enterprises benefited from this sort of patronage: injections of speculative capital, from which there was no immediate hope of return.

It is well known that the first books were heavily influenced by the established manuscript tradition. This is evident both in the organization of material on the page and in the design of the first generation of moveable types. The desire that the finished artefact should replicate a fine manuscript as closely as possible is also evident in the practice of leaving spaces on the bare sheets of printed text for the addition of illuminated capitals and hand rubrication of the text. But the new technology risked shipwreck when this imitative tradition extended too far. It was all well and good to have books imitate manuscripts in their physical appearance. What made less sense was that print shops should attempt to replicate the world of manuscripts in the organization of production, with multiple small presses almost everywhere there had been a mediaeval copy shop: in every regional capital, every episcopal see. It took time to understand the different dynamics of print: that once aristocratic venture capital had receded and the enterprise needed to be

---

[1] Richard H. Rouse and Mary A. Rouse, *Manuscripts and their Makers: Commercial Book Producers in Medieval Paris, 1200–1500* (London, 2000).

self-financing, the printed book would be economic only if produced in bulk. The market could no longer sustain consumer expectations of individually customized items based on the cultural expectations of the manuscript book trade.

This first brush with harsh economic realities brought a major restructuring of the book trade in the period 1490–1520.[2] The industry had, in the classic manner of a successful vogue technology, overexpanded. This explains the large number of places where books were printed in the incunabula age but which do not then have a press again until the latter part of the sixteenth century, if then. In England St Albans, Westminster and Oxford are all represented in incunabula publications before English book production becomes wholly centred on London. The last decade of the fifteenth and the first two decades of the sixteenth century was the period when the book world achieved commercial maturity, a process that required a drastic concentration and simplification of the centres of production. This was the period that saw the emergence of the dominant centres of European print: Paris and Antwerp in northern Europe, Venice and Rome, Basle and Cologne.

This was also the era in which the book took on its mature form. The printed book evolved into an artefact far more self-confident in its own distinctive physical form, and far less slavishly modelled on the manuscript. During this period the title-page became established as a standard feature of the book, rather than the text beginning, as it would with a manuscript, on the first leaf. Books also began to carry the identification of the printer and the place of publication on the title-page, rather than at the end, in the colophon (though this older practice was often maintained as an additional feature). Books also began to show the year of publication on the title-page.

Equally important, though less obvious from the physical appearance of the book, was the emergence of a mature commercial structure to sustain the new book world. This represented an important coming of age, as the book moved from a heavy dependence on financial patronage – often provided by aristocratic patrons with little realistic hope of return – to a more straightforward business model. This was far from easy. In the period before 1520 books remained, for the most part, prestige objects, outside the reach of most consumers. The publication of a book required a considerable investment and a heavy outlay before there was any realistic hope of return. This return was also often painfully slow, as

---

[2] This re-organization is evident enough from an inspection of the publication data embedded in the Incunabula Short-Title Catalogue database, though to my knowledge this phenomenon has not yet been systematically analysed.

booksellers and merchants undertook the difficult task of bringing the texts to potential purchasers who might be dispersed over a wide geographical area. The complex economics of the new business were not unlike those of long-distance trading ventures, which often involved a similarly large cash investment against speculative profit: for with books too, those who misjudged demand might have to carry disastrous losses in a fickle market. It is not surprising, therefore, that many of those who invested in the publishing of books in this first era of print were often men who had large experience in other branches of trade. It sometimes required deep pockets to sustain even large firms through market fluctuations: it was an economic cycle that favoured the emergence of the larger printing dynasties that did in fact come to play an increasingly large role in the developing print world.

In this uncertain climate, those involved in the production of books could not be sustained by the excitement of exploration alone; they began to look, as did all trades in the mediaeval guild world, for a measure of protection for those prepared to risk entrepreneurial investment in expensive projects. This was the origin of the system of privilege, whereby a printer or author would apply for the exclusive right to publish a book or class of literature for a stated period of years.[3] Such privileges were both highly sought after and keenly defended. The power to grant privilege became an important attribute of the governing power: indeed, for kings, bishops and city magistrates, the dispensation and enforcement of such privileges now became their major role in nurturing the publishing industry, rather than being patrons in the sense of investing their own money.

The system of privilege developed quickly in most parts of Europe that had a mature printing industry, and it was a system that worked well, allowing publishers to invest the large sums over the long period that a book might be in the press, without the fear that the work would be undercut or the market spoiled by pirate editions. Penalties for breach of privilege were often draconian. In France, the classic formula was that the offender would be published by confiscation of the book published in breach of a privilege and an unspecified fine. This was sometimes reinforced with the provision that the injured party might also recover all his 'expenses, damages and interest'.[4] Occasionally a printer breaking

---

[3] The classic study is Elizabeth Armstrong, *Before Copyright: The French Book-Privilege System 1498–1526* (Cambridge, 1990).

[4] 'Confiscation et amende arbitraire, despens, dommages et interests'. The privilege was often printed in summary on the reverse of the title-page, where it was least susceptible to being removed.

a privilege might be threatened with the confiscation of his printing equipment, or even corporal punishment. But in fact penalties for breach of privilege seem not to have been frequently invoked, because the system was largely self-regulating. In the small gossipy world of the print shops it was not easy to disguise one's own workmanship, and professional solidarity would not extend to supporting an interloper who violated the regulatory framework. In fact, all the established members of a print fraternity had a strong mutual interest in ensuring commercial stability. It is an important reminder that most pressure for the regulation of the print industry came, as one could expect in any part of mediaeval guild society, from within. When later in the century, and under pressure from the Reformation, governments began to explore systems of textual censorship, they were able to build around this already efficient system of industrial self-regulation.

The system of privilege was designed to reduce risk in an industry still feeling its way towards the full potential of the new technology. This was a system that permitted, above all, the publication of big books. Most books in the pre-Reformation period were large: long and often complex texts, published mostly to serve established markets that had been major consumers of manuscript books. These included legal texts and customaries; treatises on medicine; schoolbooks and works of theology; editions of the classical authors. In the first generation books were printed almost exclusively in large formats, that is in folio: these were books intended to be consulted in a fixed location, such as a library. The last years of the fifteenth century, however, saw increased experimentation with small formats: books intended to be carried about. These books were, in the nature of things, less expensive than the lofty folios, and published with a different sort of clientele in mind: they signalled that publishers were beginning to conceive of a larger public for books than the established consumers of the manuscript age.[5] The last decades of the fifteenth century also saw growth in the realms of cheap, ephemeral print. The potential of the new technology for purely ephemeral print had been recognized from the first years of the development of the new technology. Single-sheet indulgence certificates were amongst the first work of the Gutenberg press, and such work was no doubt a staple of the

---

[5] For the crucial contribution to this development of the famous Aldine press of Venice, see H. George Fletcher, *In Praise of Aldus Manutius. A Quincentenary Exhibition* (New York, 1995). Martin Davis, *Aldus Manutius. Printer and Publisher of Renaissance Venice* (London, 1995).

local jobbing presses in the first incunabula age.[6] However, by the end of the century cheap print was beginning to expand its range. The period after 1490 saw the publication of what might legitimately be called news pamphlets.[7] These were very often in the first instance official publications, issued to justify royal actions to the larger political nation. The fact that these texts were often taken up and republished for purely commercial reasons suggests that there was a lively market for this sort of news, a market that the Reformation would also exploit very effectively. Many of these news pamphlets were short, and in quarto format, often decorated with an eye-catching title-page woodcut: attributes that we will come to associate with the Reformation *Flugschriften*. The publication of these news pamphlets also signalled increased use of the vernacular, a feature also evident in an increasing number of larger books. These included genres that had successfully made the transition from manuscript to print, such as the popular chivalric romances. The publication of such works in increasing numbers was a sign that the publishing industry had recognized the commercial possibilities of readers outside the scholarly community, particularly the growing market in recreational reading.

The evolution of the book market towards this maturity of commercial practice and diversification of genre included many features that were common to the European book world as a whole. The shape and physical appearance of a Latin book published in Basle would have much in common with one published in Venice or Paris. All were subject to similar market disciplines of price and distribution. Nevertheless, embedded within this common pattern were many significant regional variations.[8] In particular, the important restructuring and consolidation of the industry that occurred between 1490 and 1520 did not happen in the same way throughout Europe. In some of Europe's major cultural zones, this period saw the establishment of one dominant centre of print: in France, Paris; in the Netherlands, Antwerp. In the relatively small book world of England, by the beginning of the sixteenth century print was exclusively concentrated in the capital, London, a situation that would be maintained with little variation throughout the century. England was also unusual in that it played little part in the international

[6] Albert Kapr, *Johann Gutenberg. The Man and his Invention* (Aldershot, 1996), pp. 189–97, 238–40.

[7] Seguin, 'L'information à la fin du XVe siècle en France'. Jean-Pierre Seguin, *L'information en France de Louis XII à Henri II* (Geneva, 1961).

[8] These issues are explored with detailed statistical analysis in Pettegree and Hall, 'The Reformation and the Book: A Reconsideration'.

trade in Latin books, a trade which was a cornerstone of the dominant position established by both Paris and Antwerp, and by Basle for the Swiss Confederation. Elsewhere, the other major language regions of the emerging European print world evolved without a dominant centre. This was true of both Spain and Italy, where Venice and Rome were import-ant without swamping other centres of print culture in the peninsula. It was true most of all of the German-speaking lands of the Empire. Here a number of major cities all maintained robust printing cultures: Cologne, Nuremberg, Leipzig, Vienna and Augsburg all established important roles as regional nodal points, while Cologne also played a significant part in the international Latin trade. The distinctive development of the German cultural area no doubt owed something to political circum-stances, particularly the lack of a strong central political authority; the robust localism of German economic life and social organization also no doubt found its echo in this very fragmented print world. The conse-quences were felt particularly in a different, and very much less rigid, culture of regulation. It was far more difficult to suppress rival publica-tions if an alternative centre of production lay just outside the political jurisdiction (this applied also to some extent in Italy).

This had important implications for the role of print culture in the Reformation. It is undoubtedly very important for the particular role of the book in the German Reformation that the evangelical movement was first incubated in the one part of the European book world least suscep-tible to the system of controls that had emerged to protect and shape book publishing in the incunabula age. Local systems of privilege and regulation were respected in Germany when they benefited the printers (as was the case elsewhere). But faced with the overwhelming commer-cial opportunity posed by the evangelical excitement of the 1520s, German publishers could seize it in a far more uninhibited way than, for instance, the printers of Paris and London. It would prove to be a crucial distinction.

Boomtown Wittenberg

While it is a commonplace that the book made the Reformation (albeit one this study is intended to test), it is equally certain that the Reforma-tion changed the book. This was never more the case than in the first generation, and in Luther's home town of Wittenberg. In this we have to recognize, as in the Reformation itself, the predominant role of Luther. Martin Luther was a writer of extraordinary power and versatility – from the point of view of his publishers this second characteristic would prove to be almost as important as the first. Yet in all the mountainous literature on Luther's published works it is rarely acknowledged how shrewdly Luther shaped his writing for the market place. For a theologian trained to a more formal tradition of technical debate this was already extraordinary. In fact Luther embraced the technology of print with a quite unique understanding of its yet unrecognized potential, working closely with printers and publishers to nurture the market to serve the needs of the new movement.

In the process Luther and his publishers propelled Wittenberg to the front rank of German publishing centres – a phenomenon that defied the commercial logic of the city's rather isolated eastern location, somewhat off the main nodal points of the European trade network. Wittenberg had no printing industry at all before 1502, the year of the foundation of the university.[9] Although from this date a succession of small printers settled in the city, none attempted anything more ambitious than the publication of routine schoolbooks for the use of the students and professors. In the years before 1517 Wittenberg's printers remained very much in the shadow of nearby Leipzig, which had developed a thriving community of printers. Leipzig was also, because of its mediaeval trade fair, a major centre of the book trade in north and eastern Germany. It was therefore to Leipzig that Luther instinctively turned to bring his earliest works to the market, for all that Leipzig, the principal city of Ernestine Saxony, was not allowed publicly to embrace the Reformation: a circumstance that would in the longer term prove fatal to its local primacy in the publishing trade.

The instantaneous success of the *Sermon on Indulgences* (1518) alerted Wittenberg's business elite to the potential profits that would flow from Luther's new public profile: profits that would, unless the printing industry was rapidly expanded, fall to printers in Leipzig, Erfurt and elsewhere.[10] One of the first of the new arrivals was Melchior Lotter, who in 1519 was induced (in fact by a personal appeal from Luther) to establish in Wittenberg a branch of his prosperous Leipzig operation. The established firm of Johann Rhau-Grunenberg also profited from Luther's patronage, though this veteran of the less sophisticated age before the Reformation would increasingly incur Luther's wrath for his

---

[9] For what follows, Hans Volz, 'Die Arbeitsteilung der Wittenberger Buchdrucker zu Luthers Lebzieten', *Gutenberg Jahrbuch* (1957), pp. 146–54. Helmut Claus, 'Wittenberg als Druckerstadt', in *Recht lehren ist nicht die geringste Wohltat. Wittenberg als Bildungszentrum, 1502–2002* (Wittenberg, 2002), pp. 75–201. John Flood, 'The Book in Reformation Germany', in Jean-François Gilmont (ed.), *The Reformation and the Book* (Aldershot, St Andrews Studies in Reformation History, 1998), pp. 21–103.

[10] Josef Benzing, *Lutherbibliographie. Verzeichnis der gedruckten Schriften Martin Luthers bis zu dessen Tod* (Baden-Baden, 1966), nos. 90–104.

shoddy workmanship.[11] The year 1523 witnessed the arrival of the famous Hans Lufft, whose workshop would grow to be one of the cornerstones of the Wittenberg industry for the next sixty years. Alongside these newcomers it is highly indicative that the new opportunities of book publishing also attracted the interest of some of the most substantial members of Wittenberg's business elite: men like Thomas Döring and Lucas Cranach.[12] Although now known almost exclusively for his painting, Cranach had in fact built his fortune through a wide range of economic ventures: he held a local monopoly in both sweet wines and spices for his apothecary trade (no mean privilege for a university town). The wily Cranach quickly saw money in books. He already had an established place in the business through his large painting workshop, and its effective monopoly on the design and execution of any woodcuts required by publishers for illustrations or title-page decoration. It is indeed to Cranach's workshop that we owe one of the distinctive features of early Wittenberg imprints, their beautiful title-page border frames. Distinguished both for their clarity of line and sophisticated conception, these title-page borders became part of the distinctive livery of Wittenberg publications, and played no small part in their success in the market place.[13]

Cranach was also able to exploit his longstanding friendship with Luther to ensure that his business received a good proportion of Luther's new compositions to bring to the market. In a letter to Spalatin of 1525, Luther reported that he was handing over to Cranach the manuscript of his *Christliche Schrift an Wolfgang Reissenbusch* to print in the hope that he might get some peace from other printers clamouring for his manuscripts.[14] When the market threatened to become overheated in the mid-1520s, Cranach withdrew from direct involvement in the print shops, though he still retained a firm interest in the trade through his role in the production of woodcuts.

Cranach's exploitation of his advantageous position in Wittenberg's business elite would no doubt have been more resented had not the market in these early years been so elastic. Between 1518 and 1523 some 600 editions were published in Wittenberg, an astonishing figure when

---

[11] As for instance in Luther's letter to Spalatin of August 1521, where he complained of Rhau's careless workmanship and poor typefaces. See Preserved Smith, *The Life and Letters of Martin Luther* (Boston, 1911), p. 124.

[12] On Cranach see John Flood, 'Lucas Cranach as Publisher', *German Life and Letters*, 48 (1995), pp. 241–63.

[13] *Cranach im Detail. Buchschmuck Lucas Cranachs des Älteren und seiner Werkstatt* (Wittenberg, 1994).

[14] Flood, 'Cranach as Publisher', p. 244.

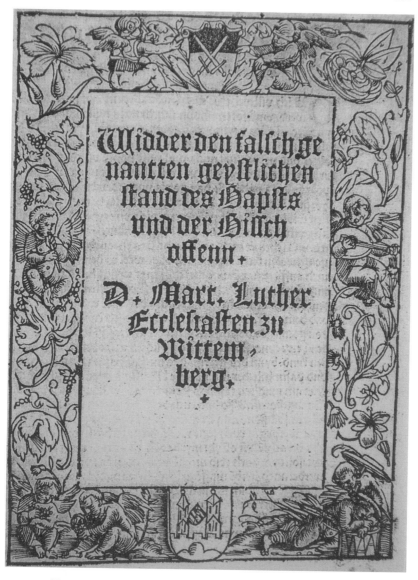

Figure 6.1. The livery of the new literature. The characteristic and distinctive title-page designs developed in the Cranach workshop helped make the Reformation *Flugschriften* instantly recognizable to their audience.

one thinks that ten years earlier the annual output of books would not have reached double figures. Some of these books were also published in editions far larger than normal. The customary size of an edition is generally estimated at between 1,200 and 1,400 copies. But for Luther's *To the Christian Nobility of the German Nation* in 1520 Melchior Lotter published a first edition of some 4,000 copies: a publisher had to be extremely confident of his market to justify an order of this size.[15] Yet demand for Luther's works had already shown that such confidence was well justified. Many of Luther's new works sold out in a matter of days; the most popular went through many reprints in the course of a few months.

For publishers this was an experience unprecedented in the brief history of the printing industry. For Luther's works offered both a guarantee of success and an exceptionally rapid return on investment capital. Previously, publishers might reckon on publishing enough copies to supply the market for two or three years, and they knew from bitter experience that many books took far longer for the print run to be exhausted. A large amount of capital was necessarily tied up in both the production process (especially in the provision of paper) and in ware-housing stock. The cost of transporting books to a widely scattered market also introduced a large differential between the price paid to the printer and the retail price paid by the purchaser. These were the harsh economic realities that dictated that larger projects (particularly the grander Latin editions with a Europe-wide sale) could only be undertaken by the more securely capitalized houses.

The extraordinary demand for Luther's writings completely subverted these cautious economics. The virtuous economic conjunction that gave guaranteed, quick profits applied even to the most complex publishing project undertaken in these years, Luther's translation of the New Testament.[16] This ambitious folio was on a scale not yet attempted in Wittenberg, and to see the project through Luther had turned to three of the industry's most substantial figures: Melchior Lotter, Thomas Döring and Lucas Cranach. The latter two presumably supplied the capital and Lotter the printing expertise; Cranach's workshop also executed the full-page woodcut illustrations (twenty-one in all) that became such a distinctive feature of this and subsequent editions. The project

[15] See Luther's letter to Lang, Wittenberg, 18 August 1520, quoted in Smith, *Life and Letters*, p. 86.
[16] Heimo Reinitzer, *Biblia deutsch. Luthers Bibelübersetzung und ihre Tradition* (Wolfenbüttel, 1983). John Flood, 'Martin Luther's Bible Translation in its German and International Context', in Richard Griffiths (ed.), *The Bible in the Renaissance* (Aldershot, St Andrews Studies in Reformation History, 2001), pp. 45–70.

was five months in the printing house, at one point being printed on three presses simultaneously to ensure that it did not miss the autumn Frankfurt fair, where it was eagerly awaited: anxious times even for its well-heeled sponsors. They need not have worried. The September Testament was an immediate success, and another edition was immediately set in train. This was the beginning of an extraordinary publishing phenomenon that swiftly embraced all of Germany, and from 1523 extended to books of the Old Testament, published in parts as Luther and his colleagues finished the work of translation. By the time the work was finally complete in 1534 Germany's publishers had brought out some 200 editions of the New Testament and parts of the Old.[17]

This success was all the more remarkable because this was not a cheap book: a bound copy of the Luther New Testament would cost up to a gulden, a substantial sum even for a comparatively prosperous family.[18] But this was apparently no disincentive. For many citizens, indeed, that price may have increased the allure: the more substantial the outlay, the more tangible the commitment to the new Gospel principles. Some purchasers went to considerable additional expense to bind and embellish the newly purchased Bible in a manner befitting its status in their new religious life. For Wittenberg's publishers such godly principles were the route to considerable prosperity, when one considers that over 100,000 copies of Luther's New Testament are reckoned to have been printed in Wittenberg alone during the reformer's lifetime.[19]

Luther rejoiced at the success of his writings, though they brought him no direct financial benefit, and the insistent clamour for new texts occasionally strained his patience. At one point the printers approached Luther with the offer of an annual honorarium in return for the exclusive right to publish his new writings: the proffered sum would have doubled his annual income.[20] The reformer preferred to maintain his independence, though he was certainly aware of his power in the market place. Luther did his best to sustain the trade by dividing his writings between the different printing houses; necessarily, since to be deprived of access to these projects could spell financial ruin. Such was the fate of Melchior

---

[17] Listed in Reinitzer, *Biblia deutsch*, pp. 116–27.
[18] This was the equivalent of the cost of a pig ready for slaughter. The unbound sheets would have cost 10½ groschen, just under half this sum (1 gulden = 24 groschen). Flood, 'Martin Luther's Bible Translation', p. 51. Of course the complete Bible would have been much more expensive. In 1543 Joachim von Alvensleben paid 5 gulden for a bound copy of Luther's 1541 Bible, the equivalent of 5 per cent of a pastor's annual income (Ibid.).
[19] Flood, 'Book in Reformation Germany', p. 69.
[20] The printers offered 400 gulden per annum. Luther's annual salary was 300 gulden.

Lotter, when in 1525 he allowed his notorious temper to get the better of him, and he beat a bookbinder's apprentice so badly that the boy's life was endangered.[21] Although he escaped with a heavy fine, the more serious punishment was the withdrawal of Luther's patronage. Rather than face certain ruin the disgraced printer soon left Wittenberg.

This incident only served to underline Luther's vital importance to the enterprises that were swiftly transforming the local economy. One must bear in mind that the printing phenomenon also created a host of jobs in ancillary trades: bookbinders, booksellers and wholesale merchants supplying the market in other parts of Germany. The growth of printing also created a healthy demand for paper, a shortage of which could shipwreck the best-organized business. (One is not surprised to learn that the ever prudent Cranach had also invested in a local paper mill.) Wittenberg's economy also benefited from the rapid expansion of the university, as students flocked from all parts of Germany and beyond, attracted by Luther's renown and the growing reputation of the university's professors. In some years students made up a third of the town's population, and innkeepers, landlords and tradesmen all benefited from the influx. The pace of economic growth inevitably brought some painful adjustments. Rents and the price of food and consumables increased dramatically, doubling in the course of the first forty years of the century.[22] This sort of inflation dealt a cruel blow to any local residents who had nothing to sell to the newcomers. There were frequent complaints at the opulent lifestyle of the students, many of whom came from prosperous burgher families.

But these were the problems of success. Wittenberg's new celebrity transformed both its status and its economy and the new wealth drawn into the town was soon evident in the city's physical appearance. New houses were built for the fast-growing population, and the town's principal streets were substantially remodelled as the most prosperous citizens invested in rebuilding to create houses that properly reflected their new economic status. One can still stand in front of the parish church on the main square and look across at Markplatz 1, the fine four-storey house in the new Renaissance style with which Lucas Cranach advertised the success of his multi-faceted business career. In boomtown Wittenberg none had more reason to praise the success of the Gospel teaching than those who catered to the buoyant trade in books and learning.

---

[21] Volz, 'Arbeitsteilung', p. 148.
[22] Helmar Junghans, *Wittenberg als Lutherstadt* (Göttingen, 1979), p. 107.

Geneva

The extraordinary economic growth that Wittenberg experienced as the home of Luther's Reformation would be echoed a generation later by Calvin's impact on Geneva. Ultimately Geneva would play for the French Reformation a role not unlike that of Wittenberg for Luther's movement, and printing would play a major part in this. It would illustrate again one salient part of the power of printing: that political factors could shape the growth of a major printing industry in a location that made no clear economic sense.

Geneva is a case in point. Before the town's volatile citizenry adopted the Reformation, Geneva was a city of modest size and commensurate economic and political importance.[23] Sandwiched in the foothills of the Alps, some way distant from the major arteries of trade that connected Italy to the south with France and the Empire, Geneva was a city of perhaps 10,000 inhabitants, dependent on a modest passing trade and the economic opportunities of a limited hinterland. A relative latecomer to the Reformation, the city converted to Protestantism as part of a citizen revolution against the rule of the local bishop. But even with its independence secured, the city seemed destined to remain in the shadow of three politically powerful neighbours: France, Savoy and the Swiss city state of Bern, its sometimes resented protector and sponsor of the revolution of 1532. Its transformation from this essentially provincial status owed everything to its reluctant reformer Jean Calvin. Like Luther, Calvin was a writer of genius and imaginative power. Like Wittenberg, Geneva became a magnet for students and new residents attracted by the reputation of its reformer. Like Wittenberg, Geneva was transformed in the process.

The printing industry in Geneva developed, as had also been the case in Wittenberg, from extremely modest beginnings. Although printing was established in Geneva at a comparatively early date (1478), the printers of the incunabula age mostly disappeared in the first decades of the sixteenth century. In the harsh business climate of the decades after 1490s Geneva could not compete with the powerful regional printing centres of Basle and Lyon. Printing revived only with the coming of the Reformation, though for some time the output of the Genevan presses remained modest: between 1536 and 1550 the production of books in the city was essentially the work of only two printers,

---

[23] William Monter, *Calvin's Geneva* (New York, 1967).

Jean Girard and Jean Michel.[24] Both, however, were highly competent craftsmen, and they were able to bring to the market a large number of vernacular texts, many of them the small polemical pamphlets with which Calvin and his colleagues pursued in these years the unlikely goal of the conversion of France.

In the next ten years Geneva's print industry underwent an enormous expansion, as new printers arrived to swell the number of those active in the city. This transformation can be attributed to three main factors. One, undoubtedly, was Calvin's growing renown as an author and preacher.[25] In the years after his return to Geneva in 1541 Calvin had consolidated the reputation earned by the success of his *Institutes* with an extraordinary outpouring of original writing. Many of these new works were intended principally for his own Genevan church, others were small pamphlets destined for importation into France. But what is most striking is the sheer range of Calvin's literary activity, from works of Latin controversy, defending doctrines and reformer friends, to biblical commentaries, sermons, works of pastoral comfort and vicious anti-Catholic polemic. As with Luther, when one considers the totality of Calvin's work, one does not know whether to admire more his extraordinary versatility or his astonishing productivity. In most years Calvin published as many as four or five newly composed works; this in addition to his frequent revisions of the *Institutes* (a work of more than 400,000 words in its final version), and his biblical commentaries, edited by faithful secretaries from the lectures given in the Auditorium. Together these add up to a formidable output. In the years after 1544 Calvin's new compositions seldom fell below 100,000 words; in the early 1550s, when the major commentaries were mostly published, he sometimes published double this, or more.[26] If one takes into account the frequent reprints and new editions, then Calvin's literary works alone would have been enough to sustain a considerable printing community.

Yet Calvin was also responsible for orchestrating two other major publishing projects that would stand alongside his own writings as the

---

[24] Francis Higman, 'French-Speaking Regions', in Gilmont, *The Reformation and the Book*, pp. 110–12. G. Berthoud, 'Les impressions genevoises de Jean Michel (1538–1544)', in J. -D. Candaux and B. Lescaze (eds.), *Cinq siècles d'imprimerie genevoise* (2 vols., Geneva, 1980), vol. I, pp. 55–88. A third printer, Michel du Bois, was active in Geneva for the single year 1540–1.

[25] For Calvin as preacher see chapter 3. On Calvin's work as author see now Jean-François Gilmont, *Jean Calvin et le livre imprimé* (Geneva, 1997). The indispensable work of reference for editions of Calvin's work is Jean-François Gilmont and Rudolphe Peter, *Bibliotheca Calviniana. Les oeuvres de Jean Calvin publiées au XVIe siècle* (3 vols., Geneva, 1991–2000).

[26] Gilmont, *Calvin et le livre imprimé*, pp. 371–6.

bedrock of the Genevan industry: the French Bible and the Genevan psalms. The first edition of the Olivetan translation of the Bible was published at Neuchâtel in 1535, and this was already a considerable publishing success.[27] But Calvin found the translation unsatisfactory, and shortly after his return to Geneva he embarked on the work of revision. When completed in 1551, the revised text became the standard for the French Protestant movement, appearing in numerous Genevan editions in a variety of formats. Calvin was less directly involved in preparing translations of the metrical psalms, but his encouragement of de Bèze helped ensure that this vital liturgical text was also available for the buying public.

With the vast torrent of works pouring from the pens of Genevan authors – not just Calvin but Viret, Farel and others were all engaged in the vernacular campaign of the 1540s – Girard's operation was clearly too small to cope with the volume of works available, and the surging demand from the readership. The turning point came at the end of the decade with the arrival of Jean Crespin and Robert Estienne.[28] Both men were from distinguished backgrounds: Crespin stemmed from a patrician family in Arras, Estienne was a member of one of the leading printing dynasties in Paris. Their establishment of new printing firms (Crespin initially in partnership with Conrad Badius, son of the famous Paris printer Josse Badius) brought to Geneva the sophistication and capital resources of the metropolitan centre of French print culture. Their arrival was the beginning of a massive emigration of print workers from France to Geneva. In the next ten years at least 130 settled in the city, bringing a huge new injection of experience and expertise.

It was a vital aspect of this new emigration that the newcomers brought with them not only superior expertise, but considerable capital resources. Within a few years of their arrival both Crespin and Estienne were able to establish businesses on a larger scale than anything previously known in the city. Both ran four presses (the maximum permitted by the city council) and disposed of a far wider range of typefaces than the more modestly financed operation of Girard. Calvin was delighted, and gave the newcomers his enthusiastic support. The output of the Genevan presses moved into a new order: from an average of nineteen editions each year in the 1540s to something over double this in the following decades. These bare figures to some extent disguise the extent

[27] B. T. Chambers, *Bibliography of French Bibles. Fifteenth- and Sixteenth-Century French-Language Editions of the Scriptures* (Geneva, 1983), no 66.

[28] Jean-François Gilmont, *Bibliographie des éditions de Jean Crespin, 1550–1572* (2 vols., Verviers, 1981).

of the transformation, since this latter period included a far higher
number of substantial projects that might occupy the press for up to
six months at a time.

The exile movement had transformed Geneva's printing industry, as it
had the economy of the city as a whole. Immigration, it now appears,
nearly doubled the population of the city in the space of twenty years.[29]
Such an influx caused enormous social disruption. The city became
overcrowded and fractious, the indigenous population inevitably resentful at the threat posed by the newcomers to their jobs and housing. But
the impact on the local economy was dramatic, not least because so
many of the immigrants were able to bring with them considerable
capital resources. How this should have been so is something of a puzzle.
The French authorities tried to keep a close eye on those who had fled
abroad, and decreed the summary confiscation of any property they had
left in France. The critical factor seems to have been that the Genevan
exile was very gradual. This enabled those planning to leave France to do
so only after careful planning. The printer Estienne is a case in point –
the transfer of his business to Geneva was prepared over the course of
four years. This was vital if the exiles hoped to realize anything ap-
proaching the real value of their assets. When the exile movement
resulted from a sudden political perturbation (as in the Netherlands in
1567 or France after the St Bartholomew's Day massacre) so much
property would come on the market that prices plummeted. Potential
purchasers were keenly aware that those anxious to disappear were not in
the position to drive a hard bargain. One solution in such a case was to
leave behind members of the family not directly implicated, who could
carry on the trade until a more propitious time to sell up and realize
assets.[30]

The arrival of the immigrant refugees in the 1550s cemented Geneva's
supremacy in the world of Francophone Protestant print, a market that
was expanding rapidly as Calvin's influence made itself increasingly felt
back in his homeland. Here, however, the comparisons with Wittenberg
begin to recede, for the Genevan printing industry was much more
strongly regulated than the German market of the previous decade, in
terms of both production and distribution. Despite the buoyant growth

[29] Naphy, *Calvin and the Consolidation of the Genevan Reformation*, p. 21.
[30] For echoes of such arrangements, see A.L.E. Verheyden, 'Une correspondance inédite
addressée par les familles protestantes des Pays-Bas à leurs coreligionnaires d'Angleterre
(11 nov. 1569–25 fév. 1570)', *Bulletin de la Commission Royale d'Histoire*, 116 (1951), pp.
95–292. These letters, confiscated by the authorities before they could reach their
intended recipients in England, also evoke movingly the personal and emotional
hardships faced by families divided in this way.

in output in the decade after 1550, bringing the books to their potential readers remained deeply problematic. Only gradually did the Genevan printers evolve the network of underground communications and travelling salesmen (colporteurs) necessary to furnish a successful commerce in forbidden books. The organization of this trade was largely the work of Laurent de Normandie, a member of Calvin's inner circle whose extensive business interests and organizational flair were laid out generously in the service of the Reformation. The full extent of Laurent de Normandie's operations is revealed to historians by the survival of his account books, which present a meticulous record of his transactions with suppliers, travelling salesmen and booksellers in France.[31] The colporteurs were often provided with stock on credit against payment on their return; some, of course, would never return. The inventory of remaining stock after de Normandie died in 1569 also reveals the phenomenal size of his operation. More systematic distribution through France was accomplished partly through de Normandie's own bookshops in Lyon, Orleans, Paris and Meaux. His papers also reveal connections with other booksellers in Montauban, Reims, Orleans, Pau, Metz, Sisteron, Lyon and Hainault.

Laurent de Normandie's marketing operation was one aspect of the Genevan church's extraordinary capacity for organization. Another aspect, perhaps less attractive, lay in the close control of production within Geneva. As confessional divisions hardened in the second generation of the Reformation, most printing centres attempted to institute a system of censorship by prior inspection, rather than merely punishing those guilty of being responsible for a disapproved text after it had gone on sale (when it was seldom possible to recover all the copies printed). The more rigorous process of inspection of manuscripts before they went to press seldom worked effectively in practice. The interests of the printers keen to exploit a commercial opportunity would always be in conflict with the reluctance of the designated censors to find time for what could be a tedious and humdrum task. In Geneva, however, the system was rigorously enforced. Calvin set the tone, and most of his colleagues at some point took a turn inspecting the proffered texts. The inspection was often close: Acace d'Albiac's verse translation of the book of Job was allowed to proceed in 1552 once he had removed three verses marked for excision on the manuscript.[32] Other texts were banned outright.[33]

---

[31] Schlaepfer, 'Laurent de Normandie', pp. 176–230.

[32] Gilmont, *Calvin et le livre imprimé*, p. 327.

[33] Ingeborg Jostock, 'La censure au quotidien: le contrôle de l'imprimerie à Genève, 1560–1600', in Andrew Pettegree, Paul Nelles and Philip Connor (eds.), *The Sixteenth Century*

It is hard to see that the operation of this system actually operated to the church's long-term advantage. The years of the most rigorous regulation (after 1560) corresponded to the most rapid decline in Geneva's market share in the French Protestant book world.[34] There were other structural reasons for this decline, but the willingness of printers located elsewhere to print texts barred in Geneva certainly played its part. In the last resort the most effective form of regulation was the power wielded by Calvin, when he bestowed his own works on favoured printers. Like Luther before him, Calvin was able to use his status as star author to shape the Genevan book world, not least through the personal support he gave to setting up the two powerful printing combinations of Crespin and Estienne. Through this initiative Calvin was able to ensure that Genevan print matched the best in Europe in terms of typographical style and quality. This played a large part in Geneva's conquest of the market in the years after 1550.

Geneva's other outstanding achievement was to establish through its clandestine network of distribution a new market model for the age of confessional conflict. For Wittenberg this had hardly been an issue; demand for Luther's books had been intense, and access to the purchaser hardly constrained. Genevan print functioned in a very different market place, a world in which curious readers were forbidden under the harshest penalties to possess these books. The phenomenal success achieved by the Genevan booksellers in subverting these controls, in effect setting up a distribution network in parallel to the open market in books across Europe, created a model that would be replicated everywhere when the trade in Protestant books was inhibited in the second half of the sixteenth century.

The book in the market place

Thus far we have considered the economics of the Protestant book world largely from the point of view of the major centres of production. We have seen that the star authors of Wittenberg and Geneva were enormously influential in shaping the production of Reformation books

---

French Religious Book (Aldershot, St Andrews Studies in Reformation History, 2001), pp. 210–38.
[34] The figures for market share come from the data collected for the St Andrews French book project. On the problems faced by the Genevan book industry during this period, see Hans Joachim Bremme, Buchdrucker und Buchhändler zur Zeit des Glaubenskämpfe (Geneva, 1969).

in places where the industry could grow very rapidly in response to enormous demand for books by the major reformers. The success of Protestant print also prompted a major change in the climate of regulation. In the first age of print the structure of regulation had been devised largely to protect the producer. Printers and authors wished to explore a variety of ways to expand the known markets for books in the law courts, universities and centres of administration. Extending the market beyond tried and tested users of books inevitably involved risk: the system of privilege helped to ensure that the risk takers were appropriately rewarded. The new book world of the Reformation changed this dynamic very profoundly. New types of book were circulating in ever larger numbers. Small books, in particular, were particularly challenging: large quantities could be transported swiftly to curious readers; relatively small traders could carry a large variety of titles. In these circumstances a new climate of regulation emerged. The stress was now not so much on protecting the producers, but on insulating the readers from pernicious content. This created a challenging new world for printers. The rewards of involvement in the trade in evangelical books could be great – as the printers of Wittenberg and Geneva both experienced. But the risks were also far greater.

Printing is not an activity that can be easily concealed. First the press must be constructed, or purchased. Then, more difficult, since this was a highly specialized occupation, the type must be obtained. Lastly, one must procure ink, paper and skilled workmen. Even a small, one-press workshop employed a lot of people: the typesetter, two pressmen, a proofreader, a lad or two to dampen the paper in preparation for printing and to stack the printed sheets. It also required a lot of space. As each sheet came off the press it was hung up to dry, before being taken down and stacked (this is seldom illustrated on contemporary illustrations of print shops). The text would then be printed on the reverse of the sheet the following day. As a book took shape, the shop must have been crammed with piles of sheets waiting to be assembled into quires and then the finished text. For larger projects, such as a folio Bible, this would require many cubic metres of temporary storage.

The chances that this could all be done unobserved – from the provision of paper and types to bringing the finished artefact to the market – were fairly remote. Nor were the printer's problems then at an end. Most print communities were tightly knit and gossipy. Skilled workmen moved from one shop to another, and specialist types were loaned back and forth: printers knew each other's work well. If the authorities took offence at a particular publication they could usually identify any local

(B)

(A)

Figure 6.2. The printer's workshop. The familiar illustration from Ammann's *Ständebuch* (A) shows the finished sheets being stacked, but not being hung up to dry. As the more realistic illustration (B) of 1642 shows, this must have required a lot of space.

printer responsible by taking a copy round the print shops. The signature style of the guilty party would usually be obvious to his competitors. They, indeed, might take the initiative in denouncing him, particularly if the disapproved project breached their copyright, or if they hoped to gain (perhaps by inheriting a valuable privilege) from a competitor's destruction.

These practical realities did much to inhibit the publication of disapproved books. If a printer were tempted, or induced, to engage in such an enterprise, then it was far better to print small books, which would be in and out of the shop in the minimum time, leaving no incriminating evidence. There is virtually no documented case of books of any size or length being brought out in conditions of secrecy. All such projects were published abroad, like the early English Protestant Bibles or the well-organized Genevan industry. Even for the most ephemeral work it was best to use a common typeface, no decorative initials, and disguise any individualities of style or typographical arrangement.

Best of all, however, was to find safety in numbers. It was far harder to pursue individual printers, and single them out for punishment, once the mass of material on the market became overwhelming. In this way a pamphlet surge, such as that in Germany in the 1520s and France and the Netherlands in the 1560s, created a dynamic quite exceptional in the normally orderly world of print. There were still risks: in these times of extreme political volatility, who knew what retribution the authorities might exact if policy shifted, or control was re-established. But sixteenth-century people knew the power and safety of the crowd, and in this respect members of the printing fraternity were no different.

'Pamphlet moments' created a very particular market: not unlike the bubble of a rising stock market, when a particular stock or class of stocks becomes suddenly fashionable.[35] The new literature sparks curiosity, bringing more onto the market; the collapse of the normal mechanisms of control induce other more cautious producers to enter the market; the world is suddenly full of books. Eventually the market reaches saturation, but in the meantime the profits that can be made are very large.

The economics of the sixteenth-century book trade have never yet been systematically studied. We have relied thus far on very fragmentary information. Inventories of the stock of deceased printers and of the value of other book collections give an idea of wholesale value.[36] To

---

[35] John Cassidy, *Dot.con. The Greatest Story Ever Sold* (London, 2002).
[36] Runnalls, 'La vie, la mort et les livres de l'imprimeur-libraire parisien Jean Janot'.

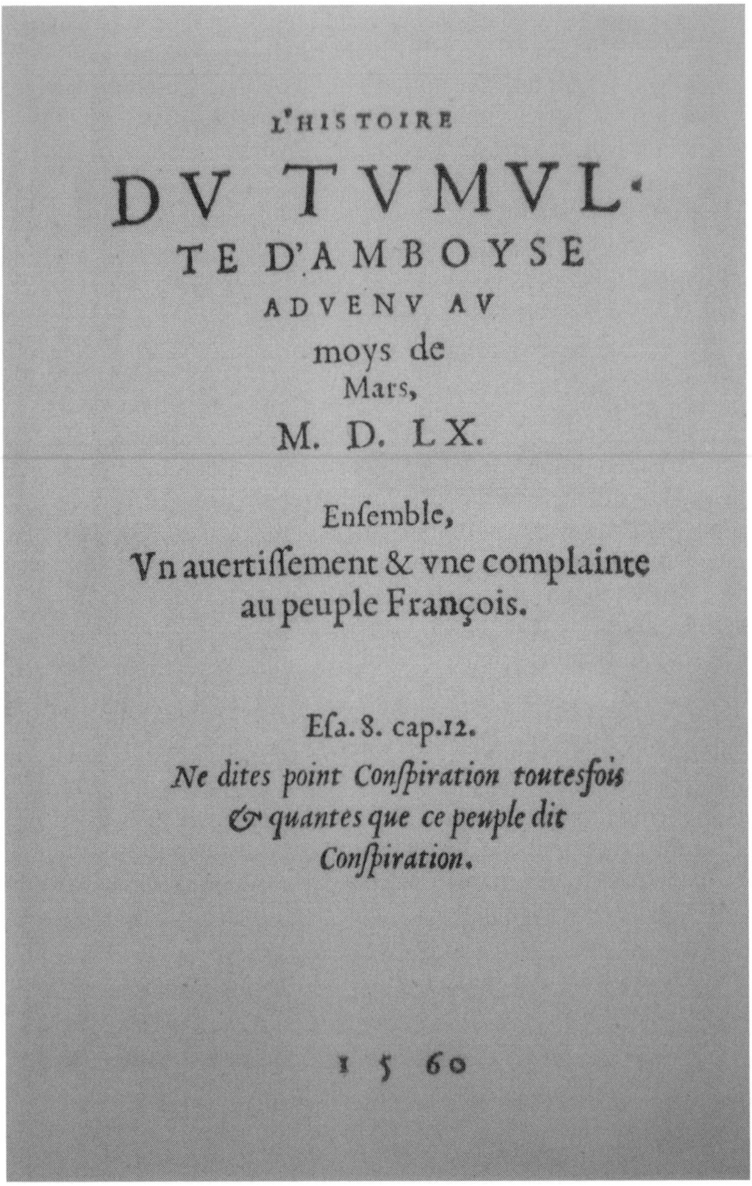

L'HISTOIRE

DV TVMVL·
TE D'AMBOYSE
ADVENV AV
moys de
Mars,
M. D. LX.

Enfemble,
Vn auertiffement & vne complainte
au peuple François.

Efa. 8. cap.12.
Ne dites point Confpiration toutesfois
& quantes que ce peuple dit
Confpiration.

1 5 60

Figure 6.3. *(cont.)*

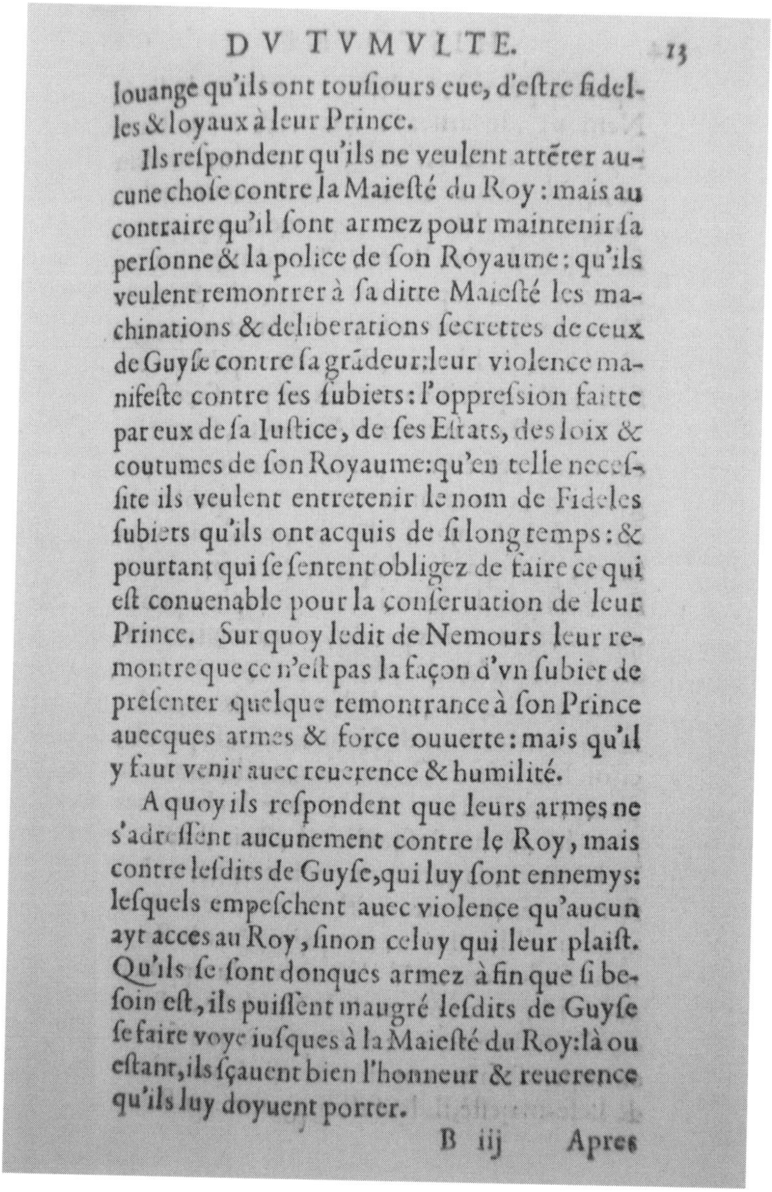

DV TVMVLTE. 13

Iouange qu'ils ont touſiours euc, d'eſtre fidel-
les & loyaux à leur Prince.

Ils reſpondent qu'ils ne veulent attēter au-
cune choſe contre la Maieſté du Roy : mais au
contraire qu'il ſont armez pour maintenir ſa
perſonne & la police de ſon Royaume: qu'ils
veulent remonrrer à ſa ditte Maieſté les machinations & deliberations ſecrettes de ceux
de Guyſe contre ſa grādeur;leur violence ma-
nifeſte contre ſes ſubiets: l'oppreſsion faitte
par eux de ſa Iuſtice, de ſes Eſtats, des loix &
coutumes de ſon Royaume:qu'en telle neceſ-
ſite ils veulent entretenir le nom de Fideles
ſubiers qu'ils ont acquis de ſi long temps : &
pourtant qui ſe ſentent obligez de faire ce qui
eſt conuenable pour la conſeruation de leur
Prince. Sur quoy ledit de Nemours leur re-
monrre que ce n'eſt pas la façon d'vn ſubiet de
preſenter quelque remonrrance à ſon Prince
auecques armes & force ouuerte:mais qu'il
y faut venir auec reuerence & humilité.

A quoy ils reſpondent que leurs armes ne
s'adreſſent aucunement contre le Roy, mais
contre leſdits de Guyſe,qui luy ſont ennemys:
leſquels empeſchent auec violence qu'aucun
ayt acces au Roy,ſinon celuy qui leur plaiſt.
Qu'ils ſe ſont donques armez à fin que ſi be-
ſoin eſt, ils puiſſent maugré leſdits de Guyſe
ſe faire voye iuſques à la Maieſté du Roy:là ou
eſtant,ils ſçauent bien l'honneur & reuerence
qu'ils luy doyuent porter.

B iij   Apres

Figure 6.3. (*cont.*)

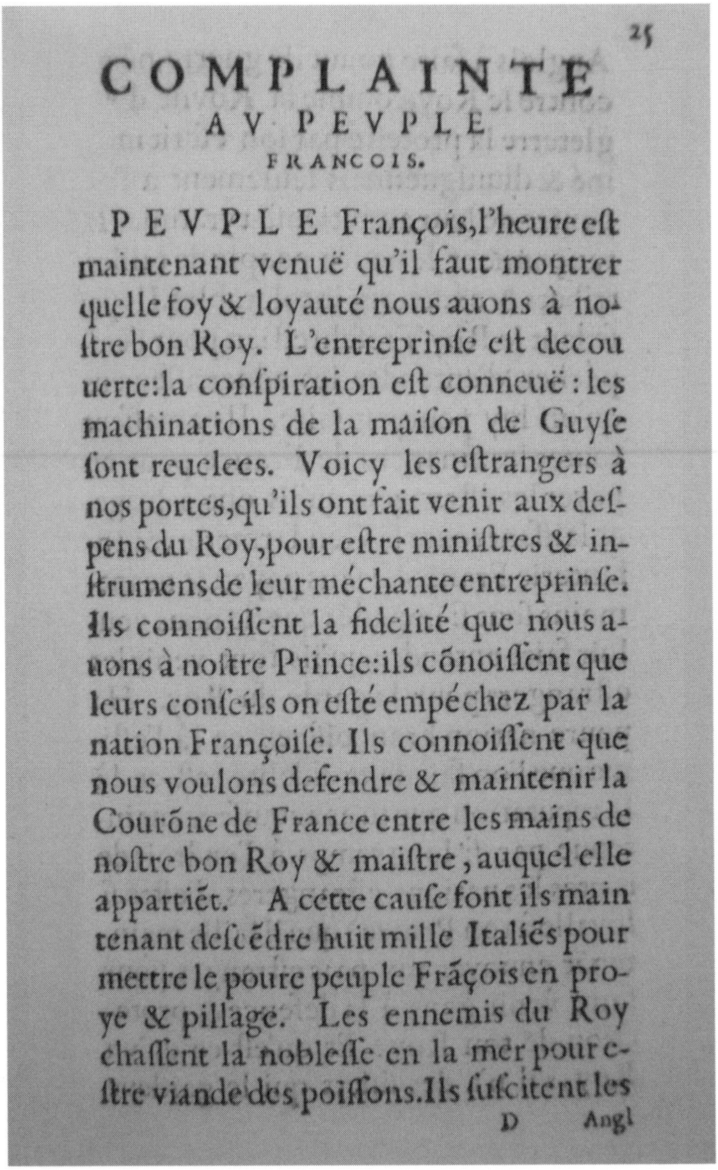

25

COMPLAINTE
AV PEVPLE
FRANCOIS.

PEVPLE François,l'heure est
maintenant venuë qu'il faut montrer
quelle foy & loyauté nous auons à nostre bon Roy. L'entreprinse est décou
uerte:la conspiration est conneuë : les
machinations de la maison de Guyse
sont reuelees. Voicy les estrangers à
nos portes,qu'ils ont fait venir aux despens du Roy,pour estre ministres & in-
strumens de leur méchante entreprinse.
Ils connoissent la fidelité que nous a-
uons à nostre Prince:ils cônoissent que
leurs conseils on esté empéchez par la
nation Françoise. Ils connoissent que
nous voulons defendre & maintenir la
Courône de France entre les mains de
nostre bon Roy & maistre , auquel elle
appartiét. A cette cause font ils main
tenant descédre huit mille Italiés pour
mettre le poure peuple Fráçois en pro-
ye & pillage. Les ennemis du Roy
chassent la noblesse en la mer pour e-
stre viande des poissons.Ils suscitent les
                                        D   Angl

Figure 6.3. Levels of anonymity. Unlike the Caen and Wittenberg books illustrated earlier, the printer of this dangerously seditious book adopts the plainest sort of typefaces with no incriminating decorative initials or identifying printer's device.

determine prices paid by purchasers we normally rely on standard multipliers of these wholesale figures. In all this data there are clear indications that small books were disproportionately profitable. In 1566 a book pedlar working in Overijssel paid a printer one gulden to print for him one thousand copies of three Beggar songs, a unit cost of one fiftieth of a stuiver per copy. If he exchanged each copy for the smallest coin available this was still an enormous profit.[37] This also hints at the other large profits available for printers who sold small books, like volumes containing a few psalms, for one or two stuivers a piece.

There were other benefits to the producer from the trade in small books. Not only was the profit potentially very healthy, the return on investment (of paper and wages) was very rapid: a small pamphlet or broadsheet represented no more than a day's work. Sometimes, as in the example cited above, the entire edition was paid for by the client, which meant that the printer bore none of the risk. In 1522 and 1523 the Cathedral Chapter at Utrecht commissioned a local printer to publish on their behalf an advertisement for the local indulgence trade (no doubt to restore its popularity after Luther's recent criticisms). Five hundred copies were ordered for the equivalent of 105 stuivers.[38] It is quite possible in this case that these small publications were intended not for sale but to be distributed free of charge, and this practice was far from uncommon in the age of polemical print. As Protestants emerged from the shadows, they signalled their increasing confidence by distributing broadsheets or pamphlets around the buildings and houses of the town, often at night. The most famous example was the placard of 1534, with its provocative denunciation of the Mass which so inflamed Francis I.[39] This process of 'sowing' books through the streets, as it was known, became an epidemic during the crisis of the Dutch Revolt. In May 1566 a handbill printed in Vianen appeared overnight in the four chief towns of Brabant.[40] The level of organization revealed by this simultaneous distribution was also a potent demonstration of the growing power of the Calvinist opposition: this, of course, was also part of the point being made.

The practice of attempting to influence public opinion by anonymous leafleting clearly continued throughout the Reformation century. In

[37] Alastair Duke, 'Posters, Pamphlets and Printers. The Ways and Means of Disseminating Dissident Opinion on the Eve of the Dutch Revolt', *Dutch Crossing*, 27 (2003), p. 31.
[38] Ibid., p. 30.
[39] Robert Hari, 'Les placards de 1534', in G. Berthoud (ed.), *Aspects de la propagande religieuse* (Geneva, 1957), pp. 79–142, with a facsimile of one of the few surviving copies.
[40] Duke, 'Posters, Pamphlets', p. 33.

1590 Claude de Rubys, an author who supported the Catholic League in their campaign against the succession of Henry of Navarre as king of France, published a response to a tract which, according to the indignant title-page, had been 'spread in days past through the streets of Lyon, by those conspiring to deliver the town into the power of the heretics'.[41] Interestingly the offending book which had inspired this onslaught, Michel Hurault's *Anti-Espagnol*, was a fairly substantial work of almost fifty pages. It may have been a sign of desperation for the League's opponents in Lyon that they had resorted to distributing the work in this way, but it involved a substantial financial outlay.

The printing and distributing of libellous pamphlets evoked the long-established practice of pursuing personal disputes by displaying handbills (usually handwritten) in public places.[42] There was also a far more mundane traffic in printed broadsheets, usually commissioned by local authorities to relay government proclamations and advertise regulations. Because such commissions were wholly paid for by the council, such work – reliable, regular and easy – was much sought after by printers. The total size of this trade in official broadsheets was probably quite large. We will never know with any certainty since the rate of survival of such mundane publications is extremely low. Once a proclamation was made or an ordinance expired, the remaining stock was disposed of, the paper used to pad the binding of books or for more mundane domestic purposes. In such circumstances rare discoveries of examples of these broadsheet publications are extremely valuable.[43]

The progress of this shadowy mundane everyday trade is not without relevance for our investigation of religious printing. In ordinary times work for official bodies was the lifeblood of many print shops, particularly the smaller regional firms. The loss of such trade might be fatal to their business; it certainly provided a strong economic incentive to avoid involvement in publishing books that might bring official disapproval. On the other hand, when these constraints were loosened, printers could turn their attention very quickly to other forms of ephemeral print.

The market in cheap print in fact epitomizes very well the two sides of the sixteenth century print world. In times of calm this was a

[41] [Claude de Rubys], *Response a l'Anti-Espagnol, semé ces jours passez par les rues et carrefours de la ville de Lyon, de la part des Conjurez, qui avoyent conspire de livrer ladicte ville en la puissance des heretiques* (Lyon, 1590).

[42] Fox, *Oral and Literate Culture*, pp. 299–344.

[43] See, for instance, the marvellous collection of the Archives Municipales of Troyes (now deposited in the Troyes Bibliothèque Municipale): Troyes AM, liasse Layette 20, Reg. P1.

well-organized, regulated industry with well-developed mechanisms of financing, marketing and control. It served a steadily growing market, with goods of high quality in a range of genres and styles. It was one of the ornaments, as well as an increasingly important part of the sinews, of sixteenth century society. On the other hand, the industry possessed a brooding, latent capacity for explosive growth in conditions of unusual economic or political opportunity. It was precisely this combination that inspired the printing phenomenon of the Reformation.

7   Pamphlets and persuasion

On the basis of the foregoing discussion we can now be reasonably satisfied that the production of books in the sixteenth century was deeply shaped by the organization of the market – both the structure of the printing industry, in a series of discrete and quite distinct national markets, and a sophisticated transnational system of distribution and marketing. These industry issues conditioned the book world at all levels: the market in scholarly books, as much as the production and sale of pamphlets. Our purpose now must be to try and locate the book in the culture of persuasion.

There can be little doubt that books had a vast and important role to play in shaping the new religious cultures of the sixteenth century. Books were bought in vast quantities, and religious books dominated the market at all levels: at both ends of the spectrum and almost all points in between. From the learned Latin biblical commentaries of Calvin, Brenz and Oecolampadius, to the 'godly ballad', with a whole host of Bibles, catechisms, works of devotion and *Flugschriften* in the middle ranges, the market in religious books dominated the sixteenth-century book world. None doubted their impact in forming opinion – certainly not Luther and his colleagues, who wrote so indefatigably and lavished praise upon the 'new' invention; certainly not the Catholic authorities who tried to limit their circulation by censorship and proscription. But in some senses the book has suffered precisely because its influence seems so obvious. In the context of this present investigation it is, however, necessary to pause and ask more directly what part books played in shaping opinion – and indeed at what point in the process of conversion and opinion forming they were most likely to be influential. With questions of this order, we get into deeper waters.

The questions are, at first sight, deceptively simple. Why did people buy books? The answer, or at least the assumption, that has under-pinned all use of sixteenth-century texts in scholarship is that people bought them to read them. They were valued primarily for the words they contained, for the arguments they laid out. This is certainly the reason authors wrote. They wrote to persuade; and when their arguments found resonance, they assumed that their books had hit their target. Yet if we subject this basic assumption to any level of scrutiny it begins to seem at the very least, questionable; not least because it in no way conforms to our own experience of engagement with the world of print. I myself have many books I have not read – and will never read, in the sense of consecutive reading, cover to cover; that ideal reading process is one I reserve largely for fiction and recreational reading, or books I am obliged to read for specific professional reasons (for instance, for review). But consecutive, narrative reading is not my normative experience of books. Quite a lot of reading material passes through my hands and is either stored or discarded unread – this is particularly the case if we expand our understanding of the print world to include all that print material that comes our way as magazines, newspapers or leaflets, some of which we purchase, some of which we come by free.

If we simply confine our thoughts to books and print material that we pay for – in other words in which we have invested some sort of hope or expectation – there are a large variety of reasons why we purchase books which have little or nothing to do with reading them. We buy as a badge of identity (the programme at a sports fixture) or as a memento (the opera programme). We buy books as a mark of professional status (the row of texts in the lawyer's office), to signal social aspiration (Stephen Hawking's *A Brief History of Time*), or as a fashion statement (Hawking again). We buy for reassurance (books of reference), through a sense of obligation, to honour someone we admire. We buy out of idle curiosity; we buy as gifts. Sometimes we buy simply because people like us buy books.

Many times we buy books of which we already know the contents; sometimes we even buy books, for any number of the reasons stated above, that we have already read. This is the case even though people much less frequently re-read books than in previous book-reading generations: among adults[1] the habit of repeat reading has now been largely displaced by other modern media such as film and television where repeat viewing plays an important (and much enjoyed) part of the recreational experience. Other times we buy books that we will never read at all. We still may value them greatly – we have quite an intimate relationship with many unread books. But the essential point is this: there are a whole host of reasons we buy books other than as the primary channel to the information they contain.

---

[1] Though not of course among children.

I think it is relatively easy to accept that in our own age the buying of books is a culturally complex decision, even if, because a book represents a relatively insignificant financial outlay, it is often not usually deeply considered. How much of this can – or should – be applied to our understanding of sixteenth-century book culture? It is immediately clear that books then existed in a wholly different cultural context. Books were much less common, and much more expensive relative to disposable income. Certainly, fewer people owned books, and those that did owned smaller collections. A purchase, it might be thought, was far less likely to be frivolous or whimsical: the purchasing of books would be a far more focused and purposeful disposal of limited surplus income.

There is, of course, a great deal of truth in this. Systematic study of many sixteenth-century library collections shows that they often had an extremely tight occupational or thematic focus. But that does not yet mean that we can assume that books were purchased wholly, or primarily, to be read. The greater expense involved could mean that books were frequently valued for their prestige as objects: in this case the mere fact of ownership marked out the owner as a man of status. This was certainly true of the manuscript age, but continued to an extent into the age of print. It has been noted, for instance, that when an inventory of a house's contents and furniture was compiled by a notary in the sixteenth century, Books of Hours were listed not with other books, but with devotional paintings, tapestries and crucifixes owned by the deceased. In other words, 'within the domestic space in which they were found, devotional works appear to have functioned as much as religious objects as they did as religious books'.[2] This point has a more general application even in the larger private collections. Much of my recent research has been undertaken in French municipal libraries, collections often especially rich in old books dating from the confiscations of the property of Catholic religious houses at the time of the French Revolution. Sometimes we are allowed to view several hundred at a time (a rare luxury in this conservation-conscious age); when we do, we are immediately struck by the enormous variety and luxury of sixteenth- and seventeenth-century bindings. Many passed into the hands of their previous religious owners through pious donation; they thus represent objects from many thousands of private laymen's libraries. They were clearly loved and cherished, embellished far beyond the value of the original cost of the text. Who can say what part of the finished article its owner most valued?

---

[2] Paul Nelles, 'Three Audiences for Religious Books in Sixteenth-Century France', in Andrew Pettegree, Paul Nelles and Philip Conner, *The Sixteenth Century French Religious Book* (Aldershot, St Andrews Studies in Reformation History, 2001), p. 266.

It could be suggested that – leaving aside such conscious embellishment – for the most part the purchase of books in the sixteenth century steered a middle way between the extremes of the manuscript age and modern consumer society. Books had become sufficiently common that they would no longer figure among the most prized possessions; they were sufficiently expensive that their purchase would always be a considered act. This contains a grain of truth. In sixteenth-century inventories of private houses, books (with the exception of precious works like the Books of Hours mentioned above, or a family Bible) were seldom given an individual valuation, though their aggregate value might be significant. But what of pamphlets? These were sufficiently cheap that the purchase could be a relatively unconsidered or insignificant outlay. In these circumstances the range of motivations we have postulated for the modern book purchaser may indeed come into play.

The crowd made text

Why did people buy pamphlets in the sixteenth century? This was the first age in which a wide variety of cheap printed matter was widely available; print began, in consequence, to impact on a far wider range of social groups. The best available evidence suggests that the cheapest pamphlets (that is, books that comprised up to one folded sheet of paper, eight pages in quarto and sixteen in octavo) cost the equivalent of one or two pence in most currencies. This brought books well within the range of most people with any level of disposable income. In the same period an artisan might earn 8d for a day's work, so the purchase of a pamphlet represented the cost of three or four hours' work. A pamphlet might be exchanged for a chicken or a pound of wax.[3] This makes the point that books were affordable, but expresses the point in a slightly misleading way. For to cast comparisons in such terms always carries the implication that large books were purchased by those with large disposable incomes, and small books by those with limited resources.[4] In fact, there is a great deal of evidence that small books were bought by people who could also afford large books.

This is certainly true of the first generation of the Reformation in France and the Netherlands, when Protestant print was forbidden. Books were sold in small formats because they were more easily transported and concealed, not because the purchasers were men of low

---

[3] Edwards, *Printing, Propaganda and Martin Luther*, p. 16.
[4] '[The cost was] not insignificant, but certainly within reach of the "common man", the pamphlets' intended audience.' Ibid.

income.[5] In fact, the process of clandestine distribution added greatly to the price.[6] This is a special market. But there is plenty of evidence that can be found that even when circulation was not inhibited, pamphlets also found a ready market among classes of readers who were also buying more expensive books.

This is a conclusion to which we would be drawn both by the simple mathematics of production, and by the evidence of surviving copies. It has been estimated that the pamphlet wars of the 1520s generated at least 6,000 separate publications in the German-speaking lands. If we estimate, conservatively, an average edition size of 1,000 copies, this implies a market suddenly flooded with around 6 million books. Given an assumed rate of male literacy of around 30 per cent this must imply multiple purchases by those who could read – Mark Edwards suggests a figure of twenty pamphlets for every literate member of the Empire.[7] (Of course this assumes that those who purchased books were by and large people who could read them.)[8] In the two years 1589 and 1590 the Paris presses turned out around 2 million copies of pamphlets in support of the Catholic League: this in a city with a total population of 500,000 which for much of the time was under siege and cut off from a wider market.[9] If these figures indicate a pattern of repeat purchasing, this is confirmed by patterns of survival. Many of these little books survive now bound together into collections, and many of these collections were quite obviously made up contemporaneously, by their first owners. This is true particularly of the small octavo pamphlets in which publishers issued French royal edicts throughout the sixteenth century. Lawyers and others with an interest in certain classes of law bound them together as an impromptu, customized reference book. But this is also the way in which many pamphlets survive, including the *Flugschriften* of the first Reformation generation. Why were they collected in this dignified way?

---

[5] Books were often concealed up sleeves. In 1526, for instance, a shoemaker from Maastricht who was in dispute with a Carmelite drew a book 'eytter sijnen mouwe'. W Bax, *Het Protestantism in Luik en Maastricht, 1505–1557* (The Hague, 1937), p. 80. For other examples see A. Johnston, 'Eclectic Reformation: Vernacular Evangelical Pamphlet Literature in the Dutch-Speaking Low Countries, 1520–1565' (University of Southampton Ph.D. dissertation, 1986), p. 24.

[6] The best estimate is that an additional 100 per cent margin over the usual retail mark-up would have been considered reasonable to compensate for the additional dangers and difficulties of supply. Bremme, *Buchdrucker und Buchhändler zur Zeit der Glaubenskämpfe*, pp. 41–5.

[7] Edwards, *Printing, Propaganda and Martin Luther*, p. 39.

[8] Of which more below.

[9] Denis Pallier, *Recherches sur l'imprimerie à Paris pendant la Ligue (1585–1594)* (Geneva, 1975).

The answer here may lie partly in the cultural expectations of their owners. Many purchasers of *Flugschriften* may have been buying cheap print, other than purely utilitarian texts, for the first time. Binding collections together was a way of making the object respectable: making it more like their concept of a book. In this way the new literature was repackaged to make it more fit for a library. The Bibliothèque Mazarine in Paris has several thousand sixteenth-century pamphlets bound together in this way, in groups of twenty or more. The organization is thematic, or chronological, or both. These *recueils* represent not just a convenient method of storage, but an attempt to organize the barrage of ideas created by the Reformation.

Sometimes, it is clear, these bundles of titles were put together in the printer's shop. This is true, for instance, of the quarto political manifestos of the leadership issued by Condé on behalf of the Huguenot churches at the outbreak of the French Religious Wars. There are around twenty different titles, and all could have been purchased individually; in fact around 95 per cent of surviving copies are bound into sets that include most or all the titles, though there is no standard order, and the different *recueils* are made up of different combinations of the several editions put out by the printer.[10] Analysis of the surviving examples suggests that the printer/bookseller probably had baskets of each title, which he replenished with new editions according to need, and from which his assistants made up copies of the whole collections as and when required by purchasers. We see a precedent for this bookshop practice in the pre-Reformation Books of Hours, where purchasers would expect to be able to add, according to taste, a mixture of small texts which would be placed after the basic Hours: perhaps a life of St Margaret, or a popular text like the *Fifteen Sayings of our Lord on the Cross*. This would create a customized, individual collection for use in worship and devotion.

In the case of the Condéan collection, the motives for purchase would be quite varied. There were many reasons why supporters (or opponents) might want to own a complete set of the pronouncements of the Huguenot leadership at the onset of the fighting. But on both sides of

[10] The Gibier tracts are listed in Louis Desgraves, *Elie Gibier imprimeur à Orléans (1536–1588)* (Geneva, 1966); the different editions of these popular works are more precisely identified in Jean-François Gilmont, 'La première diffusion des Mémoires de Condé par Éloi Gibier en 1562–1563', in P. Aquilon and H.-J. Martin (eds.), *Le livre dans l'Europe de la Renaissance. Actes du XXVIIIe Colloque international d'études humanistes de Tours* (Paris, 1988), pp. 58–70. A revised and updated version of this article also appears in a recent volume of Gilmont's collected papers: *Le livre et ses secrets* (Louvain-la-Neuve and Geneva, 2003), pp. 191–216.

the emerging divide the Condéan material would have been purchased partly as a work of reference, by those who already knew where they stood on the central issues of allegiance. The language of persuasion in which the Condéan pamphlets were couched was for these purchasers largely redundant. In this case, to many purchasers this collection of pamphlets was almost like a single book, although the fact that the pamphlets were issued separately gave it enhanced value over a single, longer text. The presence of twenty individually dated works recreated the fast-moving play of events; it emphasized the fact that the Huguenots had sought repeatedly to find solutions; it underlined their essential reasonableness. The fact that these are individual books gives the whole collection added value in its particular political context.[11]

Some groups of pamphlets were, in fact, *only* sold together, even when the individual works were given separate title-pages and appear bibliographically distinct. Sometimes the collection was issued with a separate first gathering and collective title-page that called attention to all the titles in the ensuing collection.[12] These works create complex problems for bibliographers, particularly when they have subsequently become unbound and survive only in parts. But works of this sort, thankfully, are comparatively rare: most pamphlet collections were created either in the bookshop or the bindery, in this latter case usually to an individual scheme created by their purchaser. In this way the pamphlet was brought into the mainstream of the book-owning experience. A literature of protest was domesticated.

If this practice was common, as the evidence suggests, then it undoubtedly has important implications for the way we understand the cultural impact of pamphlet literature. In this scenario, pamphlets had a dual life – as individual artefacts and as part of a collective body of material. Which was more important to the way they were 'read'? Their impact came partly from what they said, but the impact was heightened by the multiplication effect of reinforcement. A case was made not just because the individual arguments were strong, but because many voices were making them. Their impact was greater than had they been a single text, because they created an impression of cacophony and irresistible pressure. They were the crowd made text.

---

[11] This was lost when the manifestos were republished as a single book later in the decade. But by this point the works had lost the contemporary urgency of their first publication.

[12] As, for instance, the *Remonstrances faictes en la court de parlement et assemblées des estats de Bretagne* (Nantes, 1596), a collection of eight separate remonstrances. Copy Rennes Bibliothèque Municipale: Rés. 37206.

This expression must not be misunderstood. I do not seek to imply that these works emanated from the crowd. On the contrary, they were overwhelmingly the work of educated men – often the same authors turning out a great number of very similar works. What I am seeking to demonstrate is that pamphlets collectively took on a different life from their status as individual texts. It was the superabundance, the cascade of titles, that created the impression of an overwhelming tide, an unstoppable movement of opinion. Certainly, this was the reaction of contemporaries. In official comment on the pamphlet campaigns of the Reformation it is precisely the sheer quantity of such material suddenly swamping the market that seems to have been most worthy of remark, not what any of them individually were saying. Attempts to summarize their arguments tend to rely on the broadest impressions and seldom quote individual works. Pamphlets and their purchasers had together created the impression of irresistible force. This is why their publication was important even if they had nothing new to say, and why they were purchased by people who already knew that they agreed with what they contained. Their force lay in the power – or the appearance – of collective, irresistible might.

Pamphlet moments

The sixteenth century gave birth to many thousands of small religious books. Many were part of the everyday life of established churches, and we will turn to these types of books in due course; they certainly played an important part in creating and reinforcing religious allegiance. But at specific moments in the sixteenth century pamphlet literature played a part in the primary task of creating new churches: it accompanied an upsurge of fresh thinking, and encapsulated some of the core messages of the new movements. There are two such moments that require our special attention. The first, obviously, is the period of the first wave of evangelical pamphleteering in the 1520s. The second is found in the period of violent confrontation between the new Reformation insurgency and Catholic regimes in northern Europe in the 1560s. In both, there can be little doubt that pamphlets played a vital role in shaping events.

In some critical respects the Reformation dates not from the publication of the ninety-five theses in October 1517, but from Luther's decision the following year to publish a defence of his views in German. The theses on indulgences had been penned first in Latin. While they remained exclusively in the realm of scholarly debate Luther could defend his right, as a scholar and an academic, to advance speculative ideas. He had certainly recognized the sensitivity of the interests that might be stirred up by his propositions; the copy he had dutifully despatched to Albrecht of Brandenburg was accompanied by a covering letter of appropriate obsequiousness.[13] The degree of public interest initially astonished him, and he was particularly unnerved by the decision of the Nuremberg printer Conrad Scheurl to publish the theses also in German. Luther's letter to Scheurl of March 1518 where he addresses these issues is worth quoting at length:

> Greetings. I received both your German and Latin letters, good and learned Scheurl, together with the distinguished Albrecht Dürer's gift, and my Theses in the original and in the vernacular. As you are surprised that I did not send them to you, I reply that my purpose was not to publish them, but first to consult a few of my neighbours about them, that thus I might either destroy them if condemned or edit them with the approbation of others. But now that they are printed and circulated far beyond my expectation, I feel anxious about what they may bring forth: not that I am unfavourable to spreading known truth abroad – rather this is what I seek – but because this method is not that best adapted to instruct the public. I have certain doubts about them myself, and should have spoken far differently and more distinctly had I known what was going to happen.[14]

What precisely did Luther mean, when he worried that 'this method' was not the best for spreading the truth? Was he expressing the view that the medium of print was not appropriate for such public debate; or that the translation of a work intended solely for an academic audience was not the best way of making his case to such a public? Probably the latter, because when he wrote to Scheurl Luther had already decided to write a separate work in German addressing the controversy over indulgences. The *Sermon on Indulgences* appeared before the end of the month, and was an immediate success.[15] The sermon repays close attention, not least because it is clear that Luther had thought carefully about the style and structure appropriate to explain these issues to a wider public. The material is organized concisely in twenty articles, the style homely and at times colloquial, the condemnation of his critics blunt and direct. Luther had clearly already discovered that talent for colourful invective that would be such a leading characteristic of the *Flugschriften* era, and little would change in the years to come. Luther was a natural polemicist, the

---

[13] Quoted in Smith, *The Life and Letters of Martin Luther*, pp. 42–3.
[14] Ibid., pp. 43–4.
[15] It went through twenty-five editions in three years, and was published in a large number of locations throughout the German-speaking lands. Benzing, *Lutherbibliographie*, nos. 90–104.

impact of his popular writings underpinned by his extraordinary intellect and a clarity of thought born of his real command of the theological issues. It was this ability to encapsulate the core of the case in clear comprehensible language, while decoupling it from the technical theological moorings, that marks out his special genius.

March 1518 was a seminal moment in other ways. In January the chapter of the Dominican order in Saxony had gathered in Frankfurt-an-der-Oder and, as one might have expected, mounted a robust defence of Tetzel, the indulgence seller at the eye of the storm. Flushed with this success Tetzel had moved to have the 106 articles of his defence printed, and several hundred copies were dispatched for sale in Wittenberg. Here, however, the students of the university made short work of them. The bookseller with Tetzel's stock was jeered in the market place and his books were seized and burned.[16] Luther disapproved, but it was clear even from this early date that the conflict would be fought with weapons other than words. Two years later Luther would take a leaf from the students' book, and ceremonially burn the Papal Bull condemning his heresies.

The 'pamphlet moment' of the Lutheran Reformation would last a further eight years. Between 1518 and 1526 the German Empire experienced a quite unprecedented torrent of publications: perhaps as many as 6 million copies of around 6,000 separate editions. For the first time, too, this was a market dominated by small books: by books in German, most published in the comparatively unfamiliar format of quarto, rather than the scholarly Latin and the more stately folio. Contemporaries had a clear sense that something quite spectacularly new had erupted into the previously measured world of learning. One cannot know how much sheer curiosity drove many purchases and how much sheer opportunism governed the behaviour of those in the publishing industry who switched their production to feed the new public appetite for religious print. But we do know that any printers who, for local political reasons, were excluded from the new markets, resented it bitterly. In divided Saxony the Wittenberg printers flourished, while those in Leipzig, where Duke George remained stubbornly loyal to the old faith, were forbidden to publish heretical books. In 1524 the town council petitioned the duke on behalf of the suffering printers. The members of the local publishing industry had suggested that they were in danger of losing 'house, home and all their livelihood' if they were not allowed

---

[16] James Atkinson, *Martin Luther and the Birth of Protestantism* (London, 1968), p. 153.

to print or sell anything new that is made in Wittenberg or elsewhere. For that which one would gladly sell and for which there is demand they are not allowed to have or sell. But what they have in overabundance [Catholic treatises] is desired by no one and cannot even be given away.[17]

Even allowing for the tradition of heartrending hyperbole that is characteristic of all special pleading by tradesmen's guilds in the sixteenth century, this seems a fair statement of the fact of the case. In the years after Luther's quarrels first became a public issue, the evangelicals utterly dominated the book market. Luther himself accounted for a remarkably high proportion of the works published. Many of his publications were instant bestsellers, selling out in a matter of days or weeks: many went through multiple editions. Mark Edwards estimates that the total quantity of Luther's works available during his lifetime must have exceeded 3 million copies: the largest proportion of this was undoubtedly during the pamphlet fury of the 1520s.[18] Luther's works benefited from the particular cachet of his celebrity status, but evangelicals who took up his cause in print also found a ready audience. Between 1518 and 1525 Edwards has counted 1,465 German editions of the works of Martin Luther, but between them the seventeen next most popular evangelical authors account for another 807 editions. Over Luther's lifetime evangelical authors writing in support of his teachings account for another 2.5 million copies on the market.

At one level these figures may seem to demonstrate the overwhelming primacy of Luther, but the support of these other authors was undoubtedly of huge importance to the success of the Reformation movement. Partly this was for the obvious reason that the intervention of these other figures represented the active engagement of men who were themselves influential in other major cities; their publishing activity was but one part of a wider public engagement on the part of the Reformation. But it also mattered greatly that Luther was not presented as a single lonely voice, but as part of a community. Luther's criticism of the established church was so fundamental and outspoken that it was easy for polemical enemies to present him as an isolated figure: the witness of other evangelical pamphleteers gave the lie to this charge. How important this could be is evident from a pamphlet published by Lazarus Spengler, the Nuremberg city secretary, and one of the small but significant number of lay pamphleteers who wrote in favour of the Reformation. Spengler was the anonymous author of the pamphlet, *Why Dr Martin's teaching*

---

[17] Quoted in Edwards, *Printing, Propaganda and Martin Luther*, p. 14.
[18] Ibid., p. 39.

should not be rejected as unchristian but rather be regarded as Christian. In enumerating six reasons why Luther should be regarded as a true Christian teacher, Spengler is an important witness for the appeal of the early evangelical movement (although, clearly, he was himself part of the bourgeois elite). For Spengler, 'No teaching or preaching has seemed more straightforwardly reasonable, and I also cannot conceive of anything that would more closely match my understanding of Christian order as Luther *and his followers'* teaching and instruction' (my emphasis). Luther, then, was part of a community of belief, and Spengler goes on to emphasize this point with a highly significant remark: 'Up to this point I have also often heard from many excellent highly learned people of the spiritual and worldly estates that they were thankful to God that they lived to see the day when they could hear Doctor Luther and his teaching.'[19]

How are we to interpret this remark? How had Spengler 'often heard' such favourable things of Luther? From the pulpit? From casual conversation with friends in the Nuremberg ruling elite or in the market place? From pamphlets? This is perhaps impossible to know – the most plausible reconstruction is likely to involve a degree of mutual reinforcement between these various media. But from whatever source, Spengler had gathered some very precise impressions of Luther. He admired the fact that Luther spoke out according to the dictates of his conscience, and with no prospect of material gain (this was contrasted with the conduct of the indulgence pedlars). He believed that Luther's position as monk, teacher and doctor required him to speak his conscience on issues of salvation. Finally, Luther had based his teaching on the Gospel set forth in Scripture: he had offered the *Rein Evangelium.*

Spengler is an important witness, if hardly a representative of the 'common man'. Other lay authors tended to offer more generalized and often quite emotive praise of Luther as a holy man, 'a light of Christendom', even the great prophet of a new age. Both Hans Sachs and Laux Gemigger had absorbed Luther's dire warnings about the imminence of the end-time. For Gemigger, 'Luther was sent by God to teach us God's word and good morals and to drive out the Antichrist here on earth.'[20] Here is Luther as holy man, the Luther of the first, powerfully evocative portraits by Lucas Cranach: the simple monk, apostle of truth. Yet, as we have seen above, this was only part of the truth. Sachs and others might be powerfully affected by a vision of the prophet crying in the wilderness; for men of the ruling classes like

[19] Quoted in ibid., p. 53.
[20] Ibid., p. 52. On Sachs, see Russell, *Popular Pamphleteers*, pp. 165–80.

Spengler it was precisely the opposite characteristics that made Luther plausible: his unimpeachable claim to be part of a community of learning, a man of established authority within the ordered hierarchy of learned men. Yet both, when they set pen to paper to register their support for Luther, apparently drew on the same repertoire of texts. Sachs certainly read *To the Christian Nobility of the German People*, Luther's great hymn to the German ruling classes, and imbibed a wide-ranging agenda of social change and reform. Spengler was brutally scathing about 'fairy-tale preachers' who had disquieted the consciences of the people with their praise of external ceremonies. Both dipped eagerly into the eclectic mixture of messages emanating from the ferment of debate raised by the public scandal of Luther's great matter.

The period 1518–24 was characterized in Germany by a very peculiar convergence of cultural and social media. Luther dominated the conversation of the learned; he also dominated the news agenda. It was important in this respect that Luther's teaching was heard not only as the echo of distant controversies, in far-off Wittenberg and Rome, but richocheted round the Empire. The public interest stirred by Luther was greatly enhanced by his public appearances: in Heidelberg for the meeting of the Augustinian Chapter, the confrontation with Cajetan in Augsburg, the Leipzig Disputation, the Diet of Worms. Many would have seen Luther, or known someone who had; many citizens of the German cities would have felt engaged by the controversies in a very direct way. The twists and turns of Luther's conflict can be followed as a series of peaks and troughs in the polemical storm, a series of publishing sensations following quickly one after another: the *Sermon on Indulgences*, the great manifestos of 1520, Luther's address at the Diet of Worms. This alone went through twenty-five editions.[21] It was important too that these controversies were experienced not only through printed matter imported from Wittenberg, but taken up also by local authors and local printers. Through this process Luther's teaching could be interpreted and made relevant to local circumstances and local controversies.

This point is reinforced if we ask what, most of all, people made of Luther's teaching. At one level, as we have indicated in our discussion of preaching, the eclecticism of the early evangelical movement was part of its appeal. But within this context of a general engagement with contemporary issues and grievances, Luther also benefited from a brutal simplification of his central theological message. For Luther's supporters

---

[21] Benzing, *Lutherbibliographie*, nos. 905–30.

what seems to have made the greatest impact was the excoriating criticism of the corruptions of the priesthood (and particularly the papacy) and the doctrine of Scripture alone. The concept of justification by faith could, for men of education, have the same transforming effect as it had for Luther himself. Martin Bucer would date his conversion from hearing Luther expound justification at the Heidelberg Disputation, and reading Luther on justification had a similar impact on the painter Albrecht Dürer. But for most laypeople justification was too difficult to fathom. In this respect the experience of the Ghent baker Lieven de Zomere is highly revealing. De Zomere owned at least two books by Luther (and claimed to own many more). When he had heard of the *Babylonian Captivity*, Luther's classic exposition of justification, he had gone to see a local cleric, who had read him 'een quaterne'. But he had given up because 'de materie te hooghe was'.[22]

This experience was probably not uncommon – even if not everyone would have gone as far as the enthusiastic baker in supplying themselves with such a weighty and expensive tome (the *Babylonian Captivity* was somewhat out of the mainstream of Luther's pamphlet literature). The doctrine of Scripture alone, in contrast, was powerful not only because of its radical rhetorical simplification, but because it was reinforced in virtually every medium: through preaching, through the image of Luther, book in hand, in the portrait woodcuts, through the pamphlets on the streets, and finally of course through the publication of the Bible itself. The appearance of the September Testament in 1522 was an instantaneous publishing sensation. It had been well prepared by the pamphlet and preaching campaign for *Rein Evangelium*, and was itself the triumphant vindication of this principle. In turn, the text of Luther's Bible quickly made itself felt in the pamphlet literature. In the seminal study published by Bernd Moeller, one can see the rapid conquest of the market by Luther's translation reflected in the New Testament citations included in pamphlets published between 1522 and 1525. Already in 1522, 23 per cent of the pamphlets examined cite Luther's translation (presumably those published at the end of the year). This rises to 44 per cent in 1523, and 72 per cent in 1524. Even a significant number of Luther's Catholic opponents cite his translation.

If we are seeking an explanation why justification by faith did not find more resonance, then the contrast is instructive. Luther's teaching on justification relied exclusively on high-register media: either his own, more complex writings, or the mediation of these texts through the

---

[22] P. Fredericq, *Corpus documentorum haereticae pravitatis neerlandicae* (5 vols., Ghent/The Hague, 1889–1902), vol. IV, p. 113.

pulpit. The Scripture principle, in contrast, was not only more easily grasped, it was everywhere made flesh: in the pulpit, on stage, in the Bible itself, in the ubiquitous pamphlets. Here the scale of the pamphleteering phenomenon in support of the Reformation created its own momentum. It became, by its sheer scale, a public event: an unavoidable public issue for men like Spengler, a tantalizing and alluring new world for men like Lieven de Zomere. In the case of de Zomere it is interesting that he was clearly an avid purchaser of pamphlets even though he did not read – or at least read well. He would not have been the only one. The *Flugschriften* in their distinctive format and livery were instantly recognizable in the market place: an object of curiosity for the educated, a fascinating window onto a previously closed world for those of meaner understanding. Even if one could not read or understand the messages they contained, the *Flugschriften* represented a means of sharing a public excitement that one had first become aware of through the pulpit preaching, or the gossip on the street. But purchase might also be the first step in a process of personal involvement that led eventually to commitment.

The pamphlet literature of the Lutheran Reformation offered one further enticement: it provided the frisson of danger, a taste of the forbidden, disapproved or controversial, without, in fact, being dangerous. Although men like Duke George of Saxony might forbid their printers to take part in the production of Lutheran literature, the market was too swamped to exercise effective control. Within the German Empire, possession of pamphlets might carry a sense of danger, but it was essentially safe. The situation was very different in those parts of Europe where the secular authorities had moved to inhibit the trade in Lutheran books before the evangelical movement had achieved a critical mass of public support.

Proxy evangelists

Outside Germany Luther's message was heard in a very different cultural context. True, as in the German cities, interest in the controversies raised by the Wittenberg reformer was intense, particularly among intellectuals, lay and clerical, who felt that Luther's criticisms of indulgences converged with their own agenda of reform. This was the spirit in which Erasmus first experienced news of Luther's writings: cautious, yet supportive. Luther's works were widely read and discussed in Latin in the university towns of northern and western Europe; some readers were moved to voice their sympathy. But more powerful voices were also quickly raised against Luther. The extremity of the public passions raised by Luther in Germany found no resonance elsewhere; indeed, the news of these events only added to the sense of danger that had been crystallized by the growing radicalism of Luther's attack on the church hierarchy. As Luther's quarrel hurtled towards outright confrontation and condemnation, conservative forces in France, England and the Low Countries found it far easier to overpower those who privately sympathized. The double condemnation of Luther by Pope and Emperor might have done little to still the turmoil in the Empire, but it gave the clerical and lay authorities elsewhere in Europe all the encouragement they needed to forbid all teaching of the German heresies.

This general mobilization of learned opinion against Luther had the most serious consequences for the early development of the Reformation outside Germany. Those intellectuals who still cherished a hope for local reform opted to pursue their objectives through discreet lobbying within the established church structures. Meanwhile the move to the publication of evangelical works in the vernacular – essential to creating a critical mass of support for a widespread public debate – was swiftly inhibited by official prohibition. In England, France and the Netherlands, those who appropriated the pulpit for a bold public statement in favour of the Wittenberg reformer were brutally dealt with. The two Augustinians executed in Brussels in 1523 were the most prominent victims, and their fate was enough to cow many others into submission; through the decade, other less celebrated men would also suffer for too foolhardy support of the evangelical agenda. These highly public statements of official rejection of the German heresies were reinforced by strong action to control the venting of heretical views in public. The Netherlands, where Charles V faced the most obvious evidence of widespread public interest in Luther, witnessed the most systematic and draconian measures. These edicts, articulated in a series of rising severity from the first prohibition of 1521 (from 1529 possession of heretical literature could be punished by death), are very revealing for the official view of the multiple conduits that sixteenth-century society offered to the dissemination of heresy. Naturally, in the literate urban society of the Netherlands, preaching and printing were the main focus of attention. In the codification of previous edicts issued in 1551, all clerics were ordered to keep a vigilant eye out for any of their brethren infected by heresy. But the problem did not end there. This edict took cognizance of the danger posed by theological autodidacts:

We forbid all lay persons and others to communicate and dispute on the Holy Scriptures publicly or in secret, particularly on doubtful or difficult matters, or otherwise to teach from the Holy Scripture, unless they are theologians and properly instructed in theology, approved by a learned university, or others admitted thereto by the local ordinary.[23]

In the realm of the book, the busy, vibrant work of Netherlandish publishing was subjected to close regulation. No one was to print works by forbidden authors, nor to 'paint or have painted, buy or sell, have, hold, keep or hold any pictures, paintings or scandalous figures of the Virgin Mary, or the saints canonized by the holy church, or the clerical estate'. The edict is particularly revealing about the range of literature and published works through which it was believed that the heretical doctrines could be inculcated:

Seeing that the foresaid sects and errors have proceeded principally by the huge diversity of books published by forbidden and heretic authors, so we ordain that no one of whatever quality, state, nation or condition, shall print or cause to be printed anywhere in our lands, any books, refrains, ballads, songs, letters, prognostications, almanacs or any other material old or new concerning Holy Scripture or other matter, without prior permission.[24]

Pre-publication inspection by theologians of the university was prescribed for all printed matter. In the Netherlands the problem of control was particularly acute, because of the size and diversity of the local print industry. Authorities in France and England faced a less challenging prospect: in France the dominant Paris book trade was both heavily regulated and heavily dependent on the goodwill of the various organs of government (crown, Parlement and university) for work. Little unorthodox publishing of any sort was attempted in Paris before the mid-century crisis severely weakened the power of the state. In England the small London publishing fraternity was relatively easy to control.

As a result of quick, decisive action, the Reformation in all of these places was largely controlled and subdued: with some difficulty and consequent increased brutality in the Netherlands, with greater ease in France and England. The authorities felt the need for constant vigilance in case heresy should raise its head, particularly in France, where it might insinuate itself into the body politic through the support for a purportedly non-confessional evangelical agenda by influential figures at court. But public support for the Reformation was, from the first, rendered impossible. The crucial medium of the pulpit was denied the reformers. Those who proclaimed support for the Reformation in public risked the full force of the law.

---

[23] J.N. Bakhuizen van den Brink and W.F. Dankbaar (eds.), *Documenta Reformatoria* (Kampen, 1960), pp. 76–81.
[24] Ibid.

For the purpose of this present investigation this different, and very difficult, context for the dissemination of the evangelical message is especially interesting. Deprived of the range of public media that had caused the explosion of public interest in the Reformation in Germany, could the Gospel message survive? The difficult, dangerous years of clandestine evangelism in fact provide us with an effective laboratory in which to test the effectiveness of the book without the support of public preaching. Could the Reformation thrive, 'by print alone'? Could it justify the obvious sense of its potency felt by those Catholic authorities that sought to repress it?

It must immediately be recognized that this more hostile environment changed the book. The evangelical book in France and the Netherlands eschewed the confident, self-advertising quarto format of the *Flugschriften*, emblazoned with the woodcut title-page embellishments characteristic of the genre. Evangelical publishing in French and Dutch in the years after Luther's movement was proscribed adopted a wholly different livery. Books were almost invariably published in the more discreet (and more easily concealed) octavo. They contained virtually no visual embellishments. The title-pages were made up almost wholly of text, with no use of decorative borders or printers' devices. They very often concealed their content behind an uncontroversial anodyne title. None of the works of Luther published in French (or English) before 1540 give any hint of his authorial responsibility. Some were so effectively disguised that the connection with Luther has only recently been revealed.[25] In the Netherlands Luther's writings were sometimes brought before the reading public embedded in other works that purported to be the writings of a local, ostensibly orthodox author.[26] At least one of these texts, the *La summe de l'escripture saincte* enjoyed considerable success in three different language cultures, French, Dutch and Italian.[27]

---

[25] The *Livre tresutile de la vraye et parfaite subjection des chrestiens* (1525), which turns out to be a translation of *On the liberty of a Christian man* of 1520. Francis Higman, 'Les traductions françaises de Luther', in J.-F. Gilmont (ed.), *Palaestrina typographica* (Aubel, 1984), pp. 11–56, reprinted in Francis Higman, *Lire et découvrir. La circulation des idées au temps de la Réforme* (Geneva, 1998), pp. 200–32.

[26] A. G. Johnston, 'Lutheranism in Disguise: the corte instruccye of Cornelis van der Heyden', *Nederlands archief voor Kerkgeschiedenis*, 68 (1988), pp. 23–9.

[27] Francis Higman, *Piety and the People. Religious Printing in French, 1511–1551* (Aldershot, St Andrews Studies in Reformation History, 1996), S26–28. Known in Dutch as *De summa der godliker scrifturen* (1523), in Latin as *Oeconomica christiana* (1527) and in Italian as *El summario dela sancta Scriptura* (1534), this very popular text was in fact an extract from Luther's *Von weltlicher Obrigkeit*.

Even with these layers of disguise, the publication and dissemination of such literature carried with it a considerable degree of danger. Possession of a forbidden text was taken as prime facie evidence of heretical beliefs, and for the small number of local printers prepared to risk involvement the penalties were severe if the carefully anonymized books could be traced back to them. Most evangelical books, in consequence, were printed abroad and smuggled back to their readers; a partial exception was the survival of clandestine Protestant printing in Antwerp, although this came to a shattering end with the exposure and execution of two printers involved in the trade in the early 1540s. Even so, the quantities of books involved were small compared to the vast boisterous print world of German Reformation print. According to one scholar, even with the participation of Antwerp only around 170 Protestant works were published in Dutch between 1520 and 1540, and for England the figures would have been considerably smaller (most, in fact, were also printed in Antwerp). Recent bibliographical analysis of French Protestant printing gives a similar figure to that for the Dutch world.[28]

In what might otherwise be thought quite an effectively managed policy of control, the authorities made what in retrospect seems a serious error. This was to include among the canon of forbidden texts vernacular translations of the Scripture. In France this represented a signal victory for conservative forces, but an equally serious blow to the Paris publishing industry, thus excluded from a lively and growing part of the market in quality books. The reasoning behind the decision of the Parlement of Paris to ban such vernacular translations is easily comprehensible, particularly when in Germany the attack on Catholic institutions had been pressed forward under the beguiling slogan of 'Pure Gospel'. But the effect of such a ban was to make the Scripture text ever more emphatically evangelical property. The result was that, in England, France and the Netherlands, the development of new translations of Scripture became an enterprise wholly dominated by evangelicals, even if the interest in possessing such a text extended far beyond the circles of those who fully endorsed the Protestant agenda. It must be remembered here that all European cultures had a lively tradition of vernacular Bible translations that pre-dated the Reformation; indeed, for the most part it long pre-dated the invention of print.[29] Only in England had the

---

[28] Higman, *Piety and the People*. The data presented in Higman's bibliography will be augmented by the work of the St Andrews French Book project.

[29] John Sharpe and Kimberley van Kampen (eds.), *The Bible as Book. The Manuscript Tradition* (London, 1998). For Germany, John Flood, 'Martin Luther's Bible'. For France, Chambers, *Bibliography of French Bibles*.

association with heresy (in this case the Lollards) stifled the publication of vernacular Scripture in the first age of print. By frustrating the continuation of these ventures, Catholic authorities in France and elsewhere in effect resigned this critical part of an important shared tradition.

Bible translation became a cornerstone of the repressed evangelical movements of western Europe. It also became an economic lifeline for printers struggling with the far more taxing economics of managing a business dependent on clandestine distribution networks. In both Geneva in the 1540s and Emden in the 1550s (the centre of Dutch clandestine evangelical print after the break-up of the Antwerp operation), Bible publication became a lucrative bulwark of an expanding business. Through the 1540s and 1550s the output of reproved texts increased steadily; networks of distribution became more sophisticated, and harder to disrupt. A mark of increasing confidence and defiance of authority is that these heretical works published abroad began, particularly in the case of Genevan publications, to adopt quite recognizable printers' devices. The need to identify the brand to potential purchasers gradually began to outweigh the dangers to those detected in possession of them. By 1551, the French crown's efforts to control the spread of heretical print had a note of desperation. A new edict against heresy (the Edict of Châteaubriant) attempted to outlaw any contact with Geneva:

We expressly forbid all our subjects to write, to send money or otherwise to favour those who have gone out of the kingdom to reside in Geneva or in other countries notoriously separated from the Union of the Church . . . All carriers of letters coming from Geneva will be arrested and punished if it is found that the said letters are directed towards the end of diverting our subjects away from the truth . . . All goods whether movable or immovable of those who have retired to Geneva to live and reside separating themselves from union with the Church, are declared confiscate to us.[30]

These detailed provisions hint at the increasing difficulty of controlling a trade that had so fully infiltrated the normal arteries of commerce. By the end of the decade heretical books would be sold with insolent defiance on the streets, on market stalls and in bookshops. The evangelical excitement of 1520s Germany was about to be reignited.

Before turning to later events, it is worth pausing to assess the impact of this generation of clandestine literature. How effectively had books been able to function as proxies for evangelism in a climate of hostility and repression? The evidence is mixed. On the one hand, official efforts

---

[30] E. and E. Haag, *La France protestante: pièces justificatives* (reprint edn, Geneva, 1966), pp. 17–29. Duke, Lewis and Pettegree, *Calvinism in Europe Documents*, p. 64.

to control the infiltration of evangelical ideas in print had had a degree of success, at least for the first twenty years. Thereafter the establishment of well-organized centres of printing outside the borders of a state's political jurisdiction had greatly complicated the task. On the other hand, books, though they could inspire and motivate a limited number of determined autodidacts, still proved most effective when they played a supporting role among other media of evangelical agitation. Books could be particularly important in helping to sustain the faith of those who had committed themselves to a group, who met together for mutual support (usually Bible reading) and sometimes worship. These conventicles were a particular concern to the authorities, not least because they functioned very effectively as distribution points for heretical literature. The first leader of the Reformed conventicle in Antwerp, Gaspar van der Heyden, received consignments of books from Emden, which he then sold on to members of the group. He asked the Emden church for specific titles that might address pressing local problems (like the competition posed by Anabaptists) and for more copies of the psalms – though he thought that for small books these were too expensively priced.[31]

Despite these constraints the leaders of the exile churches were undoubtedly more comfortable with books being used in the more managed environments of the conventicles than facing the unpredictable consequences of solitary reading. The proxy evangelism of clandestine literature kept the Reformation alive, but at a price, since many self-trained adepts arrived at views that could not be contained within the developing orthodoxies of the new movement. In this respect the exile churches played a vital role, in that potential converts, excited to the possibilities of the new teaching, might through a period abroad experience the full pedagogic impact of these mother churches: the preaching, catechismal instruction, the worship service. The narratives of the French and Dutch churches are full of the life histories of future leaders and martyrs who came to a mature understanding of their faith in this way. Jean Le Maçon was a man who, like Calvin before him, had turned from the study of the law to seek enlightenment in Geneva and Lausanne. He returned to France to take up the ministry to the new Calvinist church in Paris.[32] Gilles Verdickt from Elversele in Flanders came from a more humble artisan background. Having first been brought to the knowledge of the truth by his brother, he travelled to

---

[31] Pettegree, *Emden and the Dutch Revolt*, pp. 59–60. Duke, Lewis and Pettegree, *Calvinism in Europe Documents*, p. 135.

[32] *Histoire ecclésiastique des églises réformées au royaume de France* (3 vols., Paris, 1883–9), vol. I, pp. 117 ff.

Emden and Zurich to complete his theological education, before returning as minister to the church in Brussels.[33] There is no doubt an element of stylizing pedagogy in these martyr narratives, but the process of first enlightenment, deepened by periods of study and training abroad, is plausibly reconstructed. Such events created the core of committed believers that prepared the French and Dutch evangelical communities for the opportunities that would emerge in the decades that followed.

Two tribes

The six years from 1559 witnessed an astonishing transformation for the evangelical cause in northern Europe. First, and with remarkable speed, Protestant regimes were established in the two British kingdoms: in England through the accident of dynastic succession, in Scotland through a brief and remarkably bloodless military insurrection. Meanwhile both France and the Netherlands embarked on a prolonged period of political and religious instability. In France the death of first Henry II and then his eldest son plunged the political elite into destructive feuding and gave encouragement to the growing Calvinist congregations. In the Netherlands a similarly urgent problem of uncontrolled religious dissent gave an added edge to noble grievances against the absentee Spanish king, Philip II.

In both France and the Netherlands the political crisis was fuelled by an apparently unstoppable tide of public agitation expressed in a variety of media. Those attempting to defend the political status quo commented with increasing frustration and hopelessness on the extraordinary upsurge of pamphlets, broadsheets, scurrilous rumours and songs. They deplored both the ubiquity of this literature and its tone. Meanwhile, for as long as the pulpits were closed to them, the preachers of the new movement taught elsewhere: in private houses and barns, in fields and churchyards. As the movements grew in confidence, these meetings were inevitably accompanied by the loud triumphant singing of psalms.

How do we judge the contribution of books to this vast turbulent movement of protest and religious renewal? Firstly, it must be remarked that this second pamphlet moment was both long prepared and intense. Faced with the new opportunities provided by the weakening of traditional authority, the dissident church movements were able to build

---

[33] Adriaen van Haemstede, *Historie des Martelaren die om de getuigenis der evangeliche waarheid hun bloed gestort hebben* (reprint edn, Utrecht, 1980), pp. 634–8.

quickly on the foundations created by the preparation in exile. In the case of France, something over one-third of all Protestant works published in French during the sixteenth century appeared in the six years 1560–65, the period immediately before, during and after the first Religious War. In the case of the Netherlands, the peak of production was reached in 1566, a year of intense publishing activity when political agitation gave way to a fleeting opportunity for church building.

Also remarkable about these years is the speed with which the publishing industry evolved to meet the new opportunities of the times. In the case of both France and the Netherlands the traditional centres of exile publication were quickly superseded by new centres of production nearer to home. With events moving so swiftly, both Emden and Geneva were inconveniently distant for the most contemporary literature; in both cases, too, the local governments harboured misgivings about the increasingly radical sentiments expressed in much of the literature. Besides, the strength of demand, the size of the potential market, and the temporary banishing of controls meant that local publishers were all eager to establish a share in the market. In France this led to the creation of new centres of Protestant printing in France: in Caen for the populous Normandy churches, in Orleans for the political manifestos, and in Lyon. In the Netherlands it stimulated a revival of Protestant print in Antwerp. Several of these printers took advantage of the new freedoms to appropriate title-page devices that identified their work as part of the growing literature of the Calvinist congregations.

This was both shameless and commercially motivated. Caen printers chose devices that imitated (sometimes even copied) those of the popular Genevan suppliers of the staples of Calvinist worship, such as Jean Crespin. Meanwhile Harmen Schinkel of Delft went as far as to commission a re-cut counterfeit of the printer's mark of the Emden publisher Gilles Ctematius, to this point chief purveyor of vernacular Dutch literature to the Reformed communities.[34] This was commercially brutal, particularly to those publishers in the exile towns who had sustained the cause in much more difficult trading circumstances over the previous two decades. But it was undoubtedly effective. In the crowded bookshops and street stalls the desired heretical books would be clearly identified visually, without the printers having to take the final step of adding their own names and addresses. In both France and the Netherlands the civil powers felt they were being drowned in a torrent of

---

[34] H. de la Fontaine Verwey, 'Meester Harman Schinckel, een Delftse boekdrukker van de 16de eeuw', *Oud Delft*, 3 (1964), pp. 5–78, here p. 37.

seditious print, much produced locally, and extremely responsive to the twists and turns of fast-moving events.

What can we say of the role, tone and content of the printed polemic of Protestantism in this new period of opportunity? First, we can observe that print functioned in this environment as it functioned best: as part of a broad, cross-media movement of public agitation and debate, and in circumstances where the constraints on production, sale and possession of the literature were weakened, or indeed rendered largely powerless. Nevertheless, there were significant differences, both from the first generation *Flugschriften* campaign and between the experiences of France and Germany. Both French and Dutch printing kept to the octavo format established as normative during the exile period. This was familiar to the readership, and was established as the most convenient format for use (not least in congregational gatherings). A rare exception to this rule were the political manifestos of the Huguenot leadership published in Orleans, in quarto: presumably here the intention was to appropriate the associations of the more 'official' format. In both France and the Netherlands also the corpus of pamphlet literature was characterized by far more intermingling of religious and political issues. This was partly because, fairly obviously, the religious question was now the central political issue. The repeated pleas for toleration were only relevant in this developed political context, with fixed and antagonistic confessions competing for supremacy. In the Netherlands the pleas for toleration were balanced with protestations of loyalty to the absentee king, a loyalty that was ever more threadbare as the opposition took on an increasingly radical turn through the summer and autumn of 1566. This political literature was, as Alastair Duke points out, a relatively new phenomenon.[35] Until this point there seems to have been little desire to air political grievances in print, perhaps because such issues were normally resolved by bargaining among the political elite behind the scenes. It was actually a sign of weakness when such agitation moved from the shadowy corridors of the royal palace into the popular prints, with consequences that soon came to appal the aristocratic leadership of the revolt.

In France, the leaders of the opposition movement recognized no such restraint. The depth of hostility and mutual detestation that marked relations between the contending parties was already evident in the brutal polemic that followed the death of Henry II in 1559. The

---

[35] Duke, 'Posters, Pamphlets and Printers'. Alastair Duke, 'Dissident Propaganda and Political Organisation at the Outbreak of the Revolt of the Netherlands', in Philip Benedict, Guido Marnef, Henk van Nierop and Marc Venard (eds.), *Reformation, Revolt and Civil War in France and the Netherlands, 1555–1585* (Amsterdam, 1999), pp. 115–32.

principal targets were Francis, Duke of Guise, and his brother, the Cardinal of Lorraine, whose blood connection to the young king (through his wife, Mary Queen of Scots, their niece) allowed them to seize control of government. Outrage at the power of the Guise merged with opposition to the policy of repression. This convergence was epitomized by two popular and notorious pamphlets of the day, the *Estates of France Oppressed by the Guise*, a forensic destruction of the Guise regime, and a vituperative attack on the cardinal, *The Tiger of France*. This was the work of the young Huguenot jurist François Hotman, and sought to defend those involved in the ill-judged Conspiracy of Amboise, a failed coup against the Guise that led to the wholesale arrests and executions of those implicated. Once again we see a highly trained mind, a man capable of some of the most thoughtful theoretical writing on French government, engaging with gusto in the street fighting of the print world.[36]

The Huguenot leader, the Duke of Condé, was also arrested and condemned to death for his part in the conspiracy. His life was saved only by the sudden death of Francis II in December 1560. This second providential royal death raised Huguenot agitation to a new peak of febrile excitement. The tone of these months of triumph and anticipation is well captured by the correspondence of Calvin and de Bèze. Both felt that God had placed the destiny of France in their hands: the conversion of their homeland lay before them.[37] The following year was a time of astonishing optimism, activism and relentless pressure on both the government and the Catholic population. The output of the presses reached a new peak, with over 300 editions of Protestant works, a third of which addressed directly the critical issue of freedom of worship. Meanwhile in many cities public demonstrations brought civil authority near to collapse; everywhere new adepts swelled the congregations.

This is not to say that all parts of the movement were marching in step. In particular, if one examines more closely this growing torrent of literature, it is possible to experience a certain dissonance between the printed word and other expressions of Protestant activism in these years. True, some of the religious tracts adopted a certain military tone in the choice of titles (*Baston de la foy, Glaive de Goliath*). There was also popular demand for reprints of some of the more rumbustious

---

[36] Kelley, *François Hotman*, pp. 112–16.

[37] See Calvin's letter to Sturm of December 1560, and de Bèze's celebratory verse after the death of Francis II, both reproduced in Duke, Lewis and Pettegree, *Calvinism Documents*, pp. 80–1.

anticlerical tracts from the first age of reform. But there was also considerable appetite in the churches for serious literature exploring the essentials of faith: works by Calvin, Viret and others, but also new short contemporary works such as the *Sommaire recueil des signes sacrez*.

There is some distance between these sober evocations of Protestant piety and the atmosphere of the streets. Nor was this bridged by the political manifestos of the church leadership, with their protestations of duty and obedience should freedom of worship be conceded. Faced with the honeyed words of de Bèze and his colleagues, Catherine de' Medici might with justice have confronted them with reports from Rouen, Lyon and elsewhere of the increasingly frequent and violent confrontations between bands of committed supporters of the rival churches.[38] Print, it seems, does not in this case tell the whole story. While books and pamphlets made the case for peace based on mutual toleration, the congregations, inspired by their preachers and their own sung attestations of victory and community, pressed for the abolition of the hated Mass.

The spirit of the times is in some respects more effectively captured by the literature published in this period in defence of the old church. For – and this is a fundamental difference between the first generation of the German *Flugschriften* and this later period – in this conflict, defenders of Catholicism made good and effective use of the press. In France this had been the case from the first years of Luther's protest, as members of the clergy took up their pens to defend the doctrines and practices of the church from Luther's criticisms. Most were doctors of the Sorbonne, and many found an effective vernacular voice to go alongside their Latin writings. Their publications proved the inspiration for those who now came forward to defend their church in its time of maximum peril in the 1560s. These Catholic authors, for the most part learned theologians, were oppressed by the sense of a double danger: the Huguenot heresy on the one side, and on the other a sense that a weakened crown would concede too much. They rallied their congregations in works of passionate bravura and excoriating rhetoric.

These French Catholic defences of the church, which have recently been the subject of more attention from scholars, demonstrate how well the defenders of the old church had learned the power of the new rhetoric of religious polemic.[39] In these works there is little attempt through patient advocacy to win back those tempted by the new faith;

---

[38] Benedict, *Rouen during the Wars of Religion*, pp. 49–70.

[39] Luc Racaut, *Hatred in Print. Catholic Propaganda and Protestant Identity during the French Wars of Religion* (Aldershot, St Andrews Studies in Reformation History, 2002).

there is little exploration of common ground with those who, while deluded in doctrine, nevertheless share common concerns for the restoration of true religion. Rather the Huguenots are mercilessly denounced as followers as a perverted, deformed parody of religion. The intention is not to win converts, but to warn Catholics of the awful consequences of flirting with such a corrupt travesty of worship.

One of the new generation of Catholic authors, Antoine du Val, set out the intentions of this literature with admirable clarity: 'We have collected this little book to guard and arm you against them [the Protestants]. By reading it, you will learn their false doctrine, their life and diabolical jargon, to be contrary to their pretence and false discourse.'[40]

To this end these learned authors deployed a variety of arguments and libels that emphasized the irredeemable mendacity of Huguenot worship, and the threat that it posed to the French state. The Huguenot assemblies (which often, before they were officially permitted, took place at night or in concealed places) were the cover for sexual orgies. Worse, the babies that resulted from these illicit couplings were then killed and consumed during the Eucharist: this was an inventive variation of the mediaeval blood libel against the Jews. Another comparison that drew on the mediaeval past was that of the Albigensian heresy, put down with great violence in the thirteenth century. Jean Gay, author of the *Histoire des scismes et heresies des Albigeois*, urged that the time was right for a new crusade. Huguenot disavowals of sedition were repudiated with contempt, their Reformation characterized as a deformation that turned all order topsy-turvy. They were accused of the fickle and changeable whims of women. In short, Protestantism was the source of division, chaos and disorder. If France was to be saved, it must be expelled.

This was powerful stuff, given added force by the fact that many of the effects alleged were demonstrably true. The onset of Protestantism had plunged France into chaos. Whether readers believed the more exotic claims as to what took place in the secrecy of congregational worship is a more difficult question. What is certainly without doubt is that by 1572 many Catholics so loathed Protestants that they turned on them with eager fury when opportunity presented itself on St Bartholomew's Day.[41]

Between 1560 and 1565 the polemical battle between Catholics and Protestants was waged with an unprecedented ferocity in France. Never before in the Reformation century had two contending parties made their case to the reading public with such force, or with evident lack of

---

[40] Antoine du Val, *Mirouer des Calvinistes*, sig. A3r. Quoted in Racaut, *Hatred in Print*, pp. 42–3.
[41] Diefendorf, *Beneath the Cross*.

mutual sympathy. These reflections have prompted a lively discussion as to whether this literature overreaches the boundaries of a polemical debate: whether, in fact, this literature should be characterized in modern terms as propaganda. This is a distinction that is important to maintain, for all the loose use of the latter term in general discussions of the Reformation period, for polemic possessed qualities of engagement and persuasion that are absent in propaganda. Miriam Usher Chrisman encapsulates the distinction thus:

Polemic can be defined as a controversial argument, a discussion in which opposite views are presented and maintained by opponents. It connotes a two-way process, a dialogue, although it may be a dialogue between the deaf. Propaganda lacks that quality of interchange. It is one-sided, a systematic attempt to propagate a particular opinion or doctrine. Its purpose is to influence men's opinions and attitudes and thus their actions and behaviour.[42]

This is well put, and points up a clear difference in tone and intention between the generation of Luther and that of the Religious Wars. While much of the polemical writing of Luther's day was rumbustious in tone, making liberal use of ridicule and *ad hominem* attacks, it still vigorously maintained the prospect of reconciliation, or at least a personal change of mind. It could not be otherwise in a church where so many of the first generation of ministers were former Mass priests. By the 1560s the conflicts in northern Europe were being fought out in a very different context. Divisions between Protestant and Catholic were now entrenched. Reconciliation was a real prospect only for a handful of idealist intellectuals. French polemicists engaged the battle for souls in full knowledge that the differences between contrasting visions of the true church were unbridgeable.

In this context the literature of the conflict took on a new urgency. Much of the writing emanating from the period could well be accommodated within the model developed by Norman Davis to define the notion of propaganda. In discussing the totalitarian states of the twentieth century, Davis advances the five leading characteristics of propaganda:

1 The rule of simplification: reducing all data to a simple confrontation between 'Good and Bad', 'Friend and Foe'.
2 The rule of disfiguration: discrediting the opposition by crude smears and parodies.

---

[42] Miriam Usher Chrisman, 'From Polemic to Propaganda', *Archiv für Reformationsgeschichte*, 73 (1982), p. 173.

3 The rule of transfusion: manipulating the consensus values of the target audience to one's own ends.

4 The rule of unanimity: presenting one's viewpoint as if it were the unanimous opinion of all right-thinking people: drawing the doubting individual into agreement by the appeal of star-performers, by social pressure, and by 'psychological contagion'.

5 The rule of orchestration: endlessly repeating the same messages in different variations and combinations.[43]

Some of this, of course, could be applied to much of the literature of persuasion discussed in this book. Effective communication in an age before mass literacy inevitably required the constant use of repetition (Davis's rule of orchestration); one would not associate this with the same technique applied in modern news management. But the presentation of religious choice as a simple confrontation between good and evil was a technique of which both sides were guilty. The Protestants achieved much with the dialectic use of paired opposites, from Luther on, though the device seems to have been taken to new levels in the age of religious war. Thus Protestants characterized their arch-foe, the Duke of Guise: 'This one has changed God in to Satan, Christ into Bel, peace into war, the blessing into the wrath of God, a legitimate government into tyranny'.[44] The Catholic author Robert Ceneau put it more succinctly: 'Either all Calvinist or totally faithful, in short either totally white or black'.[45]

This was a rhetoric that left little room for reconciliation, and in France there would be none. Successive bursts of fighting interspersed by massacres and forced conversions left Balkanized communities. Catholics and Protestants lived largely in separate towns and villages, in mutual distrust and hostility.[46] Elsewhere the new confessional states seldom found room for a tolerated minority. Protestant and Catholic alike sought sanctuary from bruising confessional battles in states that increasing derived a sense of their own identity from their religious allegiance. The way was prepared for the next phase of church building: a deepening of the religious culture through the identification of individual Christians with their own state church.

---

[43] Norman Davies, *Europe: A History* (London, 1997), p. 500.
[44] *Advertissement a la royne mere du roy* (1561), sig. B3v. Quoted in Racaut, *Hatred in Print*, p. 45.
[45] Robert Ceneau, *Response catholique*, sig. A7r. Quoted in Racaut, *Hatred in print*, p. 44.
[46] Conner, *Huguenot Heartland*.

8   New solidarities

By 1580 Europe's confessional boundaries were essentially fixed. The British kingdoms of England and Scotland were secure under the control of Protestant monarchs; in France a Calvinist minority was entrenched, but it was clear the nation would never be converted. In the Netherlands the Protestant north would never be recovered by Spain; the southern provinces would gradually assume a distinct Catholic identity. In Germany the oldest Lutheran states were now entering their third generation since the adoption of a Protestant church order. The Scandinavian kingdoms had also settled to life with a Lutheran state church. Only in eastern Europe would the tides shift in a significant manner, as the Habsburg victories of the 1620s allowed the suppression of the previously dominant Protestant estates of Hungary and Bohemia. That was for the future. For the moment the reality of a confessionally divided Europe was a generally accepted fact of European life and politics.

It would be wrong, however, to believe that this relative stability, so clear in retrospect, had calmed the passions raised by the first Reformation conflicts. On the contrary, relations between the faiths remained fractious and unstable, coloured above all by fear. On the Protestant side, this was understandable enough. In 1580 memories of the terrible massacres of Paris (1572) and Antwerp (1576) were still fresh, a reminder of Catholic perfidy, and the imminent danger that hard-won freedoms could still be dashed away. The military campaign in the Netherlands still held many perils for the insurgent provinces, and ultimately for England and France's Huguenots as well. Behind all these dangers lay the distant and relentless figure of the Spanish king, Philip II, a monarch whose military resources had never seemed more overwhelming or more dangerous. Where his armies could not reach, then conspiracy and assassination threatened a new poisonous turn to the confessional battle; since the assassinations of the French Religious Wars and numerous plots against the English queen, none of Europe's crowned heads could feel entirely secure, and several would indeed meet violent deaths. On the Catholic side, too, international politics were complicated by constant anxiety: that armies were overextended by the double conflict against heretic and Turk, perhaps even that the Protestant tide had not reached its flood. In Germany, the attempt to carry the strategically vital archbishopric of Cologne into the Protestant camp was a reminder that the Peace of Augsburg was a fragile basis for long-term harmony. For Germany's Lutheran states there was also the creeping, insidious threat of Calvinism, the enemy within, a conflict which stirred some of the greatest theological passions of the latter part of the sixteenth century.

These were uncertain times, though in the daily round of parish life the pace of change had finally begun to recede. Churches now fixed and securely established could bend their efforts towards the care and Christian education of their flock. This was an age when many national churches attained a sort of equilibrium. At the same time, the world beyond the parish continued to provide dark and ominous reminders of the fragility of God's providential blessings. In 1572 the General Assembly of the church of Scotland ordered a national festival of atonement, a propitiary ceremony to mark their horror at the news of the St Bartholomew's Day massacre.[1] The following decade the godly in England were contributing to collections for the defence of Geneva, the fountainhead, now threatened with military ruin.[2] Nothing could be taken for granted, abroad or at home, where pestilence or bereavement could strike at any time to test the faith.

There were many reasons, therefore, why the proselytizing zeal of Europe's Protestants did not lose its urgency. On the contrary, ministers, magistrates and engaged citizens redoubled their efforts to create a Christian people, a Christian parish and a Christian family. The relative political stability made possible, in particular, a new co-operation between church and state in what many regarded, quite rightly, as a shared enterprise. A Christian people was an orderly people, and a godly magistrate could expect obedience. This partnership of church and state has become a cornerstone of interpretations of the implementation of the Reformation programme in the second half of the century, particularly for Germany, where this process has become known as confessionalization.[3] There

---

[1] David Calderwood, *The History of the Kirk of Scotland*, ed., from the original manuscript preserved in the British Museum, by Thomas Thomson (Edinburgh, printed for the Woodrow Society, 1842–9) vol. II, pp. 227–30.

[2] Simon Adams and Mark Greengrass (eds.), 'Jean Malliet, "Memoires et procedures de ma negociation en Angleterre"', in Ian Archer (ed.), *Religion, Society and Politics in Sixteenth Century England*, Cambridge, Camden Society, 5th ser., 22 (2003), pp. 137–96.

[3] For the literature on confessionalization see Heinz Schilling (ed.), *Die reformierte Konfessionalisierung in Deutschland. Das Problem der 'Zweiten Reformation'* (Gütersloh, 1986).

are several aspects of the confessionalization paradigm that are indeed
helpful, not least the sense that the process of implementation of reform
proceeded in parallel in churches of different confessions, Lutheran,
Catholic and Calvinist.[4] This is undoubtedly the case, and it is also true
that this period of church renewal from within entrenched the relationship between ministers and state government, a development that laid the
basis for the exaggerated respect for state authority characteristic of
Germany Lutheranism through to the twentieth century. Where the confessionalization paradigm falls down is by exaggerating the extent to
which parish reform was imposed by the authorities, clerical and lay, on
largely passive, or even sullen and resentful parishioners. This, at best, is
to misstate the reality of a process of continuous and gradual religious
renewal in which many parishioners were active and willing participants.
It also risks misunderstanding the ways in which sixteenth-century societies functioned. For passivity was never a leading characteristic in the
engagement of the governed with authority. All the examples we will
consider below evince an active commitment to a form of religion, for
all that this was sometimes manifested in rather different ways from that
anticipated by godly authority. This was a protean, active process, that
proceeded to no very obvious official plan: that was perhaps its underlying
strength.

Schools of Christ

The huge expansion in educational provision during the sixteenth century was one all churches sought to turn to their advantage. A large part
of the pedagogic literature in all the media we have considered – songs,
biblical drama and printed books – was destined first and foremost for
the schools.[5] The teachability of the young was one of the great weapons
of church building. Not only were schools preparing the next generation
of church leaders and godly citizens. They were also reaching through
the schools into the heart of the Protestant family. The power of childish
memory had been exploited from the emergent years of the church,
particularly in familiarizing the congregation with the new hymns and
metrical psalms. Now the same catechismal urge was extended to the
whole community.

---

[4] On the Catholic side, see now W. Reinhard and Heinz Schilling (eds.), Die *Katholische
Konfessionalisierung* (Gütersloh, 1995). Marc Forster, 'With or without Confessionalization. Variations of Early Modern German Catholicism', *Journal of Ecclesiastical History*, 1
(1998), pp. 315–43.
[5] Parente, *Religious Drama and the Humanist Tradition*.

The reformers invested enormous hopes in the powers of religious education. Systematic instruction of the community was to proceed through the use of catechisms: instructions in the fundamentals of faith by way of question and answer. The reformers were inclined to claim the catechism, if not as an original invention of the Reformation, then at least as an aspect of the early church piety recovered after centuries of disuse. What we set before you, announced Calvin in the preface to the Geneva catechism, is what was used among Christians in ancient times before the devil ruined the church.[6] This claim has to be qualified. The mediaeval church recognized the principle of catechesis, and in the fifteenth century in particular the consciousness of the religious needs of the laity led to the composition of a large number of manuals laying out the essentials of faith. Some were intended as manuals of instruction for the clergy; others, like *L'ABC des simples gens* by Jean Gerson, were intended to be read by, or to, the laity. But, as this example suggests, the typical pre-Reformation catechism was declaratory: the Reformation catechism, constructed always in the form of question and answer, was indeed in pedagogic terms largely new.

In its developed form the catechesis of the Reformation era represented the synergy of two strands of educational practice: the mediaeval reliance on rote learning, still indispensable for all elementary education, and the Renaissance discovery of the dialogue. The dialogue, by introducing two or more characters, created a dramatic situation in which the lessons could emerge through the cut and thrust of questioning and answering. This, as we have seen, was a device the reformers quickly adopted for their polemical tracts, where the dialogue became an imagined conversation between two ostensibly equal partners.[7] This fiction added force to the persuasive power of the arguments placed in the mouth of the exponent of the evangelical case when he, inevitably, prevailed. For the catechism, this form was readily adapted to the inculcation of religious essentials. Here, by interspersing simple question prompts with larger comments or conversational observations put in the mouths of the teacher, the material could be absorbed far more easily than by mere repetition of an extended text. The interventions of the teacher also provided opportunities for summary, or to reorientate the pupil towards a new theme or subject.

Such at least was the theory. In practice, some catechisms were so long and complex that they would have strained the capacities of the aptest

---

[6] Ian Green, *The Christian's ABC. Catechisms and Catechizing in England, c. 1530–1740* (Oxford, 1996), p. 13.

[7] Erika Rummel, *Scheming papists and Lutheran Fools. Five Reformation Satires* (New York, 1993).

pupil. The concepts and terminology also made little concession to the likely knowledge of the young. Nevertheless, the extraordinary energy devoted to the composition and teaching of catechisms shows how much hope the reformers invested in this method of instruction. In this, as in so much else, Luther led the way. His two compositions of 1529, the *Deudsch Catechismus* and *Kleine Catechismus* were milestone events in the history of church formation. Whereas the first, longer catechism offers an extended defence of the developing doctrine of the new church, and may have been intended primarily for pastors, the smaller catechism has the elegant simplicity and single-minded focus on the essentials of faith that would characterize the best of Protestant writing in this genre. Luther's example stimulated an enormous outpouring of compositional energy, as local pastors throughout Germany turned their attention to the needs of their particular communities. This was laudatory, but risked a bewildering confusion of voices: at one point in the century there were at least fifty catechisms circulating in the single city of Hamburg. The second half of the century brought an attempt to enforce greater uniformity by teaching only from Luther's Short Catechism, which thus acquired canonical status. In 1580 new ordinances in Saxony required that a portion of Luther's catechism should be read every Sunday in church.

In the Reformed churches the emphasis from the beginning lay on securing a greater uniformity of practice. Calvin's Geneva Catechism achieved from the first a dominant position in the Francophone tradition. Published in 1541, it represented the product of five years of experimentation and deep thought about the needs of the community and the capacities of those to be instructed.[8] The questions, and some of the answers, are relatively short, and the material is organized to articulate the essentials of faith with clarity and according to a clear structure. The catechism is still a formidable size, and although Calvin had clearly recognized this problem, dividing the material into fifty-five 'Lord's Days' for teaching throughout the year, the need for something shorter and more accessible for those new to the faith was increasingly obvious. A popular solution was a tiered structure of catechisms, of increasing length and complexity, such as that adopted by the Dutch church in London in 1550. Here the church used both a long catechism, some parts of which would be expounded by the minister in church every week, and a shorter catechism for the use of the children. In addition

---

[8] Peter Y. de Jong, 'Calvin's Contribution to Christian Education', *Calvin Theological Journal*, 2 (1967), pp. 162–201. Thomas F. Torrance, *The School of Faith. The Catechisms of the Reformed church* (London, 1959).

there was a succinct digest of forty questions and answers, *Een korte ondersoeckinghe des gheloofs*, for those to be admitted to the church. The London catechisms proved extremely popular in the emerging Dutch Calvinist church, though they (like the London psalm translations) would later be superseded, in this case by the growing popularity of the Heidelberg Catechism. This powerful work, the creation of a group of theologians set to the task by the Calvinist Elector Palatine, quickly achieved a dominant position among German and Dutch Calvinists. In these languages and in translation it became the most published catechism of the sixteenth century.

Most Protestant churches had by the last decades of the sixteenth century moved towards use of a single official or limited range of catechisms; the exception was England, which saw an enormous outpouring of catechismal writing that continued unabated into the eighteenth century.[9] The zeal and energy of the English clerical authors, recently the subject of an exhaustive investigation by Ian Green, allow us to anatomize what these authors saw as the purposes and benefits of catechism. The first and plainest intention was to establish the basis of religious knowledge without which an individual could not hope for salvation. This went straight to the heart of the Protestant project. For without knowledge of the fundamentals of true belief man cannot have faith, and without faith he cannot be saved: 'Justifying faith presupposeth the knowledge of God and Christ, of the precepts of the Word, and promises of the Gospel', in the elegant summation of John Ball.[10] Beyond this vital theological core, catechizing enabled members of the church to attain a deeper understanding of the Scriptures and what took place during the church service, and it specifically prepared them for the solemn duty of receiving the Eucharist. It enabled them to distinguish true religion from false (a particularly important role in new or emergent churches facing competition from other sects); it promoted Christian virtue, and dissuaded members from vice.

With so much at stake it is no wonder that the churches reserved so large a space for catechism: in the formal worship service, in schools and at home. In church many Protestant traditions reserved the second afternoon service on a Sunday for the catechism, and often mid-week services as well. In schools, catechisms provided a basic tool of education from the first years of education, often grafted onto the most simple form of text, the ABC book. This compendium of a printed alphabet with simple prayers was a staple of all Protestant churches, and huge numbers

---

[9] Green, *Christian's ABC*.
[10] Ibid., p. 26.

were published.[11] In England the *ABC with the Catechism* was a jealously guarded and hugely lucrative part of the patent of the printer of the book of martyrs, John Daye. Indeed, it was probably the quick profits from these small books that allowed him to undertake as complex and lengthy project as the martyrology.

Catechizing in the home was a more difficult issue. Many authors envisaged a place for their books in the godly home, but here they faced stiff competition for the limited time available for home pedagogy, not least from the Bible, the book of books. In any analysis of the way in which the values of a godly society were inculcated, the Bible must have a special place; indeed, it is hard in any survey to do real justice to its primacy and influence. But this was a remarkable and many-faceted book, a success in so many of the categories of print that sixteenth-century readers found so fascinating. It was a travelogue and a work of history; a work of literature and poetry; it provided the model for much of the most successful drama of the age; it was a work of prophecy in an age obsessed by prophecy; it was a treasure trove for botanists, grammarians and etymologists, and a foundation text for students of the ancient languages; it was a work of jurisprudence, perhaps the sixteenth century's most influential legal text; it was certainly the century's most influential work of political thought. It provided role models for rulers and priests, for fathers and mothers, for soldiers and martyrs.

In this book the print culture of the sixteenth century was displayed in all its technical sophistication. It could be a handy pocket-sized book in tiny print, or a gloriously illustrated folio. The narrative illustrations in the Old Testament brought to life some of the greatest stories of the Christian tradition; even in the austere purged editions of the later Protestant tradition the text often came accompanied by maps, technical drawings, and ingenious diagrams of belief and unbelief.[12] It is not too much to say that in this one volume is epitomized much of what sixteenth-century book culture had to offer.

The sixteenth century placed this compendious and many-sided work directly in the hands of unprecedented numbers of people. Throughout the century and in all European vernaculars there were published at least 5,000 whole or partial editions of the Bible, a total of at least 5 million copies. Many were in small formats, and used to destruction; others

---

[11] R. Peter, 'L'abécédaire genevois ou catéchisme élémentaire de Calvin', *Revue d'Histoire et de Philosophie religieuses*, 45 (1965), pp. 11–45.

[12] Catherine Delano-Smith and Elizabeth Morley Ingram, *Maps in Bibles, 1500–1600. An Illustrated Catalogue* (Geneva, 1991). Rosier, *The Bible in Print*. Heimo Reinitzer, *Biblia deutsch. Luthers Bibelübersetzung und ihre Tradition* (Wolfenbüttel, 1983).

were a most cherished family possession, passed down through the generations.

The association of Protestantism and the Bible was close and intimate from the first years of Luther's movement; it remained central to the rhetoric of the movement and its ideology of scriptural renewal. Nevertheless, the Catholic churches, despite initial uncertainty, never wholly resigned their interest in vernacular Scripture. In Catholic Germany there was never a ban on the vernacular Scripture, though Catholic translations often drew so heavily on Luther that it is arguable that they did more to spread knowledge of Luther's version than to impede it. It was a similar case in the Francophone world, where the Louvain Bible made much use of the translations of Lefèvre and Olivetan. This Louvain Bible was itself derived from the first Catholic Bible printed in Paris after the ban on vernacular Scripture in France was relaxed in 1566. This was the work of René Benoist, whose translation was almost entirely based on the Geneva Bible.[13]

The Bible, clearly, played a vital role in the godly home. So too did music. One rather perverse indication of the popularity of the Protestant metrical psalms is the speed with which they evolved a domestic recreational counterpart, with arrangements of the psalm texts for four-part singing.[14] This is in some respects rather ironical, for a large part of the musical theology of the psalms was embedded in their simplicity of line, giving precedence to audibility and the clarity of the lyric. In this lay the contrast with the complex polyphonies of mediaeval religious music. Yet almost every major musician practising in France in the second half of the sixteenth century (some forty in all) tried their hand at harmonizing at least some of the psalms. The composer Claude Goudimel composed two complete cycles; Claude de Jeune published complete sets of harmonizations in three parts and in four. Catholic composers such as Roland de Lassus were also not immune to the charms of the psalms.[15] Some of these compositions were intended for performance, and survive into the repertoire to this day. But we know that many were intended for domestic parlour singing. This is clear not least from the practice of printing part books with two vocal lines on a single page, the music and

---

[13] Chambers, *Bibliography of French Bibles*, nos. 371–4. Emile Pasquier, *Un curé de Paris pendant les guerres de religion: René Benoist, le pape des Halles* (Paris, 1913).

[14] For examples of four-part arrangements of the psalms from many language cultures see François Lesure (ed.), *Répertoire international des sources Musicales. Recueils imprimés XVIe–XVIIe siècle* (Munich and Duisburg, 1960), 1563/8, 1592/7 (English), 1568/11, 1588/12 (German), 1569/9–11, 1577/1–3, 1578/3–4 (French).

[15] Francis Higman, 'Music', in Andrew Pettegree, *Reformation World* (London, 2001), p. 499.

text printed with two halves, one upside down, so both face towards the middle of the page. This was clearly to be used by two people placed on opposite sides of a table reading from the same copy.

Further incidental evidence of the popularity of domestic musical entertainment can be found in an early Dutch phrase book, published in London in the first years of the seventeenth century.[16] After basic grammatical exercises *The Dutch School-Master* offers phrases for a variety of business and social situations, including music making. 'What shall we do now?', the reader is prompted:

> Shall we sing a song of foure parts?
> It is well said,
> You shall sing the base,
> Maister N. shall sing the countertenor,
> I will sing the tenor,
> And mistresse N. shall sing the treble?[17]

The evening wears on. The singing inspires playing ('tune your Lute') and dancing ('you daunce very well: ghy danst seer wel'), before, exhausted, the bold user of the musical phrase book is prompted to suggest retiring to bed: a sequence which, perhaps unintentionally, seems to confirm the consistory's darkest fears of the inevitable connection between music, dancing and licentiousness.

Part-book printing with musical notation was not inexpensive, and pre-supposed a clientele both prosperous and musically literate. Indeed, if we are to confront the question of the utility of this great outpouring of energy on the education of the Christian people, we must recognize a clear differentiation between the sort of experience of religion open to those from relatively prosperous urban households, and others. These Protestant families would have access to Bibles, music and literature; their children would be instructed in schools; they would hear sermons preached by the best-qualified and best-remunerated ministers; theirs came close to the experience of Christian education anticipated by the reformers. Outside these privileged groups the range and density of media applied to this purpose would be much reduced. Here the experience of religion would be less complete. But the country parishes were not entirely neglected. Here the sermons, the catechism service and the experience of communal singing still did much to inculcate the values of the new religion. Even in the towns, of course, the most zealous instruction could not guarantee agreement among the citizens who brought

[16] Marten Le Mayre, *The Dutch School-Master* (London, 1606; facsimile edn, Scholar Press, 1972). I am grateful to Jane Pettegree for drawing this book to my attention.
[17] Ibid., sig. F5r.

their own increasingly autonomous readings to what they heard in the pulpit, or read in their books at home. Empowerment of a theologically informed laity brought its own dangers.

Battles half won

In some parts of Europe it was clear from a comparatively early date that hopes of a Protestant victory would go unfulfilled. In France the real prospect that the nation could be converted had disappeared by the end of the first round of fighting in 1563. Instead, the Calvinist congregations had to content themselves with a limited freedom of worship, and even these rights often proved difficult to defend against unsympathetic local officials, egged on by a largely hostile Catholic population.[18] This sense of embattlement coloured the religious experience of the Huguenot churches at every turn, and encouraged the development of a particular form of social self-identification: simultaneously in the community and yet maintaining distance. Several recent studies have described how French Huguenot churches cultivated an ostentatious distinctiveness that went far beyond the separation of their worship practice. They began to dress in sober, unornamented garments that acted as a tangible, visual demonstration of the superior moral code to which they had committed themselves. All, of course, were under the discipline of the local consistory, a discipline to which many submitted with a willingness that modern commentators have found difficult to fathom. If the moral discipline exercised on behalf of church members by the consistory reinforced their sense of themselves as a chosen people, this was manifested also in the choice of names for new infant members of the church. In increasing numbers they eschewed traditional saints' names in favour of Abraham, Isaac and Daniel for boys, Judith, Susanna and Sara for girls.[19] Their participation in a sealed, autonomous worship community encouraged over the course of time an increasing tendency to confine their social, and even business, relations to other members of the community. In Paris, where the sense of embattlement was enhanced by the dangerous hostility of the Catholic majority, this became particularly pronounced during the decade before the St Bartholomew's Day massacre. Leading members of the community contracted their children in marriage to fellow church members; their marriage contracts were witnessed by fellow members of the church, who naturally also stood as

[18] Penny Roberts, 'Religious Pluralism in Practice: The Enforcement of the Edicts of Pacification', in Keith Cameron, Mark Greengrass and Penny Roberts (eds.), *The Adventure of Religious Pluralism in France* (Bern, 2000), pp. 31–43.
[19] Benedict, *Rouen*, p. 105.

godparents to their infants. These contracts were drawn up by a small group of Protestant notaries. Even beyond the church elite, members of the community showed a pronounced tendency to do business together, borrow money from one another, stand as guarantors for loans, and otherwise assist each other in business dealings.[20] The more prosperous members of the community took poorer members of the church as their domestic servants; even relatively unprosperous members of the church could signal their allegiance by taking their business to tradesmen from within the congregation.

One can see how all aspects of this behaviour were likely to increase the sense of alienation from the majority Catholic population. Within the church, every aspect of this largely autonomous existence – the separate worship, the consistory discipline, the ostentatious witness through dress and deportment, even the sense of embattlement – could be framed theologically. They knew, because they were constantly taught, that at the last day only a few could be saved. The identity of the saints must have seemed very evident when the majority of their neighbours so ostentatiously rejected the Gospel. On the Catholic side, the deliberate and increasingly ostentatious isolation of the Protestants in their midst must have seemed like a deliberate provocation. Only if one recreates the atmosphere of these difficult, disputatious years can one truly understand why the Catholic population of Paris fell on their Huguenot neighbours with such fury and relish in 1572; and why so many of those who died were done to death by people who knew them well, and had clearly come to hold them in angry contempt.

After the massacre many of the formerly numerous churches in northern France virtually ceased to exist. The initial shock of the massacres was followed by a wave of abdurations, which in purely numerical terms did more to depopulate the flagging congregations than the original killings. Many others sought safety in flight, swelling the Protestant majority in the towns of the south where the Huguenots had established control in the first years of the war, and maintained it since: places like Montauban, Montpellier and Nîmes. Yet even these communities were not free from the sense of embattlement that had so shaped the Calvinist minority in Paris, Rouen and elsewhere.[21] For these southern provinces were far from the Calvinist fortress conveyed by the fanciful concept of 'the United provinces of the South'. True, the Protestants controlled many of the principal towns of Languedoc, and many of the regional

---

[20] Diefendorf, *Beneath the Cross*, pp. 127–36.
[21] Conner, *Huguenot Heartland*.

nobility had also adhered to the new religion.[22] But Bordeaux, Toulouse and Aix-en-Province remained securely Catholic; so too did many towns of medium size and many villages under the control of Catholic nobles and garrisons. Throughout the later stages of the French wars this region was constantly at the mercy of military bands of both parties, or neither. The Calvinists of Montauban or Nîmes, even if secure within their own walls, could not live a life separate from their hinterland, where pockets of Catholic strength could be found in dangerous proximity. Nor could they be sure that the long-threatened royal campaign to bring them to obedience would not finally materialize.

The sense of embattlement, then, was never absent in the religious consciousness of French Huguenots, even in their area of greatest geographical strength. This may explain their pursuit of a moral code of unusual rigour even in the Calvinist tradition. The Huguenot churches of Montauban and elsewhere waged war on ostentation in dress and many aspects of entertainment culture beloved of many otherwise godly citizens; in particular they pursued a remorseless campaign against dancing.[23] Sometimes this moral rigour could seem almost wilfully self-defeating. Even other Calvinist ministers were shocked when the ministers of Montauban sought to exclude from the communion the wife of Philippe du Plessis Mornay, influential statesman and author and the right-hand man of Henry of Navarre. Madame du Plessis Mornay had offended the ministers by the ostentation of her hairstyle, a case which highlights the difficulties facing a religious culture with two contrasting centres of gravity, located in the urban bourgeois church, and in the nobility. To the ministers ostentation was to be deplored; to the Protestant nobility, fine clothing, jewellery and plate were not only attributes of their status, but part of the necessary cash reserve which could be (and often was) liquidated for the service of the church in time of especial need.[24] Here, the Montauban ministers exhibited that almost perverse delight in conflict that was all too often a leading characteristic of a self-regarding godly minority.

In England and the Netherlands these instincts took rather longer to exhibit themselves. In the Netherlands the churches had played so integral a role in the establishment and survival of the independent

[22] Raymond A. Mentzer, Jr., *Blood and Belief. Family Survival and Confessional Identity among the Provincial Huguenot Nobility* (West Lafayette, Ind., 1994).

[23] Philippe Chareyre, "'The Great Difficulties One Must Bear to Follow Jesus Christ": Morality at Sixteenth-Century Nîmes', in Raymond A. Mentzer (ed.), *Sin and the Calvinists. Moral Control and the Consistory in the Reformed Tradition* (Kirksville, Mo., 1994), pp. 63–96.

[24] S. Amanda Eurich, *The Economics of Power: The Private Finances of the House of Foix-Navarre-Albret during the Religious Wars* (Kirksville, Mo., 1993).

northern state that initially co-operation with the lay powers had been very close. Because the Calvinist congregation abroad had provided so large a part of the finance, military supplies and even manpower for the insurgency, they were able to extract a high price for their co-operation. As each of the Holland towns went over to the rebels, the church demanded and received the best and most prominent churches to re-establish their worship. The ministers gave thanks to providence for the transformation of their prospects. 'We can never thank the Lord sufficiently for opening so large a door to his Holy Word everywhere, and especially in Holland', enthused a minister in Delft in September 1572. Nor were they slow to acknowledge the role of the emerging civil power in providing support and encouragement. 'I see that we have a more godly government than ever France or Germany have had', was the optimistic judgement of Jan van der Beke in February 1573.[25]

In these years of exuberant growth the churches faced an almost unsustainable burden of expectation. The godly core that had returned from the exile churches was small compared to the population of the towns that had now to be introduced to the new Calvinist worship service; the supply of well-qualified ministers to lead these churches was pitifully small. Ministers had to be recruited, housed and paid. The problems of appointing a properly qualified ministry revealed the first cracks in the unity of purpose that had bound the church and lay authorities through the military struggle. Inevitably the magistrates expressed a strong interest in whose voice would be heard from the powerful city pulpits. Since they paid the salaries they were in a position to prevail. But disputes over the rights of nomination in a number of towns revealed differences over quite fundamental issues. In a civil church, the ministers conceded that they could not expect a continuation of the autonomy that they had enjoyed in the exile churches. But the progressive erosion of their influence over schools and poor relief, and control over important church ceremonies such as marriage, led to a rising tide of alarm. Schools and poor relief could at least be presented as areas of mixed competence, but two issues proved to be particularly divisive: the rights of the church to exercise consistorial discipline, and the failure to suppress competing sects.

On this latter issue the tolerant tradition of the Dutch north caused the ministers endless heartache. At the height of the military danger in 1574 they had secured the abolition of the Mass, but further than this the magistrates would not go. Dutch Calvinism was forced to vie for members with a range of alternative churches whose status ranged from near open toleration to a largely unrestricted half-secrecy. Even the right of the Calvinist churches to establish the full apparatus of consistorial discipline was at some points in doubt. Elements in the States of Holland wished to forbid the establishment of consistories altogether, and although this drastic line was not maintained, it was only permitted to exercise the discipline among those who voluntarily decided to become full members of the church: and these were perilously few. The suppression of vice in society as a whole depended on the co-operation of the magistrates, who at different times showed scant regard for ministerial demands for the regulation of the Sabbath, the suppression of the taverns, and the regulation of entertainment culture. In particular, the Reformed made little headway in their attempts to suppress two forms of recreation particularly dear to the urban bourgeoisie, dancing and the theatre. Even those city governments which in other matters proved relatively amenable to the church refused to heed the ministers on these issues. Here the magistrates, in turning a deaf ear to the pulpit tirades, were speaking for the consensus. The Leiden city council refused point blank to dissolve the local Chamber of Rhetoric, and even in Dordrecht and Delft, strongholds of the church, performances continued, as did the national *rederijker* festivals.[26]

The church never lost its special place in Dutch society, but it emerged from these conflicts with a very particular character. Although the larger part of the population eschewed the competing churches and adhered, in some way, to the Calvinist congregations, only a small majority became full confessing, communicating members. In the Dutch vernacular these members (*liedmaten*) were differentiated from the broader class of sympathizers (*liefhebbers*) who attended services but neither communicated nor submitted themselves to consistorial discipline. Here the search for an inner minority – what one might call the puritan instinct – found institutional form, and in a way that reasonably suited both sides. The churches had the use of the buildings and an opportunity to shape Dutch society, but the more austere implications of the Calvinist view of the Christian life could not be imposed on the population at large. For all the angry recriminations and pulpit prophecies of social collapse, this differentiation was maintained with a reasonably good grace. The same could not be said for England, where the imperfect resolution of the Reformation process caused serious divisions in the face of English Protestantism.

[26] Ibid., p. 178.

By adhering to the principles of the earlier Edwardian reform, and placing bishops at the centre of the new church structure, the English authorities precluded the development of a full Reformed church structure (and especially the exercise of consistorial discipline). They also ensured that there would be a convenient whipping boy for urgent Protestants disappointed in the new church and impatient for further progress towards the creation of a godly society. The first major confrontation was not long awaited. The English church had, in doctrinal terms, adhered quite closely to the lodestones of the Reformed tradition. Both Calvin and Bullinger gave it their blessing; Calvin, in particular, was the unquestioned theological writer of choice for all quarters of the English church throughout Elizabeth's reign.[27] The conflict, when it erupted, came over the comparatively adiaphorous issue of ecclesiastical dress: for those disappointed in the new church, the decision to enforce the wearing of the 'popish' surplice became a metaphor for all their doubts regarding the sincerity and zeal of those who bore direction of the new church. The unfortunate bishops, charged with enforcing the queen's injunctions to require the surplice, obeyed with varying degrees of reluctance. A significant portion of the clergy, especially in London, refused to comply and were deprived. This included a large number of the church's most gifted and diligent preachers.[28] For a young church faced with the task of evangelizing a recalcitrant population it was a haemorrhage of talent they could not afford.

The vestiarian controversy established a pattern that would be repeated at different times during Elizabeth's reign, though the issue of controversy shifted with the passage of years. Each dispute would be accompanied by inevitable charges of backsliding and treachery, bad faith and opportunism. The fact that those at the eye of the storm barely differed in terms of their core beliefs did not lessen the level of personal invective. Through all of these conflicts – Field's *Admonition*, the suppression of prophesying, Whitgift's campaign to impose subscription – the clerical leadership of the godly sustained some heavy blows. They often showed indifferent judgement in their choice of a battlefield, and intemperance of language that would alienate potential supporters. That the cause of the godly was sustained through all these calamities owed everything to the emergence of a party among the laity that identified themselves with the cause: the gentry patrons who sustained the

[27] Francis Higman, 'Calvin's Works in Translation', in ibid., pp. 82–99. Andrew Pettegree, 'The Reception of Calvinism in Britain', in Wilhelm H. Neuser and Brian G. Armstrong (eds.), *Calvinus Sincerioris Religionis Vindex* (Kirksville, Mo., 1997), pp. 267–89.
[28] Patrick Collinson, *The Elizabethan Puritan Movement* (London, 1967), pp. 59–97.

suffering clergy against the harassment of their clerical superiors, and the ordinary parishioners whose patient zeal gave the puritan cause its extraordinary resilience.

For a church that set such store by recreating the primitive simplicity of the apostolic church, it was perhaps ironic that the greatest protection of the godly cause would prove to be the Byzantine complexities of church patronage. Magnates and gentry who exercised rights of preferment as part of a quasi-feudal lordship were able to use these rights to place ministers in favour of reform in strategic positions; the bishops were powerless to prevent them.[29] The ministers also owed much to the godly magistrates, who had their own obvious reasons to favour eloquent preachers who taught the duty of an earnest life of repentance and hard work. But this would have counted for nothing had the ministers not been sustained by the active support of parts of their congregations that aspired to a life of worship, prayer and devotion. In some parishes the godly came close to creating a plausible replica of the Genevan consistorial system, with the minister exercising the informal power of excommunication by excluding notorious sinners from the Eucharist.[30] This was all well and good when the bulk of the parish, and the parish officers, were willing to accept such charismatic authority. It was divisive and resented if the minister carried with him only a small portion of the parish, who began to think of themselves as a separate group, ostentatiously shunning the degenerate majority. Sometimes this might lead to the sort of social exclusivity that we have seen as a characteristic of the French Huguenot movement. One man who renounced his former puritan loyalties testified that, in his former fraternity, the name of brother was denied to any who were not of 'their own fraction and opinion', and that the godly, 'as much as they might conveniently', refused to eat, drink or do business with those not 'inclining that way'.[31]

In England, the opportunities for such exclusivity were rare. By and large the values espoused by such forward Protestants were not intrinsically different from those of society at large. All early modern communities reproved licentiousness and vagrancy, and anything that might disturb the fragile local peace.[32] The godly were exceptional only in

[29] Claire Cross, *The Puritan Earl. The Life of Henry Hastings, Third Earl of Huntingdon, 1536–1595* (London, 1966). Simon Adams, 'Favourites and Factions at the Elizabethan Court' and 'A Godly Peer? Leicester and the Puritans', in his *Leicester and the Court. Essays on Elizabethan Politics* (Manchester, 2002).

[30] Collinson, *Elizabethan Puritan Movement*, pp. 346–55.

[31] Patrick Collinson, *English Puritanism* (London, Historical Association pamphlet, 1983), p. 19.

[32] Martin Ingram, *Church Courts, Sex and Marriage in England, 1570–1640* (Cambridge, 1987).

their more active identification with the harsh prophetic voice of the pulpit orators who denounced the parish communities as sinks of wickedness. But this lack of measure, which led occasionally to ostentatious symbolic separation epitomized by the adoption of newly conceived Christian forenames (such as Praise God, Much-mercy or Sin-deny), was more likely to bring ridicule than sympathy in the parish community.[33] Even in these extreme cases, and crucially, the Godly did not advance beyond this symbolic internal distancing: they were not separatists, and never took the crucial step of creating a formally constituted new church. When the Protestant settlement in England was imperilled, and when the threat came from without, they quickly rediscovered the essential unity that bound them to other friends and neighbours.

Godly kin and godly nation

The redefinition of kin was an essential part of the rhetoric of those who sought to create a new religious identity by distancing themselves from the community around them. We have heard that the puritan group described by a disenchanted defector above denied 'the name of brother' to all who did not adhere to their faction, and such naming became a common characteristic of all the future separatist groups that eventually repudiated the broad church of the English settlement. Such appropriation of kinship is all the more important when one considers that the traditional sacraments played a relatively modest role in defining the new Protestant family. Baptism was an important rite of belonging but took place only once, and was in England and the Netherlands available to all children of the parish community. It did not define commitment to the confessing congregation under the discipline, as had been intended in the original Reformed church orders. The churches also exhibited a considerable difference in practice as to how far the extended kinship relationship of godparenting should be practised: in some Reformed traditions it was effectively repressed. The Eucharist, rescued from the pollution of the Roman Mass, also played a much more modest role in defining the godly community than might have been anticipated by the reformers. It was infrequent, often only quarterly, and only in the churches that achieved a real unity between the godly people and the parish (such as Scotland and the Huguenot towns of southern France) could it function as a rite of communal self-identification. In

---

[33] Nicholas Tyacke, 'Popular Puritan Mentality in Late Elizabethan England', in Peter Clark, Alan G.R. Smith and Nicholas Tyacke (eds.), *The English Commonwealth, 1547–1640* (Leicester, 1979), pp. 77–92.

the Netherlands, as we have seen, only a tenth of the population aspired to full communicating membership of the church: a godly core, but not in any way representative of the totality of the Christian people.

The search for the godly people thus could not end with the narrow sacramental community of the Eucharist. Rather, it radiated outwards in two directions: firstly, to a community of saints that recognized no limits of locality, nation or time. This was a congregation that united the godly both with the saints departed and with those in other godly nations. Simultaneously, however, the Protestant churches developed an alternative vision of a godly people, that united a broad cross-section of the people who felt a broad commitment to the common purpose of church and nation, irrespective of whether they also adhered to the core of the confessing church. It was this broader church of the godly nation that would sustain the cause through the crises that marked the last decades of the sixteenth century.

Central to the first definition of Christian kinship was the identification of a community of saints in the church before Luther: the creation of a collective inferred heritage. This went forward in a tremendous burst of creative energy during the 1550s, when Protestants discovered both an individual historical tradition and a new genre of pedagogic writing, the martyrology. In the Lutheran tradition the landmark works were the historical writings of Johann Sleidan and the Magdeburg Centuriators.[34] Sleidan, a career author and diplomat, was in 1542 entrusted with the task of compiling an official history of the Schmalkaldic League: official documents were put at his disposal, and he corresponded widely to create what emerged as a complete history of the Reformation movement from the time of Luther's protest against indulgences. Perhaps surprisingly, the work was not well received, even by those who had commissioned it: its implied criticism of the conduct of some of the Protestant princes sat ill with the partisan tradition of Reformation polemic.[35] But this relatively dispassionate presentation of original documents was what ensured the work its long-term success: even Catholic authors, while they deplored Sleidan's fundamentally positive presentation of Luther, made use of his repertoire of documents in their own works. The Magdeburg Centuriators took a different approach, allocating one volume to each century of the church's history. Again the Centuriators made copious use of primary documents (often

---

[34] On Sleidanus see now Alexandra Kess, 'Johann Sleidan and the Protestant Vision of History' (University of St Andrews, Ph.D. dissertation, 2004). A.G. Dickens and John Tonkin, *The Reformation in Historical Thought* (Oxford, 1985), pp. 10–19.

[35] Described in Kess, 'Johann Sleidan'.

drawing on the same sources of information as Sleidan).[36] In this case, however, the presentation of a complete church history made the essential ideological purpose – the identification of contemporary Protestant churches with the best parts of the historical Christian tradition – all the more plain.

This too was a fundamental purpose of the great Protestant martyrologies, developed in all the major Lutheran and Reformed traditions in a great burst of creative energy between 1550 and 1559.[37] The Lutheran compilation of Ludwig Rabus inevitably had a somewhat different character, since the German church could claim comparatively few who had paid the ultimate price for their faith. His witnesses included figures like Luther who had done noble service without dying a violent death.[38] The Reformed martyrologies placed far greater emphasis on the raw testimonies of those who had died to sustain the Protestant cause – often very recently. The English martyrology arose out of the experience of dislocation and defeat following the death of Edward VI and the subsequent suppression of Protestantism by Queen Mary. Although we associate it with the authorial genius of John Foxe, it was always conceived as a collective enterprise.[39] The moving spirit behind the project seems to have been Edmund Grindal who, as a leading figure in the Marian exile community, offered to take responsibility for gathering materials for an English edition, while Foxe worked on a Latin edition. In the event the task proved more complex than anticipated; on the accession of Elizabeth in 1558 Grindal returned to England with the task uncompleted, leaving Foxe to supervise the last stages of the publication of the great Latin *Commentarii*. The definitive English edition then took shape in the years after Foxe was re-established in England. In Geneva the responsibility for the French martyrology fell to the publisher Jean Crespin, a member of Calvin's intimate circle who had himself before leaving for Geneva witnessed the burning of one of the early martyrs of the French church. Crespin brought to his task an extraordinary commitment, perhaps born of this searing experience; he was also able

---

[36] Heinz Scheible, *Die Entstehung des Magdeburg Zenturien* (Gütersloh, 1966).

[37] Gregory, *Salvation at Stake*, pp. 165–80. Dickens and Tonkin, *Reformation in Historical Thought*, pp. 41–51. Jean-François Gilmont, 'Les martyrologes du XVIe siècle', in Silvana Seidel Menchi (ed.), *Ketzerverfolgung im 16. und frühen 17. Jahrhundert* (Wolfenbüttel, 1992).

[38] Robert Kolb, *For All the Saints: Changing Perceptions of Martyrdom and Sainthood in the Lutheran Reformation* (Macon, Ga., 1987).

[39] For the large and fast-growing literature on Foxe see, by way of introduction, David Loades (ed.), *John Foxe and the English Reformation* (Aldershot, St Andrews Studies in Reformation History, 1997). Christopher Highley and John N. King, *John Foxe and his World* (Aldershot, St Andrews Studies in Reformation History, 2002).

Lxx. Nadat Paulus met grooter neersticheyt de ghemeynte des Heeren als een ghetrouwe dienaer, opghebout, gheleert, vermaent ende onderwesen hadde, met woorden ende met schriften, * is hy ten laetsten te Jerusalem in den tempel ghevanghen, ghestooten en geslagen geworden van den Joden, welcke hem meynden te dooden: maer hy is van haren handen ontweldicht door een Capiteyn der krijchsknechten.

Acto. 21. c. 17

Als hy nu aldus ghevanghen was, so hebben hem de Bisschoppen en Priesters beschuldicht ende verklaghet als een oproerder ende ketter. Paulus zijn onschuldt ghedaen hebbende * heeft geappelleert ende op den Keyser beroepen. So is hy ghevanckelick te Roomen ghesonden. Daer hy † etlicke iaren lanck het woort Gods ende de Evangelische waerheyt ghepredickt heeft.

Paulus behelpt hem met de Heydensche rechten.
* Act. 25 c. 10
† Act. 28 g. 30

Ten laetsten is hy van den wreedẽ Tyrant, Nero, den Keyser, om de ghetuyghenisse des Christelicken Religioens onthooft geworden. Also heeft desen heylighen Apostel, die meer dan alle andere ghearbeydet heeft, synen loop gheeyndicht, ende heeft van den Heere ontfanghen de kroone der glorien. Ende is gheschiet (so men schrijft) na de gheboorte Jesu Christi ons Salichmakers int iaer Lxx.

IGNATIVS BISSCHOP VAN ANTIOCHIEN.

Ignatius de eerste Bisschop van Antiochien na Sint Peter, een seer vlijtich man in de godsalighe leeringhe des heylighen Evangeliums: als hy wt tlant van Syrien na Roomen ghevanckelick gheuoert wart, was hy overghelevert in de handen der krijchsknechten, die hem seer wreedelick handelden, ende hoe hy haer liefslicker aenghinck, hoe sy door zijn goetdadicheyt daghelicx teghen hem straffer werden.

Dese seyde dat hy doe eerst een leerjongher Christi Jesu wart, als hem de vervolghinghe bestreet. Te Roomen komende wort hy aldaer verwesen, voor de wilde beesten ghewoopen te worden, om van die verbeten ende verschoort te worden. Daerop seyde hy: Jck ben het koren Gods, ick sal met der beesten tanden ghemaelt ende ghekauet worden, op dat ick een suyver broot worde. Also heeft de vrome ghetuyge Christi Jesu den beesten voor ghewoopen gheweest, ende van haer verschoert geworden.

Onder tervice wort men Christus discipel.

Ontrent dese tijt, als Traianus de veerthiende Keyser van Roomen regneerde, ontrent den iare onses eenighen Salichmakers Christi Jesu. C. x. isser groote vervolghinghe ende bloetverghietinge gheschiet onder den Christenen. De oorsake deser wreetheyt was, om dat de keyser sorchde, datter eenich oproer wt de vergaderinghen der Christenen soude moghen oprijsen. Maer de Christenen verdroeghen den doot ende de vervolghinghe so ghedueldichlick dat de Heydensche Rechters daer af verwonderden. So dat Plinius Secundus een Roomsche Landtvooght den Keyser Traiano overschreef, datter daghelicx veel duysent menschen iammerlick ghedoot worden, daermen nochtans gheen boosheyt, noch yet dat teghen de Roomsche rechten is, in bevinden konden.

C. x.

Och of onse Princen dit oock aenmercken.

van alleen dat sy eenen, die Christus ghenaemt is, lof songen ende eerden: maer overspel, moort, ende ander straffelicke lasteringhen worden by haer onbetamelick ghehouden ende seer ghehaet &c. Dusdanigen lof moesten oock de Heydenen den Christenen na geven: also lieten sy haer lichten schijnen tot Gods glorie ende heerlickheyt.

C. hviij.

Polycarpus Bisschop te Smyrnen.

Polycarpus een discipel Joannis des Evangelists, een wel geleert ende godvruchtich Leeraer ende Bisschop te Smyrnen: na dat hy om den naem Jesu Christi gevangen was, heeftmẽ hem willen doen sweeren by de fortuyne des Keysers, ende dat hy Christum soude lasteren, welcke hy gheen van beyde heeft willen doen, wel wetende datmen alleen in den naem des Almachtigen Gods sweeren sal, die alleenlick een onderkenner der herten is, ende heeft op het anderde also gheantwoort: Jck diene Christum nu sessentachtentich iaren lanck, ende hy en heeft my noyt yet misdaen: hoe sal ick dan mynẽ Koninck, die my salicheyt ghegheven heeft konnen lasteren. Jck ben een Christen, ende wilt ghy de redenen des Christelicken Religioens weten, so bestelt my eenen dach ende ghy sultse hooren. De Rechter seyde maeckt dat den volcke wijs. Doe sprack Polycarpus: Jck hebbe v gheantwoort, want wy worden gheleert, dat wy den Princen en de macht, die van God gheordineert is, sulcke eere sullen bewijsen, die teghen onse religie niet en is. Het en is myn officie niet den rasenden volcke te voldoen.

Als hem de Rechter seyde, dat hy de wilde dieren bereydt hadde, so verre als hy gheen leedtwesen en thoonde ende hem bekeerde. Heeft Polycarpus gheantwoort: Laetse voortkomen, want onsen sin is onveranderlick, wy en konnen ons door leedtwesen niet bekeeren van het goet tot het quaet. Het ware beter dat sy haer selven tot het goet bekeerden, die in boosheyt volherden. Doe seyde de Rechter: Jst v niet leedt, ende veracht ghy de wilde beesten, so sal ick v met vuer verbranden. Polycarpus antwoorde: ghy dreycht my het vuer dat in eenen ooghenblick onsteken, ende lichtelick wederom wtgheblust wort, want v het eewighe vuer onbekent is, dat den boosen toekomen sal in den dach des oordeels. Maer wat vertoeft ghy? brengt voort welck v van beyde belieft.

Leedtwesen en bekeeren.

Als hem nu het volck ter doot eyschede, is hy van den Rechter overghelevert om levendich verbrant te worden, also is de vrome ghetuyghe Jesu Christi, seer oudt van daghen, door den vuere den Heere opoffert.

Ptolemeus ende Lucius.

Ptolemeus

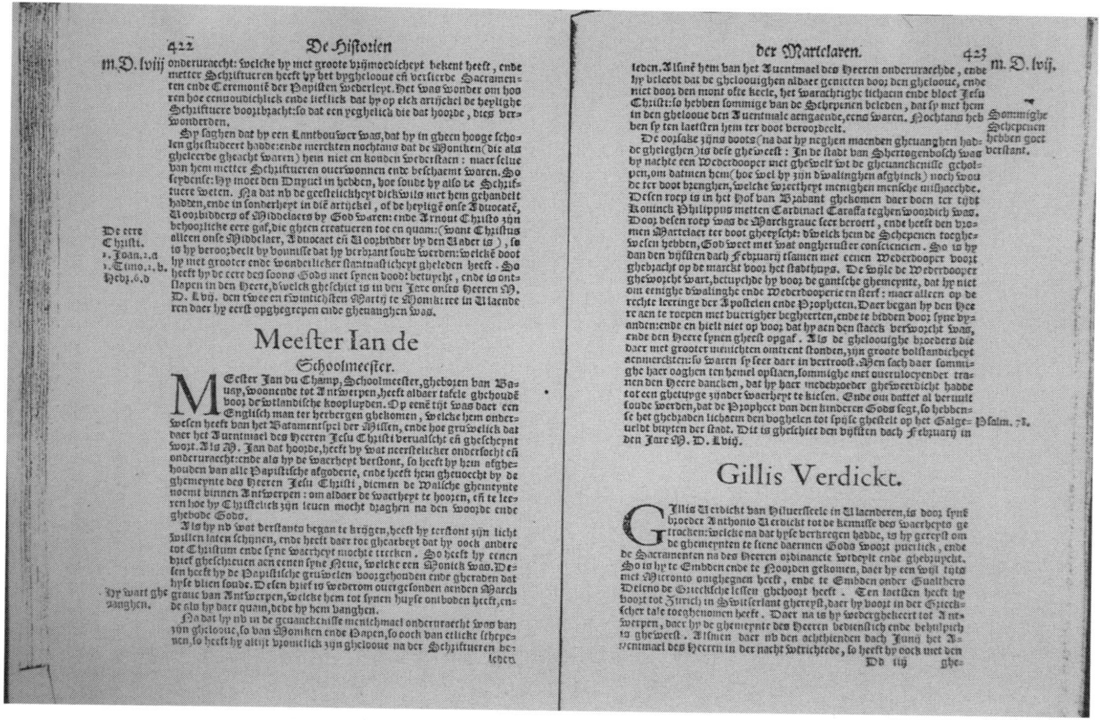

422 De Historien
m.D.lviij

Meester Jan de
Schoolmeester.

der Martelaren. 423
m.D.lviij.

Gillis Verdickt.

Figure 8.1. The Reformed martyrology. Typographical unity knits together the modern martyrs and the saints of the early church.

to rely on the extended web of Genevan connections to bring him information.[40]

Both the French and the English martyrologies took shape as enormous folio compilations of essentially contemporary material. Events that were so fresh, and personally touched those involved in the projects, obviously dominated the process of composition. Neither had yet achieved the harmonious synergy of contemporary events with the Christian heritage of the saints through all the ages – except in so far as these contemporary narratives were carefully patterned on the narratives of the early Christian martyrs. The first to offer a presentation that explicitly tied contemporary events into a narrative that flowed from the early church to the present was the least known of the Reformed martyrologies, the Dutch compilation of Adriaen van Haemstede. Van Haemstede was a minister in Antwerp, and present at a number of the executions he recorded; in fact his decision to embark on a provocative public preaching campaign may well have provoked the clampdown that saw a number of his congregation taken up and executed.[41] Van Haemstede escaped to Emden, where he set about completing his work. The result was a largely unknown literary masterpiece: a complete history of Christian martyrdom going back to the first Christian century. Inspecting one of the few surviving copies of the rare first edition (1559), one notes an especially strong visual symbolism in the organization of the text. A bold Roman type picks out the names of those treated in the text; progress through the pages then unites the fathers of the church – Stephen and the apostles, the mediaeval witnesses, with the humble saints of Brussels and Bruges: men like Adriaen de Schilder and Gilles Verdickt. The extensive use of contemporary documents, particularly the Confession of Faith presented by the victims to their examiners, also serves a pedagogic purpose. These become a form of catechism, in much the way that the accounts of events at the stake evoke a model of Christian dying for readers who not inconceivably might one day find themselves in a similar plight.

Van Haemstede's example was taken up in subsequent editions by Foxe and Crespin, both of whom build into the later definitive editions of their works an account of the first Christian centuries.[42] All the martyrologists also plunder each other's texts for examples that broaden their accounts of contemporary witnesses outside narrow national

---

[40] Jean-François Gilmont, *Jean Crespin. Un éditeur réformé du XVIe siècle* (Geneva, 1981).

[41] A.J. Jelsma, *Adriaan van Haemstede en zijn martelaarsboek* (The Hague, 1970).

[42] Andrew Pettegree, 'Haemstede and Foxe', in Loades, *John Foxe and the English Reformation*, pp. 278–94.

boundaries.[43] It is a critical step in building a sense of a church that extends to all of common faith in different European nations.

The same sense of a common identity can be observed in one of the strangest enterprises of Protestant self-identification, calendar revision. At one level, the evangelical repudiation of Catholic feast days and festivals was deadly serious, if not always popular. Protestant cities swiftly stripped from the annual round all public holidays associated with the now discredited saints: a reform which greatly increased the burdens laid on the working population, and greatly reduced their opportunities for communal entertainment. The great public dramas of Lutheran Germany might have been intended in some way to compensate for these gaps in the festive year; the Calvinist offering of the mid-week catechism service did not have the same allure.

Nothing daunted, the leaders of the Reformed churches progressed from the cleansing of the Catholic calendar to the promotion of a new Reformed calendar. The ministers of Geneva formed the vanguard of this movement, devising a scheme of new commemorations to take the place of the old saints' days in the calendars published in the popular almanacs. The days of commemoration now marked key events taken from a miscellany of historical (even classical) events, interspersed with the marking of critical moments in the unfolding of the new Protestant movement. Thus January noted the circumcision of Christ, Nebuchadnezzar's siege of Jerusalem (10th), and the conversion of St Paul; but also that on 24 January the Emperor Caligula had been assassinated, and the Duke of Somerset executed in London in 1552. On 18 February the calendar called attention to the fact that on this historically busy day the Romans celebrated the festival of fools, Noah sent out the dove that brought back the olive branch, and Martin Luther died in 1546.[44]

The Genevan calendar made scarcely any impact outside the French Calvinist communities, but it was not unique. In Germany, the year 1559 witnessed the publication of Golywurm's *Kirchen Calendar,* a more tightly focused collection of thirteen pre-Reformation and forty-nine post-Reformation martyrs. The most controversial and most scathingly treated of these alternative calendars was that published by John Foxe as part of the 1563 *Book of Martyrs.* Foxe's calendar adopted a more traditional structure, in that it kept the twenty fixed festivals of the church year that in England had survived the Protestant revisions of

[43] Watson, 'Jean Crespin', ch. 6. Pettegree, 'Haemstede and Foxe'.
[44] Eugénie Droz, 'Le calendrier genevois, agent de la propagande', in her *Chemins de l'hérésie. Textes et documents* (4 vols., Geneva, 1971), vol. II, pp. 433–56.

the church year.[45] The spaces between the ancient saints' days were filled with the names of the recent Protestant martyrs: Cranmer, Ridley and Latimer, but also more obscure individuals. In December there appeared the names of William Tracy, 'a scholer', 'a Jew' and 'Two Gray friars'. The calendar was rescued from this rather baffling parochialism by commemorations for continental reformers such as Melanchthon, Bucer and Peter Martyr. Jan Hus and Jerome of Prague were also found space, and the English Lollards were well represented.

For all the generous variety of the new commemorations, the calendar was scathingly received. The Catholic critic Harpesfield mocked Foxe as the new Pope for his energetic appropriation of the right to create new feasts; ominously, few of the Protestant admirers of the book rushed to the calendar's defence. Foxe was forced to argue, rather lamely, that the calendar had only ever been intended as a sort of index: 'for no other purpose, but to serve the use only of the reader, instead of a table, shewing the yere and moneth of every martyr'.[46] For the edition of 1570 he did indeed replace it with a more conventional index.

This did not end Protestant attempts to devise a new cleansed system of commemorations; but this was not something that could easily be imposed on a population for which the old festivals were freighted with diverse associations of far more than religious significance. In the last resort the most culturally significant Protestant involvement in the re-shaping of the calendar would come not through their own initiative but in resistance to Catholic calendar reform. The need for such a reform was widely acknowledged. While the Roman reordering of the calendar year had served Christendom well (it was the Emperor Augustus who had finally fixed the names of the months and their lengths), it was by the sixteenth century common knowledge that the calendar year had drifted away from the true seasons. The error – the difference of the true summer from the calendar date – was now of the very significant order of eleven days. But how should this drift be corrected? Various papal commissions grappled with the problem, before the matter was finally taken in hand by Gregory XIII in 1581. For decades theologians had wrestled with the technically difficult and theologically charged issue of determining the true astronomical year, and by now they had both their measurements and a solution. On 1 March 1582 Gregory signed the Bull

[45] Damian Nussbaum, 'Reviling the Saints or Reforming the Calendar? John Foxe and his "kalendar" of Martyrs', in Susan Wabuda and Caroline Litzenberger (eds.), *Belief and Practice in Reformation England* (Aldershot, St Andrews Studies in Reformation History, 1998), pp. 113–36.
[46] Ibid., p. 118.

proclaiming the new Gregorian calendar: at midnight on 4 October the calendar year would leap forward to 15 October.

The effect was, to say the least, traumatic. Europe's Catholic countries by and large fell into line: Spain, Portugal and the Italian states on the specified day, France and Flanders at the end of the year. Bavaria and the Austrian lands converted in 1583, as did Würzberg, Münster and Mainz (though each dropped a different set of ten days). But for Protestant states the Gregorian calendar was just one further example of papal arrogance and power. In the German city of Frankfurt people rioted against the Pope and mathematicians. Throughout Europe Protestant states generally rejected the reform (as did the Eastern Orthodox).[47] For over a century Protestant and Catholic Europe would march to a different time.

It is hard to think of a way in which the separation of Catholic and Protestant Europe could have been more forcefully evoked. Not only were these two separate religious worlds: they also kept to a different time. A journey from Catholic Regensburg to Protestant Nuremberg, 70 kilometres along the road, took one not only into a different state, but a different time. One could set off on 1 January and arrive on 21 December the previous year. It says a great deal for the intensity of religious passions that these absurdities were not resolved for the best part of two hundred years. England was the last major Protestant state to adopt the Gregorian calendar, in 1752.

The ill-starred attempts to create a new Protestant church year offer an important lesson: that new festivals of commemoration and remembrance could not be imposed, but could only emerge organically, with the passage of years. In England this process can be observed progressively through the reign of Elizabeth, with a pronounced increase in tempo in the last decade of the reign, after the outbreak of war with Spain. A significant step was the decision to encourage prayers and festivities on 17 November, the anniversary of the queen's accession. It proved a shrewd and popular choice, developing into a national annual celebration, marked by the ringing of church bells and other civic festivities.[48] Crownation day celebrations are recorded in different parts of England from the mid-1570s, but the most fervent honouring of the anniversary is exhibited when the Elizabethan heritage seemed under

---

[47] The exception being the northern Netherlands, where the Gregorian calendar was introduced by stages, first in Brabant, Zealand and Holland between 1582 and 1583. Groningen also made the change, but then reverted to the Julian calendar in 1594; other provinces held out until 1700/1.

[48] David Cressy, *Bonfires and Bells. National Memory and the Protestant Calendar in Elizabethan and Stuart England* (London, 1989), pp. 50 ff.

threat, after the Armada, and into the seventeenth century. The Armada itself set off a fanfare of celebratory bonfires, sermons and commemorative medals. Anniversary commemorations were somewhat inhibited by the absence of a specific day when the long campaign could most appropriately be marked, a deficiency repaired in 1605 by the discovery of the Gunpowder Plot on 5 November. This second example of Catholic malignancy and perfidy provided a perfect opportunity to remember the earlier example of God's providential protection. Protestant England had acquired a second November festival to inspire national reflection on the extraordinary gifts bestowed by a merciful God on a nation blessed, and on the memory of a blessed queen. The evocation of this increasingly idealized past became a useful partisan weapon in the years leading to the outbreak of the Civil War. For an age used to taking the temperature of common opinion by observation of the symbolism of public display, the vigour or otherwise of these celebrations spoke volumes. The dutiful ringing for Charles's marriage to Henrietta Maria in 1625 made a sobering contrast to the triumphant peals in celebration of his return from Spain in 1623 *without* a Catholic bride. There were renewed celebrations in 1628 when Charles accepted the Petition of Right.[49]

These public celebrations are a fitting climax to our survey of an emerging Protestant identity. This identity was many-sided. It could be narrow in focus, exclusive and limited, when the godly sought tangible expression for their own hopes of election. This exclusive and enclosed solidarity created tensions, as this process of definition inevitably involved impugning the religious experience of those not of the brotherhood. But the creation of a new Protestant identity did not ultimately bypass those for whom the strenuous exertions of the hotter Gospellers were uncongenial, or too demanding. This broader, more inclusive Protestant identity placed less emphasis on doctrinal precision or personal theological education. It evoked a sense of common heritage that drew together the martyrs of the ages, and fellow believers in other nations. It was incubated in an increasingly comprehensive Protestant culture that reached into every aspect of life: the school, the home, the everyday commerce of sociability. And it was at its most potent when the Protestant cause seemed most under threat, particularly if that threat was part of the dark danger of an international Catholic conspiracy.

[49] Ibid., pp. 76, 93–109.

9 The culture of belonging

We began this book by emphasizing that the decision to adhere to the new evangelical teaching was often painful, and pregnant with consequences. It meant breaking or reordering a whole web of associations and loyalties, to family, friends, workmates and even the local state power. It could mean separating oneself from comfortable regimes and familiar practices; it called into question the validity of customs practised with relish for a whole lifetime, even for generations. Sometimes the Reformation demanded an impossible choice between conflicting loyalties. Kristen Neuschel has offered an evocative picture of the dilemma posed to the French nobility who owed fealty to the leader of the Huguenot party, Louis de Condé, at the beginning of the Religious Wars. Many were devoutly committed to their Catholic faith; but all other accustomed social tradition urged the precedence of a duty of loyalty to their sworn lord. Inevitably different families, or different members of the same family, resolved these difficulties in contrasting ways. When Condé emerged as leader of the insurgent Huguenot party, some sent their excuses or boldly proclaimed a higher duty to crown and religion. Others dutifully gathered behind Condé's standard at Orleans.[1] Similar unpalatable choices faced thousands of men and women wherever the evangelical message was heard and became embedded in the local culture; many, even among those who headed the call to adhere to the new confessions, did so with grave misgivings and very mixed emotions.

The challenge of the Gospel was therefore for many of Europe's citizens hardly the elevating and uplifting experience that the reformers had anticipated. The process of separation from much that was familiar – family, friends, workmates and even home – was a profoundly alienating experience; little wonder that it generated bitterness and anger. This anger is most evident in young evangelical movements: the German and

[1] Kristen B. Neuschel, *Word of Honor: Interpreting Noble Culture in Sixteenth-Century France* (Ithaca, N.Y., 1989).

Swiss churches in the first evangelical generation, and the Calvinist churches of the 1560s. It found its most tangible expression in iconoclasm, as citizens found catharsis for their rejection of the familiar in the wanton destruction of all that the churches of their upbringing held most precious. It was a richly symbolic rite of separation from a religion by which many now felt they had been 'duped': at moments of decision or heightened political tension Protestants turned on the statues and pictures of the Catholic devotion with a previously unimaginable fury.[2]

For others the decision to repudiate the old church was eased by an apocalyptic sense of urgency: a sense that these years of social turmoil heralded the final resolution anticipated in the book of Revelation. This, it is now proposed, was a leading feature of Luther's preaching of redemption and repentance, and particularly powerful in the febrile atmosphere of Germany in the 1520s.[3] But, in fact, this sense of eschatological urgency seems to have been a relatively constant feature of the whole Reformation century; certainly it has been argued, in different contexts, for virtually every significant decade of evangelical change for the different parts of Europe.[4] Perhaps the truth is that our sixteenth-century forebears always had a greatly enhanced sense of the fragility of the human condition, and this inevitably added urgency to any situation where the fundamentals of belief and religious practice were called into question.[5]

In this age of endeavour, the urgent tone of conflict and the call for activism were best conveyed by the oral means of articulating the new teachings: by preaching and by song. Song also proved an extremely effective vehicle for the ridicule that was an essential feature of all sixteenth-century decision making that involved a measure of public participation. Even for those who could not understand the theological principles that demanded such drastic action against the current church fabric, the simpler ancillary messages – the contempt for the church hierarchy, the reviling of the idle parasitical priesthood – were easily expressed in songs.[6] Singing also encapsulated the spirit of communal

---

[2] Solange Deyon and Alain Lottin, *Les casseurs de l'été 1566. L'iconoclasme dans le Nord* (Westhoek, 1986). Natalie Zemon Davis, 'The Rites of Violence', in her *Society and Culture in Early Modern France* (London, 1975), pp. 152–87.

[3] Oberman, *Luther.*

[4] Denis Crouzet, *Les guerriers de Dieu: La violence au temps des troubles de religion, vers 1525 – vers 1610* (2 vols., Paris, 1990). Norman Jones, *The Birth of Elizabethan England. England in the 1560s* (Oxford, 1993).

[5] Bruce Gordon and Peter Marshall, *The Place of the Dead. Death and Remembrance in Late Mediaeval and Early Modern Europe* (Cambridge, 2000).

[6] On the phenomenon of anticlericalism see especially now Peter A. Dykema and Heiko A. Oberman, *Anticlericalism in Late Mediaeval and Early Modern Europe* (Leiden, 1994).

activism that was so important a part of the moment of decision making, and almost all Reformation movements embraced such a moment.

There came a time, however, when the heat of battle gave way to more sober reflection; when the decision to adhere to the new confession, or remain with the old, was made. One could not be angry, and urgent, for ever. Now, as the rubble of the old was swept away, a mood of sober reflection filled the leaders of the new churches as they recognized the scale of the task that faced them. Now began the work of creating new loyalties and invoking new solidarities.

The extent to which the new Protestant churches succeeded or failed in this endeavour has been the subject of much scholarly debate. To some extent this has been misdirected by the gloomy reflections of the reformers themselves. For now, surveying both this literature of debate and the understanding of the Reformation process developed in this book, one can recognize an inevitable disjunction between what the reformers aimed for and the manner in which the process of church building worked. The reformers saw their task in terms of teaching, in inculcating the essentials, or even a more complex understanding of the core of belief. For without knowledge there could be no faith, and without faith there was no salvation. In this endeavour they expended enormous energy, in preaching, catechizing, writing, publishing and distributing numerous works of religious instruction; and finally in the nervous surveys of their population to gauge the effectiveness of this restless activism.[7]

Here they were destined for disappointment, for the kind of understanding promoted by the Protestant clergy had never stood at the centre of the religious experience of the people. Rather, the laity had built their religious life round a culture of belonging: rich, complex and active. The essentials of faith were mediated – or possibly only inferred – around the constant enactment of the religious life as sharing: a parish religion, a civic culture, a familial experience embracing generations past.[8]

In order to succeed, the Reformation had to replace institutions and associations damned by evangelical criticism with a new complex of loved, lived solidarities. This was easiest when the process of evangelization allowed the conversion of old institutions to serve the new purpose. In some parts of Europe the parish church was simply accommodated to

---

[7] The classic presentation of visitation records is Strauss, *Luther's House of Learning*. For the debate inspired by Strauss's book and his response, see also Strauss, 'The Reformation and its Public in an Age of Orthodoxy', pp. 194–214. C.S. Dixon, *The Reformation and Rural Society. The Parishes of Brandenburg-Ansbach-Kulmbach, 1528–1603* (Cambridge, 1996).

[8] Duffy, *The Stripping of the Altars*.

the new worship, though seldom without cost to the dignity of the old Mass priest if he reappeared in the new guise of a Protestant minister. Sometimes an old institution could become the vehicle for the new evangelical scepticism. We have observed the evangelical appropriation of the Dutch Chambers of Rhetoric, and the renewed Protestant tradition of biblical drama. Communities deprived of the much loved passion plays were offered an immediate alternative: not perhaps one infused with the festive values of carnival to quite the same extent as the old mysteries, but still a powerful evocation of communal values. Communities could still stand, shoulder to shoulder, in shared recreation.

To a modern way of thinking, perhaps the most uncomfortable aspect of the argument presented here has been the frequent and generally positive evocation of collective action: the power of the crowd. To modern sensibilities the crowd is an instrument of irrationality and anarchy: the antithesis of the cool rationality of decision making which we envisage in idealized form as an essential attribute of our personal sovereignty. Hence the reverence with which we regard the secret ballot, and the overwhelmingly negative associations of mass activism, from the French Revolution to the rallies of the twentieth-century totalitarian states.[9]

The early modern world had a different, if still complex, perception of the crowd. The fear of disorder was still very real, but crowds gathered too in ceremonies of affirmation: for preaching or religious processions; to greet new rulers when they made their ceremonial entry; to witness a public execution – a ceremonial and often very solemn expulsion from the community.

The reformers recognized that the call for religious renewal represented a challenge to many communal values: hence the need to create a counter-community. This was the power of the evangelical sermon, a powerful demonstration of a new, evolving community. This was also why demonstrations at executions were so threatening, because if the crowd would no longer affirm the justice of the proceedings, however savage, then ultimately they could not continue, for the local magistrates had little authority if they lost the confidence of the community.[10]

---

[9] George Rudé, *The Crowd in the French Revolution* (Oxford, 1957). Charles Mackay, *Extraordinary Popular Delusions and the Madness of Crowds* (Amsterdam, 1845). Gustave Le Bon, *The Crowd: A Study of the Popular Mind* (Mineola, N.Y., 2002). For the beginnings of a spirited counter-argument see James Surowiecki, *The Wisdom of Crowds* (New York, 2004).

[10] David Nicholls, 'The Theatre of Martyrdom in the French Reformation', *Past and Present*, 121 (1988), pp. 49–73.

The reformers grew adept at manipulating symbols by which supporters expressed their loyalty to new communities of protest or belief. In
the Reformation world the symbols of old religious allegiance – such as
pilgrims' tokens – were reworked and reapplied. A much understudied
aspect of the sixteenth-century evangelical movement is the use of such
badges of belonging. The Protestant movement discovered the power of
such totems remarkably early, not least in the Lutheran mining town of
Joachimsthal, where abundant supplies of precious metals encouraged a
precocious and multi-faceted medal culture.[11] The earliest sixteenth-
century miners celebrated their good fortune with stamped silver impressions of traditional religious subjects, such as the Virgin and saints.
These resembled very closely the small tokens bought by pilgrims to
mark the end of their journey to Rome, Compostella or St Andrews. The
citizens of Joachimsthal were also much addicted to plague medals: a
design with a serpent on one side and the crucified Christ on the other.
By coincidence the output of the mines of Joachimsthal peaked in the
1530s, at precisely the time when the town consolidated its turn to
Lutheranism. The new circumstances inspired new medal traditions:
portraits of Luther, Hus and the Saxon Electors, or representations of
biblical themes especially beloved in the new Protestant churches, such
as Abraham and Isaac, or Christ with the Samaritan woman.

The circumstances of Joachimsthal were obviously very particular, but
the passion for totemic badges of belonging proved powerful in several of
the new Protestant churches. These found their most powerful manifestation in the Dutch Revolt, from the point at which the dissident
nobility, responding to a widely reported contemptuous remark by an
advisor of the regent, Margaret of Parma, crafted insignia of Beggars to
symbolize their new brotherhood. Here they subverted the established
esteem of the Order of the Golden Fleece, the highest honour bestowed
by the Habsburgs on the loyal Netherlandish nobility. It was both a
magnificent gesture of defiance and a symbolic changing of the guard.[12]

The Beggars' protest inaugurated a long tradition of the minting of
such tokens by the insurgent Dutch. As the revolt progressed, the
symbolism became more ornate, the medals larger and more formal.
They became more and more reminiscent of the Renaissance portrait
medals exchanged between the fifteenth-century literati, and now owned
in large numbers by major museum collections. From the Netherlands

[11] V. Katz, *Die erzgebirgische Prägemedaille des XVI. Jahrhunderts* (Prague, 1932).
[12] H.F.K. van Nierop, 'A Beggars' Banquet: The Compromise of the Nobility and the
Politics of Inversion', *European History Quarterly*, 21 (1991), pp. 419–43. Duke,
'Dissident Propaganda', pp. 122–23.

the practice spread to England, where triumphant medals were struck to celebrate the failure of the Armada.[13]

The Reformation medal tradition epitomized many aspects of the complex process we have described in this book. It provided a tangible token of the culture of belonging, a culture developed in another way by the widespread use in the Reformed churches of communion tokens, small coins stamped with the symbol of the local church and distributed to those permitted to take the Eucharist.[14] It defiantly appropriated the attributes of authority by minting coins (a closely guarded attribute of power). It was both visual and tangible: it allowed the encoding of complex messages, but its primary function was performed by possession, as a badge of belonging.

This, we have argued, was also the function of much of the visual culture of the Reformation. This was the way in which the woodcut functioned in the chain of communication. The woodcut could not teach or explain. It could amuse or provoke, but only among those who already understood the frames of reference. Its wider social impact was as a badge of identity, a tangible symbol of allegiance for those who wished to affirm the general programme of the Gospel preachers. Pamphlets, we have argued, could also function in this way. In this respect the Catholic authorities were right to regard mere possession, rather than reading or understanding, as the essential heresy.[15] The potent power of the woodcut image as badge was most systematically exploited in the widespread use made of printers' devices. In an age where the possession of forbidden books was inevitably perilous, these served as an encoded symbol of the likely contents and confessional allegiance of a book that might otherwise exercise discretion over proclaiming authorship and place of publication. It is highly significant that this age – the period of mass publication before mass literacy – made such extensive use of the printer's device.

Human beings are gregarious. We crave belonging and we fear isolation. Anyone who has heard young children unburden themselves about playground quarrels, the constant shifting of inclusion and exclusion, will feel again the power of the crowd and the fear of being ostracized that runs so deep in us all. Even in an age like our own, which

---

[13] A fine selection of medals commemorating the defeat of the Spanish Armada is available via the website of the National Maritime Museum, www.nmm.ac.uk. For another famous victory that inspired an outpouring of numismatic celebration, see P. Ch. Robert, *Souvenirs numismatiques du siège de 1552* (Metz, 1852).

[14] H. Gelin, *Le méreau dans les églises réformées de France et plus particulièrement dans celles de Poitou* (Saint-Maixent, 1891).

[15] Monter, *Judging the French Reformation*.

so values individual choice, the desire to be part of a group exercises a strong contrary attraction. In the sixteenth century the creation of new solidarities was an essential step in the process of assimilating the Reformation movement. The Reformation posed a new and often challenging dialectic, and this extended to parts of social life that in the pre-Reformation church had usually marched in harmony: family and kin; parish and community; faith and nation. Now these could be in conflict; painful choices were to be made. It was the great achievement of the Reformation century that by its end many of these critical aspects of a whole life had been brought back into harmony; and that many people in parts of Protestant Europe had found comfort in the new familiarity of Protestant living.

Bibliography

Adams, Alison and Harper, Anthony J., (eds.), *The Emblem in Renaissance and Baroque Europe* (Leiden, 1992).

Adams, Simon, 'Favourites and Factions at the Elizabethan Court', and 'A Godly Peer? Leicester and the Puritans', in his *Leicester and the Court. Essays on Elizabethan Politics* (Manchester, 2002).

Adams, Simon and Greengrass, Mark (eds.), Jean Malliet, 'Memoires et procedures de ma negociation en Angleterre', in Ian Archer (ed.), *Religious, Society and Politics in Sixteenth Century England* (Cambridge, Camden Society, 5th ser., 22, 2003), pp. 137–96.

Andersson, Christiane, 'Popular Imagery in German Reformation Broadsheets', in Gerald P. Tyson and Sylvia S. Wagonheim, *Print and Culture in the Renaissance. Essays on the Advent of Printing in Europe* (Newark, N.J., 1986), pp. 120–50.

Armstrong, Elizabeth, *Before Copyright: the French Book-Privilege System 1498–1526* (Cambridge, 1990).

Atkinson, James, *Martin Luther and the Birth of Protestantism* (London, 1968).

Aurich, Frank, *Die Anfänge des Buchdrucks in Dresden. Die Emserpresse, 1524–1526* (Dresden, 2000).

Bacon, Thomas I., *Martin Luther and the Drama* (Amsterdam, 1976).

Bakhuizen van den Brink, J. N., and Dankbaar, W. F., (eds.), *Documenta Reformatoria* (Kampen, 1960).

Bax, W., *Het Protestantism in Luik en Maastricht, 1505–1557* (The Hague, 1937).

Baxandall, Michael, *The Limewood Sculptors of Renaissance Germany* (New Haven, Conn., 1980).

Benedict, Philip, *Rouen during the Wars of Religion* (Cambridge, 1981).

'Of Marmites and Martyrs. Images and Polemics in the Wars of Religion', in *The French Renaissance in Prints from the Bibliothèque Nationale de France* (Los Angeles, 1995), pp. 108–37.

Benesch, Otto, *German Painting from Dürer to Holbein* (Geneva, 1966).

Benzing, Josef, *Lutherbibliographie. Verzeichnis der gedruckten Schriften Martin Luthers bis zu dessen Tod* (Baden-Baden, 1966).

Berthail, Marie, *Les premiers graveurs français. Un art naissant: l'illustration du livre* (Nantes, 1986).

Berthoud, G., 'Les impressions genevoises de Jean Michel (1538–1544)', in J.-D. Candaux and B. Lescaze (eds.), *Cinq siècles d'imprimerie genevoise* (2 vols., Geneva, 1980), vol. I, pp. 55–88.

Bevington, David, 'Theatre as Holiday', in David L. Smith, Richard Strier and David Bevington (eds.), *The Theatrical City. Culture, Theatre and Politics in London, 1576–1649* (Cambridge, 1995).

Bèze, Théodore de, *Abraham sacrifiant. Tragedie françoise*. Critical edition with introduction and notes by K. Cameron, K. M. Hall and F. M. Higman (Geneva, 1967).

Blume, Friedrich, *Protestant Church Music: A History* (New York, 1974).

Boonen, Jacqueline, 'Verhalen van Israëls Ballingschap en Vrijheidsstrijd', in Christian Tümpel (ed.), *Het Oude Testament in de Schilderkunst van de Gouden Eeuw* (Amsterdam, 1991), pp. 106–21.

Bordier, Henri-Léonard, *Le chansonnier Huguenot du XVIe siècle* (reprint edn, Geneva, 1969).

Bosma, Jelle, 'Preaching in the Low Countries, 1450–1650', in Larissa Taylor (ed.), *Preachers and People in the Reformations and Early Modern Period* (Leiden, 2001).

Bostoen, Karl, 'Reformation, Counter-Reformation and Literary Propaganda in the Low Countries in the Sixteenth Century: The Case of Brother Cornelis', in N. Scott Amos, Andrew Pettegree and Henk van Nierop (eds.), *The Education of a Christian Society. Humanism and the Reformation in Britain and the Netherlands* (St Andrews Studies in Reformation History, Aldershot, 1999), pp. 164–92.

Brady, Thomas, *Turning Swiss: Cities and Empire, 1450–1550* (Cambridge, 1985).

Bremme, Hans Joachim, *Buchdrucker und Buchhändler zur Zeit des Glaubens-kämpfe* (Geneva, 1969).

Broadhead, Philip, 'The Contribution of Hans Sachs to the Debate on the Reformation in Nuremberg: A Study of the Religious Dialogues of 1524', in Robert Aylett and Peter Skrine (eds.), *Hans Sachs and Folk Theatre in the Late Middle Ages* (Lewiston, N.Y., 1995), pp. 43–62.

Broomhall, Susan, *Women and the Book Trade in Sixteenth-Century France* (Aldershot, 2002).

Brown, Christopher Boyd, 'Singing the Gospel: Lutheran Hymns and the Success of the Reformation in Joachimsthal' (Harvard University, Ph.D. dissertation, 2001). Harvard University Press, forthcoming.

Bruin, Martine de, 'Het Wilhelmus tijdens de Republiek', in Louis Peter Grijp, *Nationale hymnen. Het Wilhelmus en zijn buren* (Nijmegen and Amsterdam, 1998), pp. 16–42.

Bruin, Martine de, 'Geuzen- en antigeuzenliederen', in L. P. Grijp (ed.), *Een muziekgeschiedenis der Nederlanden* (Amsterdam, 2001), pp. 174–80.

Burke, Peter, *Popular Culture in Early Modern Europe* (London, 1978).

Calderwood, David, *The History of the Kirk of Scotland*, ed., from the original manuscript preserved in the British Museum, by Thomas Thomson (Edinburgh: Printed for the Woodrow Society, 1842–9).

Campi, Emidio, 'Bullinger's Early Political and Theological Thought: *Brutus Tigurinus*', in Bruce Gordon and Emidio Campi (eds.), *Architect of Reformation. An Introduction to Heinrich Bullinger, 1504–1575* (Grand Rapids, Mich., 2004), pp. 181–99.

Campi, Emidio (ed.), *Heinrich Bullinger und Seine Zeit, Zwingliana*, 31 (2004).

Cargill Thompson, W. D. J., 'The Problem of Luther's "Tower Experience" and its Place in his Intellectual Development', in his *Studies in the Reformation. Luther to Hooker* (London, 1980), pp. 60–81.

Cassidy, John, *Dot.con. The Greatest Story Ever Sold* (London, 2002).

Chambers, B. T., *Bibliography of French Bibles. Fifteenth- and Sixteenth-Century French-Language Editions of the Scriptures* (Geneva, 1983).

Chareyre, Philippe, '"The Great Difficulties One Must Bear to Follow Jesus Christ": Morality at Sixteenth-century Nîmes', in Raymond A. Mentzer (ed.), *Sin and the Calvinists. Moral Control and the Consistory in the Reformed Tradition* (Kirksville, Mo., 1994).

Chrisman, Miriam Usher, *Strasbourg and the Reform. A Study in the Process of Change* (New Haven, Conn., 1967).

'From Polemic to Propaganda', *Archiv für Reformationsgeschichte*, 73 (1982), pp. 175–96.

Christensen, Carl C., *Art and the Reformation in Germany* (Athens, Ohio, 1979).

Princes and Propaganda: Electoral Saxon Art of the Reformation (Kirksville, Mo., 1992).

Clark, Sandra, *The Elizabethan Pamphleteers. Popular Moralistic Pamphlets, 1580–1640* (London, 1983).

Claus, Helmut, 'Wittenberg als Druckerstadt', in *Recht lehren ist nicht die geringste Wohltat. Wittenberg als Bildungszentrum, 1502–2002* (Wittenberg, 2002), pp. 75–201.

Cole, Richard G., 'Pamphlet Woodcuts in the Communication Process of Reformation Germany', in Kyle C. Sessions and Philip N. Bebb (eds.), *Pietas et Societas. New Trends in Reformation Social History* (Kirksville, Mo., 1985), pp. 103–21.

Coleman, Joyce, *Public Reading and the Reading Public in Late Mediaeval England and France* (Cambridge, 1996).

Collinson, Patrick, *The Elizabethan Puritan Movement* (London, 1967).

English Puritanism (London, Historical Association pamphlet, 1983).

The Birthpangs of Protestant England. Religious and Cultural Change in the Sixteenth and Seventeenth Centuries (London, 1988).

Conner, Philip, *Huguenot Heartland. Montauban and Southern French Calvinism during the Wars of Religion* (Aldershot, St Andrews Studies in Reformation History, 2002).

Cooke, Charles L., 'Calvin's Illnesses and their Relation to Christian Vocation', in Timothy George (ed.), *John Calvin and the Church. A Prism of Reform* (Louisville, Ky., 1990).

Cranach im Detail, Buchschmuck Lucas Cranachs des Älteren und seiner Werkstatt (Wittenberg, 1994).

Cressy, David, *Bonfires and Bells. National Memory and the Protestant Calendar in Elizabethan and Stuart England* (London, 1989).

Crick, Julia and Walsham, Alexandra (eds.), *The Uses of Script and Print, 1300–1700* (Cambridge, 2004).

Cross, Claire, *The Puritan Earl. The Life of Henry Hastings, Third Earl of Huntingdon, 1536–1595* (London, 1966).

Crouzet, Denis, *Les guerriers de Dieu: La violence au temps des troubles de religion, vers 1525 – vers 1610* (2 vols., Paris, 1990).

Dauven-Knippenberg, Carla van, 'Ein Anfang ohne Ende: Einführendes zur Frage nach dem Verhältnis zwischen Predigt und geistlichem Schauspiel des Mittelalters', in Ulrich Mehler and Anton H. Touber (eds.), *Mittelalterliches Schauspiel* (Amsterdam, 1994), pp. 143–60.

Davies, Norman, *Europe: A History* (London, 1997).

Davis, Martin, *Aldus Manutius. Printer and Publisher of Renaissance Venice* (London, 1995).

Davis, Natalie Zemon, 'The Rites of Violence', in her *Society and Culture in Early Modern France* (London, 1975), pp. 152–87.

D'Avray, David, *Medieval Marriage Sermons. Mass Communication in a Culture without Print* (Oxford, 2001).

'Printing, Mass Communication and Religious Reformation: The Middle Ages and After', in Julia Crick and Alexandra Walsham (eds.), *The Uses of Script and Print, 1300–1700* (Cambridge, 2004), pp. 50–70.

Decavele, Johann, *De dageraad van de Reformatie in Vlaanderen, 1520–1565* (Brussels, 1975).

Delano-Smith, Catherine and Ingram, Elizabeth Morley, *Maps in Bibles, 1500–1600. An Illustrated Catalogue* (Geneva, 1991).

Desgraves, Louis, *Elie Gibier imprimeur à Orléans (1536–1588)* (Geneva, 1966).

Deyon, Solange and Lottin, Alain, *Les casseurs de l'été 1566. L'iconoclasme dans le Nord* (Westhoek, 1986).

Dickens, A. G., and Tonkin, John, *The Reformation in Historical Thought* (Oxford, 1985).

Diefendorf, Barbara, *Beneath the Cross. Catholics and Huguenots in Sixteenth-Century Paris* (New York, 1991).

Dixon, C. Scott, *The Reformation and Rural Society. The Parishes of Brandenburg-Ansbach-Kulmbach, 1528–1603* (Cambridge, 1996).

Droz, Eugénie, 'Antoine Vincent. La propagande protestante par le psautier', in G. Berthoud (ed.), *Aspects de la propagande religieuse* (Geneva, 1957), pp. 276–93.

'Le calendrier genevois, agent de la propagande', in her *Chemins de l'hérésie. Textes et documents* (4 vols., Geneva, 1971), vol. II, pp. 433–56.

Duffy, Eamon, *The Stripping of the Altars: Traditional Religion in England, c.1400–c.1580* (New Haven, Conn., 1992).

Duke, Alastair, 'Dissident Propaganda and Political Organisation at the Outbreak of the Revolt of the Netherlands', in Philip Benedict, Guido Marnef, Henk van Nierop and Marc Venard (eds.), *Reformation, Revolt and Civil War in France and the Netherlands, 1555–1585* (Amsterdam, 1999), pp. 115–32.

'Posters, Pamphlets and Printers. The Ways and Means of Disseminating Dissident Opinion on the Eve of the Dutch Revolt', *Dutch Crossing, 27* (2003), pp. 23–44.

Duke, Alastair, Lewis, Gillian and Pettegree, Andrew, *Calvinism in Europe, 1540–1610. A Collection of Documents* (Manchester, 1992).

Dykema, Peter A., and Oberman, Heiko A., *Anticlericalism in Late Mediaeval and Early Modern Europe* (Leiden, 1994).

Edwards, Mark U. Jr, *Printing, Propaganda and Martin Luther* (Berkeley, Calif., 1994).

Ehrstine, Glenn, *Theater, Culture and Community in Reformation Bern, 1523–1555* (Leiden, 2002).

Eire, Carlos, *The War Against the Idols* (Cambridge, 1986).

Eisenstein, Elizabeth, *The Printing Press as an Agent of Change* (2 vols., Cambridge, 1979).

Engammare, Max, 'Calvin Incognito in London: The Rediscovery in London of Sermons on Isaiah', *Proceedings of the Huguenot Society of London*, 26 (1996), pp. 453–62.

Eurich, S. Amanda, *The Economics of Power: The Private Finances of the House of Foix-Navarre-Albret during the Religious Wars* (Kirksville, Mo., 1993).

Evenhuis, R. B., *Ook dat was Amsterdam; de kerk der hervorming in de goude eeuw* (2 vols., Amsterdam, 1965–7).

Fenlon, Iain, *The Renaissance. From the 1470s to the End of the 16th Century* (Basingstoke, 1989).

Fleming, Gerald, 'On the Origins of the Passional Christi und Antichristi and Lucas Cranach the Elder's Contribution to Reformation Polemics in the Iconography of the Passional', *Gutenberg Jahrbuch* (1973), pp. 351–68.

Fletcher, H. George, *In Praise of Aldus Manutius. A Quincentenary Exhibition* (New York, 1995).

Flood, John, 'Lucas Cranach as Publisher', *German Life and Letters*, 48 (1995), pp. 241–63.

'The Book in Reformation Germany', in Jean-François Gilmont (ed.), *The Reformation and the Book* (Aldershot, St Andrews Studies in Reformation History, 1998), pp. 21–103.

'Martin Luther's Bible Translation in its German and International Context', in Richard Griffiths (ed.), *The Bible in the Renaissance* (Aldershot, St Andrews Studies in Reformation History, 2001), pp. 45–70.

Fontaine Verwey, H, de la, 'Meester Harman Schinckel, een Delftse boekdrukker van de 16de eeuw', *Oud Delft*, 3 (1964), pp. 5–78.

Ford, James Thomas, 'Preaching in the Reformed Tradition', in Larissa Taylor (ed.), *Preachers and People in the Reformations and Early Modern Period* (Leiden, 2001).

Forster, Marc, 'With or Without Confessionalization. Variations of Early Modern German Catholicism', *Journal of Ecclesiastical History*, 1 (1998), pp. 315–43.

Fox, Adam, *Oral and Literate Culture in England, 1500–1700* (Oxford, 2000).

Fox, John, *A Literary History of France. The Middle Ages* (London, 1974).

Fredericq, P., *Corpus documentorum haereticae pravitatis neerlandicae* (5 vols., Ghentand The Hague, 1889–1902).

Friedländer, Max J. and Rosenberg, Jakob, *Lucas Cranach* (New York, 1978).

Fudge, Thomas A., *The Magnificent Ride. The First Reformation in Hussite Bohemia* (Aldershot, St Andrews Studies in Reformation History, 1998).

Gagnebin, Bernard, 'L'histoire des manuscripts des sermons de Calvin', in Jean Calvin, *Sermons sur le Livre d'Esaïe, chapitres 13–29* (Supplementa Calviniana, II, Neukirchen, 1961), pp. xiv–xxviii.

Garside, Charles, *Zwingli and the Arts* (New Haven, Conn., 1966).

Geisberg, Max, *The German Single-Leaf Woodcut, 1500–1550*, rev. and ed. Walter L. Strauss (New York, 1974).

Gelin, H., *Le méreau dans les églises réformées de France et plus particulièrement dans celles de Poitou* (Saint-Maixent, 1891).

Gesetz und Genade, Cranach, Luther und die Bilder (Torgau, 1994).

Gildersleeve, Virginia, *Government Regulation of the Elizabethan Drama* (New York, 1908).

Gilmont, Jean-François, *Bibliographie des éditions de Jean Crespin, 1550–1572* (2 vols., Verviers, 1981).

Jean Crespin. Un éditeur réformé du XVIe siècle (Geneva, 1981).

'La première diffusion des Mémoires de Condé par Eloi Gibier en 1562–1563', in P. Aquilon and H.-J. Martin (eds.), *Le livre dans l'Europe de la Renaissance. Actes du XXVIIIe Colloque international d'études humanistes de Tours* (Paris, 1988), pp. 58–70.

'Les martyrologes du XVIe siècle', in Silvana Seidel Menchi (ed.), *Ketzerverfolgung im 16. und frühen 17. Jahrhundert* (Wolfenbüttel, 1992).

Jean Calvin et le livre imprimé (Geneva, 1997).

(ed.), *The Reformation and the Book* (Aldershot, St Andrews Studies in Reformation History, 1998).

Le livre et ses secrets (Louvain-la-Neuve and Geneva, 2003).

Gilmont, Jean-François and Peter, Rudolphe, *Bibliotheca Calviniana. Les oeuvres de Jean Calvin publiées au XVIe siècle* (3 vols., Geneva, 1991–2000).

Gordon, Bruce, 'Preaching and the Reform of the Clergy in the Swiss Reformation', in Andrew Pettegree (ed.), *The Reformation of the Parishes. The Ministry and the Reformation in Town and Country* (Manchester, 1993), pp. 63–84.

'The Changing Face of Protestant History and Identity in the Sixteenth Century', in his *Protestant History and Identity in Sixteenth-Century Europe* (2 vols., Aldershot, St Andrews Studies in Reformation History, 1996), vol. I, pp. 1–23.

The Swiss Reformation (Manchester, 2002).

Gordon, Bruce and Campi, Emidio (eds.), *Architect of Reformation. An Introduction to Heinrich Bullinger, 1504–1575* (Grand Rapids, Mich., 2004).

Gordon, Bruce and Marshall, Peter, *The Place of the Dead. Death and Remembrance in Late Mediaeval and Early Modern Europe* (Cambridge, 2000).

Gould, Kevin, '"Vivre et mourir en la religion ancienne, romaine et catholique." Catholic Activism in South-West France' (University of Warwick, Ph.D. dissertation, 2003).

Green, Ian, *The Christian's ABC. Catechisms and Catechizing in England, c. 1530–1740* (Oxford, 1996).

Print and Protestantism in Early Modern England (Oxford, 2000).

Gregory, Brad S., *Salvation at Stake. Christian Martyrdom in Early Modern Europe* (Cambridge, Mass., 1999).

Grijp, Louis Peter, 'Van geuzenlied tot Gedenk-clanck', *De Zeventiende Eeuw*, 10 (1994), pp. 266–76.

Gurr, Andrew, *The Shakespearean Stage, 1574–1642* (Cambridge, 1970).

Playgoing in Shakespeare's London (Cambridge, 1987).

Haag, E., and E., *La France protestante: pièces justificatives* (reprint edn, Geneva, 1966).

Haigh, Christopher, 'Puritan Evangelism in the Reign of Elizabeth I', *English Historical Review*, 92 (1977), pp. 30–58.

English Reformations. Religion, Politics and Society under the Tudors (Oxford, 1993).

Hari, Robert, 'Les placards de 1534', in G. Berthoud (ed.), *Aspects de la propagande religieuse* (Geneva, 1957), pp. 79–142.

Hertel, Gustav (ed.), *Die Chroniken des niedersächsischen Städte: Magdeburg* (Leipzig, 1899).

Highley, Christopher and King, John N., *John Foxe and his World* (Aldershot, St Andrews Studies in Reformation History, 2002).

Histoire ecclésiastique des églises réformées au royaume de France (3 vols., Paris, 1883–9).

Higman, Francis, *Censorship and the Sorbonne* (Geneva, 1979).

'Calvin's Works in Translation', in Andrew Pettegree, Alastair Duke and Gillian Lewis (eds.), *Calvinism in Europe, 1540–1620* (Cambridge, 1994), pp. 82–99.

Piety and the People. Religious Printing in French, 1511–1551 (Aldershot, St Andrews Studies in Reformation History, 1996).

'French-Speaking Regions', in Jean-François Gilmont (ed.), *The Reformation and the Book* (Aldershot, St Andrews Studies in Reformation History, 1998), pp. 110–12.

'Les traductions françaises de Luther', in Jean-François Gilmont (ed.), *Palaestrina typographica* (Aubel, 1984), pp. 11–56, reprinted in his *Lire et découvrir. La circulation des idées au temps de la Réforme* (Geneva, 1998), pp. 200–32.

'Music', in Andrew Pettegree (ed.), *Reformation World* (London, 2001), pp. 491–504.

Hinds, Arthur M., *An Introduction to a History of Woodcut* (2 vols., New York, 1935).

Horst, Daniel, *Die opstad in Zwart-wit* (2 vols., University of Amsterdam, Ph.D. dissertation, 2000).

Huppert, George, *Public Schools in Renaissance France* (Chicago, 1984).

Ingram, Martin, *Church Courts, Sex and Marriage in England, 1570–1640* (Cambridge, 1987).

Jelsma A. J., *Adriaan van Haemstede en zijn martelaarsboek* (The Hague, 1970).

Jenny, Markus, *Zwinglis Stellung zur Musik im Gottesdienst* (Zurich, 1966).

Luthers geistliche Lieder und Kirchengesänge. Vollständige Neuedition in Ergänzung zu Band 35 der Weimarer Ausgabe (Cologne, 1985).

'Reformierte Kirchenmusik? Zwingli, Bullinger und die Folgen', in Heiko Oberman and GotFried Locher (eds.), *Reformiertes Erbe. Festschrift für Gottfried W. Locher, Zwingliana*, 19 (1991–2), pp. 187–205.

Johnston, A., 'Eclectic Reformation: Vernacular Evangelical Pamphlet Literature in the Dutch-Speaking Low Countries, 1520–1565' (University of Southampton, Ph.D. dissertation, 1986).

'Lutheranism in Disguise: the corte instruccye of Cornelis van der Heyden', *Nederlands archief voor Kerkgeschiedenis*, 68 (1988), pp. 23–9.

de Jong, Peter Y., 'Calvin's Contribution to Christian Education', *Calvin Theological Journal*, 2 (1967), pp. 162–201.

Jones, Norman, *The Birth of Elizabethan England. England in the 1560s* (Oxford, 1993).

Jostock, Ingeborg, 'La censure au quotidien: le contrôle de l'imprimerie à Genève, 1560–1600', in Andrew Pettegree, Paul Nelles and Philip Conner (eds.), *The Sixteenth Century French Religious Book* (Aldershot, St Andrews Studies in Reformation History, 2001), pp. 210–38.

Junghans, Helmar, *Wittenberg als Lutherstadt* (Göttingen, 1979).

Kapr, Albert, *Johann Gutenberg. The Man and his Invention* (Aldershot, 1996).

Karant-Nunn, Susan, 'What was Preached in German Cities in the Early Years of the Reformation? *Wildwuchs* versus Lutheran Unity', in Philip N. Bebb and Sherrin Marshall, *The Process of Change in Early Modern Europe* (Athens, Ohio, 1988), pp. 81–96.

The Reformation of Ritual. An Interpretation of Early Modern Germany (London, 1997).

Karant-Nunn, Susan C., and Wiesner-Hanks, Merry E., (eds.), *Luther on Women. A Sourcebook* (Cambridge, 2003).

Katz, V., *Die erzgebirgische Prägemedaille des XVI. Jahrhunderts* (Prague, 1932).

Kelley, Donald R., *François Hotman. A Revolutionary's Ordeal* (Princeton, N.J., 1973).

Kess, Alexandra, 'Johann Sleidan and the Protestant Vision of History' (University of St Andrews, Ph.D. dissertation, 2004).

King, John N., *English Reformation Literature. The Tudor Origins of the Protestant Tradition* (Princeton, N.J., 1982).

Koepplin, Dieter and Falk, Tilman, *Lukas Cranach. Gemälde – Zeichnungen – Druckgraphik* (Basle, 1974).

Kolb, Robert, *For All the Saints: Changing Perceptions of Martyrdom and Sainthood in the Lutheran Reformation* (Macon, Ga., 1987).

Kümin, Beat, 'Masses, Morris and Metrical Psalms: Music in the English Parish, c. 1400–1600', in Fiona Kisby, *Music and Musicians in Renaissance Cities and Towns* (Cambridge, 2001), pp. 70–81.

Leaver, Robin A., *'Goostly psalmes and spirituall songes'. English and Dutch Metrical Psalms from Coverdale to Utenhove, 1535–1566* (Oxford, 1991).

Luther's Works. American edition, ed. Jarislav Pelikan (54 vols., Philadelphia, 1955–86).

D. Martin Luthers Werke: Kritische Gesamtausgabe (68 vols., Weimar, 1883–1978).

Le Bon, Gustave, *The Crowd: A Study of the Popular Mind* (Mineola, N.Y., 2002).

Lefèvre, Louis Raymond (ed.), *Propos rustiques de Noël du Fail* (Paris, 1928).

Lesure, François (ed.), *Répertoire international des sources musicales. Recueils imprimés XVIe–XVIIe siècle* (Munich and Duisburg, 1960).

Loades, David (ed.), *John Foxe and the English Reformation* (Aldershot, St Andrews Studies in Reformation History, 1997).

Maag, Karin, *Seminary or University? The Genevan Academy and Reformed Higher Education, 1560–1620* (Aldershot, St Andrews Studies in Reformation History, 1995).

Mackay, Charles, *Extraordinary Popular Delusions and the Madness of Crowds* (Amsterdam, 1845).

MacCulloch, Diarmaid, *Reformations. Europe's House Divided, 1490–1700* (London, 2003).

McGrath, Alister E., *A Life of John Calvin* (Oxford, 1990).

Marsh, Christopher, 'The Sound of Print in Early Modern England: The Broadside Ballad as Song', in Julia Crick and Alexandra Walsham (eds.), *The Uses of Script and Print, 1300–1700* (Cambridge, 2004), pp. 171–90.

Matheson, Peter, *The Rhetoric of the Reformation* (Edinburgh, 1998).

Mentzer, Raymond A. Jr, *Blood and Belief. Family Survival and Confessional Identity among the Provincial Huguenot Nobility* (West Lafayette, Ind., 1994).

Meuser, Fred W., *Luther the Preacher* (Minneapolis, Minn., 1983).

Meyer, Christian, 'Le psautier huguenot: notes à propos de quelques éditions antérieures à son achèvement (1554–1561)', *Bulletin de la Société de l'Histoire du Protestantisme Français*, 130 (1984), pp. 87–95.

Michalski, Sergiusz, *The Reformation and the Visual Arts. The Protestant Image Question in Western and Eastern Europe* (London, 1993).

Moeller, Bernd, 'Was wurde in der Frühzeit des Reformation in den deutschen Städten gepredigt?', *Archiv für Reformationsgeschichte*, 75 (1984), pp. 176–93. Now in English as 'What was Preached in German Towns in the Early Reformation?', in C. Scott Dixon (ed.), *The German Reformation* (Oxford, 1999), pp. 36–52.

Monter, William, *Calvin's Geneva* (New York, 1967).

'Heresy Executions in Reformation Europe, 1520–1565', in Ole Peter Grell and Bob Scribner (eds.), *Tolerance and Intolerance in the European Reformation* (Cambridge, 1996), pp. 48–64.

Judging the French Reformation. Heresy Trials by Sixteenth-Century Parlements (Cambridge, Mass., 1999).

Moore, Helen (ed.), *Amadis de Gaule, Translated by Anthony Munday* (Aldershot, 2004).

Morrall, Andrew, *Jörg Breu the Elder. Art, Culture and Belief in Reformation Augsburg* (Aldershot, 2001).

Moxey, Keith, 'Festive Peasants and Social Order', in his *Peasants, Warriors and Wives. Popular Imagery in the Reformation* (Chicago, 1989), pp. 35–66.

Muir, Lynette R., *The Biblical Drama of Mediaeval Europe* (Cambridge, 1995).

Naphy, William, G., *Calvin and the Consolidation of the Genevan Reformation* (Manchester, 1994).

Nelles, Paul, 'Three Audiences for Religious Books in Sixteenth-Century France', in Andrew Pettegree, Paul Nelles and Philip Conner, *The Sixteenth Century French Religious Book* (Aldershot, St Andrews Studies in Reformation History, 2001), pp. 256–85.

Nettl, Paul, *Luther and Music* (Philadelphia, 1948).

Neumann, Bernd, *Geistliches Schauspiel in Zeugnis der Zeit. Zur Aufführung mittelalterlicher religiöser Dramen im deutschen Sprachgebiet* (2 vols., Munich, 1987).

Neuschel, Kristen B., *Word of Honor: Interpreting Noble Culture in Sixteenth-Century France* (Ithaca, N.Y., 1989).

Nicholls, David, 'The Theatre of Martyrdom in the French Reformation', *Past and Present*, 121 (1988), pp. 49–73.

Van Nierop, H. F. K., 'A Beggars' Banquet: The Compromise of the Nobility and the Politics of Inversion', *European History Quarterly*, 21 (1991), pp. 419–43.

Norman, Corrie, 'The Social History of Preaching: Italy', in Larissa Taylor (ed.), *Preachers and People in the Reformations and Early Modern Period* (Leiden and Brill, 2001).

Nussbaum, Damian, 'Reviling the Saints or Reforming the Calendar? John Foxe and his "kalendar" of Martyrs', in Susan Wabuda and Caroline Litzenberger (eds.), *Belief and Practice in Reformation England* (Aldershot, St Andrews Studies in Reformation History, 1998), pp. 113–36.

Oberman, Heiko A., *Luther. Man between God and the Devil* (New Haven, Conn., 1989).

O'Connor, John, *Amadis de Gaule and its Influence on Elizabethan Literature* (New Brunswick, N.J., 1970).

Olin, John, (ed.), *The Catholic Reformation: Savonarola to Ignatius Loyola* (New York, 1992).

Olson, Jeannine E., *Calvin and Social Welfare. Deacons and the Bourse française* (Selinsgrove, Pa., 1989).

Pallier, Denis, *Recherches sur l'imprimerie à Paris pendant la Ligue (1585–1594)* (Geneva, 1975).

Panofsky, Erwin, *The Life and Art of Albrecht Dürer* (1943; rev. edn, Princeton, N.J., 1971).

Parente, James A., *Religious Drama and the Humanist Tradition: Christian Theater in Germany and the Netherlands, 1500–1680* (Leiden, 1987).

'Drama', in *The Oxford Encyclopedia of the Reformation* (4 vols., New York, 1996).

Parmelee, Lisa Ferraro, *Good newes from Fraunce: French Anti-League Propaganda in late Elizabethan England* (Rochester, N.Y., 1996).

Parker, Geoffrey, *The Dutch Revolt* (London, 1977).

Parker, T. H. L., *Calvin's Preaching* (Edinburgh, 1992).

Parker, Kenneth L., and Carlson, Eric J., *'Practical Divinity': The Works and Life of Revd Richard Greenham* (Aldershot, St Andrews Studies in Reformation History, 1998).

Pasquier, Emile, *Un curé de Paris pendant les guerres de religion: René Benoist, le pape des Halles* (Paris, 1913).

Peter, R., 'L'abécédaire genevois ou catéchisme élémentaire de Calvin', *Revue d'Histoire et de Philosophie religieuses*, 45 (1965), pp. 11–45.

Pettegree, Andrew, *Emden and the Dutch Revolt. Exile and the Development of Reformed Protestantism* (Oxford, 1992).

'Coming to Terms with Victory. The Upbuilding of a Calvinist Church in Holland, 1572–1590', in Andrew Pettegree, Alastair Duke and Gillian Lewis (eds.), *Calvinism in Europe, 1540–1620* (Cambridge, 1994), pp. 160–80.

'Haemstede and Foxe', in David Loades (ed.), *John Foxe and the English Reformation* (Aldershot, St Andrews Studies in Reformation History, 1997), pp. 278–94.

'The Reception of Calvinism in Britain', in Wilhelm H. Neuser and Brian G. Armstrong (eds.), *Calvinus Sincerioris Religionis Vindex* (Kirksville, Mo., 1997), pp. 267–89.

'"The Law and the Gospel". The Evolution of an Evangelical Pictorial Theme in the Bibles of the Reformation', in Orlaith O'Sullivan (ed.), *The Bible as Book. The Reformation* (London, 2000), pp. 123–35.

'Protestantism, Publication and the French Wars of Religion. The Case of Caen', in Robert J. Bast and Andrew C. Gow, *Continuity and Change. The Harvest of Late-Mediaeval and Reformation History* (Brill, 2000), pp. 163–79.

'Protestant Printing during the French Wars of Religion. The Lyon Press of Jean Saugrain', in Thomas A. Brady, Katherine G. Brady, Susan Karant-Nunn and James D. Tracy (eds.), *The Work of Heiko A. Oberman. Papers from the Symposium on his Seventieth Birthday* (Brill, 2003), pp. 109–29.

Pettegree, Andrew and Hall, Matthew, 'The Reformation and the Book: A Reconsideration', *Historical Journal*, 47 (2004), pp. 1–24.

Pettegree, Andrew, Nelles, Paul and Connor, Philip (eds.), *The Sixteenth Century French Religious Book* (Aldershot, St Andrews Studies in Reformation History, 2001).

Pettegree, Jane, 'Shoemakers and Dutchmen: Brothers under the Skin. The Shoemaker's Holiday and Thomas Dekker's Vision of Protestant International Brotherhood' (unpublished paper, St Andrews Reformation Studies Institute, 2003).

Pidoux, Pierre, *Le psautier huguenot du XVIe siècle. Mélodies et documents* (2 vols., Basle, 1962).

'Les origines de l'impression de musique à Genève', in J.-D. Candaux and B. Lescaze (eds.), *Cinq siècles d'imprimerie genevoise* (2 vols., Geneva, 1980), vol. I, pp. 97–108.

Pineaux, Jacques, *La poésie des protestants de langue française du premier synode national jusqu'à la proclamation de l'édit de Nantes (1559–1598)* (Paris, 1971).

'Poésie de cour et poésie de combat: l'admiral Gaspard de Coligny devant les poètes contemporains', *Bulletin de la Société de l'Histoire du Protestantisme Français*, 118 (1972), pp. 32–54.

Potter, G. R., *Zwingli* (Cambridge, 1976).

Pratt, Waldo, *The Music of the French Psalter of 1562* (New York, 1966).

Racaut, Luc, *Hatred in Print. Catholic Propaganda and Protestant Identity during the French Wars of Religion* (Aldershot, St Andrews Studies in Reformation History, 2002).

Reid, W. Stanford, 'The Battle Hymns of the Lord. Calvinist Psalmody of the Sixteenth Century', in Carl S. Meyer (ed.), *Sixteenth Century Essays and Studies*, (St Louis, Mo., 1971), vol. II, pp. 36–54.

Reimann, H., 'Zwingli – der Musiker', *Archiv für Musikwissenschaft*, 17 (1960), pp. 126–41.

Reinhard, W., and Schilling, Heinz (eds.), *Die Katholische Konfessionalisierung* (Gütersloh, 1995).

Reinitzer, Heimo, *Biblia deutsch. Luthers Bibelübersetzung und ihre Tradition* (Wolfenbüttel, 1983).

Robert, P. Ch., *Souvenirs numismatiques du siège de 1552* (Metz, 1852).

Roberts, Penny, 'Religious Pluralism in Practice: The Enforcement of the Edicts of Pacification', in Keith Cameron, Mark Greengrass and Penny Roberts (eds.), *The Adventure of Religious Pluralism in France* (Bern, 2000), pp. 31–43.

Robinson-Hammerstein, Helga, 'The Lutheran Reformation and its Music', in her *The Transmission of Ideas in the Lutheran Reformation* (Blackrock, Co. Dublin, 1989).

Rosier, Bart A., *The Bible in Print. Netherlandish Bible Illustration in the Sixteenth Century* (2 vols., Leiden, 1997).

Rouse, Richard H., and Mary A., *Manuscripts and their Makers: Commercial Book Producers in Medieval Paris, 1200–1500* (London, 2000).

Rubin, Miri, *Corpus Christi. The Eucharist in Late Mediaeval Culture* (Cambridge, 1991).

Rublack, Hans-Christoph, 'The Song of Contz Anahans: Communication and Revolt in Nördlingen, 1525', in R. Po-Chia Hsia (ed.), *The German People and the Reformation* (Ithaca, N.Y., 1988), pp. 102–20.

Rudé, George, *The Crowd in the French Revolution* (Oxford, 1957).

Rummel, Erika, *Scheming Papists and Lutheran Fools. Five Reformation Satires* (New York, 1993).

Runnalls, Graham A., *Répertoire des mystères français imprimés (1486–1630)* (Edinburgh, 1997).

'La vie, la mort et les livres de l'imprimeur-libraire parisien Jean Janot d'après son inventaire après décès (17 février 1522 [n.s.])', *Revue Belge de philosophie et d'histoire*, 78 (2000), pp. 797–850.

Rupp, Gordon, 'Luther against "The Turk, the Pope and the Devil" ', in Peter Newman Brooks (ed.), *Seven-headed Luther* (Oxford, 1983), pp. 255–73.

Russell, Paul A., *Lay Theology in the Reformation. Popular Pamphleteers in Southwest Germany, 1521–1525* (Cambridge, 1986).

Saunders, Alison, *The Sixteenth-Century French Emblem Book. A Decorative and Useful Genre* (Geneva, 1988).

Scarisbrick, J. J., *The Reformation and the English People* (Oxford, 1984).

Schade, Werner, *Cranach: A Family of Master Painters* (New York, 1980).

Schalk, Carl, *Luther on Music: Paradigms of Praise* (St Louis, Mo., 1988).

Scheible, Heinz, *Die Entstehung des Magdeburg Zenturien* (Gütersloh, 1966).

Schilling, Heinz (ed.), *Die reformierte Konfessionalisierung in Deutschland. Das Problem der 'Zweiten Reformation'* (Gütersloh, 1986).

Schlaepfer, Heidi-Lucie, 'Laurent de Normandie', in G. Berthoud (ed.), *Aspects de la propagande religieuse* (Geneva, 1957), pp. 176–230.

Scott, Tom, *Thomas Müntzer. Theology and Revolution in the German Reformation* (Basingstoke, 1989).

Scribner, R. W., 'Flugblatt und Analphabetentum. Wie kam der gemeine Mann zu reformatorischen Ideen?' in *Flugschriften als Massenmedium der Reformationszeit* (Stuttgart, 1981), pp. 65–76.

For the Sake of Simple Folk: Popular Propaganda for the German Reformation (Cambridge, 1981).

'Oral Culture and the Diffusion of Reformation Culture', in his *Popular Culture and Popular Movements in Reformation Germany* (London, 1987), pp. 49–69.

Seaver, Paul S., 'The Artisanal World', in David L. Smith, Richard Strier and David Bevington (eds.), *The Theatrical City. Culture, Theatre and Politics in London, 1576–1649* (Cambridge, 1995).

Seguin, Jean-Pierre, 'L'information à la fin du XVe siècle en France. Pièces d'actualité imprimées sous le règne de Charles VIII', *Arts et traditions populaires* (1956), pp. 309–30; (1957), pp. 46–74.

L'information en France de Louis XII à Henri II (Droz, 1961).

Sessions, Kyle C., 'Luther in Music and Verse', in Kyle C. Sessions and Philip N. Bebb (eds.), *Pietas et Societas. New Trends in Reformation Social History* (Kirksville, Mo., 1985), pp. 123–39.

'Song Pamphlets: Media Changeover in Sixteenth-Century Publicization', in Gerald P. Tyson and Sylvia S. Wagonheim, *Print and Culture in the Renaissance. Essays on the Advent of Printing in Europe* (Newark, N.J., 1986), pp. 110–19.

Sharpe, John and van Kampen, Kimberley (eds.), *The Bible as Book. The Manuscript Tradition* (London, 1998).

Slenk, Howard, 'Jan Utenhove's Psalms in the Low Countries', *Nederlands Archief voor Kerkgeschiedenis*, 49 (1968–9), pp. 155–68.

Smith, Preserved, *The Life and Letters of Martin Luther* (Boston, 1911).

Strauss, Gerald, *Luther's House of Learning. Indoctrination of the Young in Reformation Germany* (Baltimore, Md., 1978).

'The Reformation and its Public in an Age of Orthodoxy', in R. Po-Chia Hsia (ed.), *The German People and the Reformation* (Ithaca, N.Y., 1988), pp. 194–214.

Surowiecki, James, *The Wisdom of Crowds* (New York, 2004).

Tailby John E., 'Sachs and the Nuremberg *Fastnachtspiel* Tradition of the Fifteenth Century', in Robert Aylett and Peter Skrine (eds.), *Hans Sachs and Folk Theatre in the Late Middle Ages* (Lewiston, N.Y., 1995), pp. 187–95.

Taylor, Larissa (ed.), *Preachers and People in the Reformations and Early Modern Period* (Leiden and Brill, 2001).

Thayer, Anne T., *Penitence, Preaching and the Coming of the Reformation* (Aldershot, St Andrews Studies in Reformation History, 2002).

Todd, Margo, *The Culture of Protestantism in Early Modern Scotland* (New Haven, Conn., 2002).

Torrance, Thomas F., *The School of Faith. The Catechisms of the Reformed Church* (London, 1959).

Trevor-Roper, Patrick, *The World through Blunted Sight* (revised edn, London, 1988).

Tyacke, Nicholas, 'Popular Puritan Mentality in Late Elizabethan England', in Peter Clark, Alan G. R. Smith and Nicholas Tyacke (eds.), *The English Commonwealth, 1547–1640* (Leicester, 1979).

Verheyden, A. L. E., 'Une correspondance inédite addressée par les familles protestantes des Pays-Bas à leurs coreligionnaires d'Angleterre (11 Nov. 1569–25 fév. 1570)', *Bulletin de la Commission Royale d'Histoire*, 116 (1951), pp. 95–292.

Volz, Hans, 'Die Arbeitsteilung der Wittenberger Buchdrucker zu Luthers Lebzieten', *Gutenberg Jahrbuch* (1957), pp. 146–54.

Wagner Oettinger, Rebecca, *Music as Propaganda in the German Reformation* (Aldershot, St Andrews Studies in Reformation History, 2001).

Waite, Gary K., *Reformers on Stage. Popular Religious Drama and Religious Propaganda in the Low Countries of Charles V, 1515–1556* (Toronto, 2000).

Walsham, Alexandra, *Providence in Early Modern England* (Oxford, 1999).

Wandel, Lee Palmer, *Voracious Idols and Violent Hands. Iconoclasm in Reformation Zurich* (Cambridge, 1995).

Warnke, Martin, *Cranachs Luther. Entwürfe für ein Image* (Frankfurt, 1984).

Watson, David, 'The Martyrology of Jean Crespin and the Early French Evangelical Movement, 1523–1555' (University of St Andrews, Ph.D. dissertation, 1997).

Watt, Tessa, *Cheap Print and Popular Piety, 1550–1640* (Cambridge, 1991).

Weber, Edith, *La musique protestante de langue française* (Paris, 1979).

Weinstein, Donald, *Savonarola and Florence* (Princeton, N.J., 1970).

White, Paul Whitfield, *Theatre and Reformation. Protestantism, Patronage and Playing in Tudor England* (Cambridge, 1993).

Wilson, Jean, *The Archaeology of Shakespeare* (Stroud, 1995).

Reformation Appealing to bringing closer to one Apocalypse.?

Index